TOMBOYS!

to Nile and Coal,
for their independence and tomboy spirit
K.B.

to my Bears,
for inspiration and laughter, always
l.y.

TOMBOYS!

Tales of Dyke Derring-do

---

edited by
Lynne Yamaguchi
& Karen Barber

Alyson Publications, Inc.
LOS ANGELES

Cover and book design by Lynne Yamaguchi. Front cover photograph courtesy of Karen Barber: "Down the Shore, New Jersey, 1968."

Typeset and printed in the United States of America.

Published by Alyson Publications, Inc.,
P.O. Box 4371, Los Angeles, California 90078.

This book is printed on acid-free paper.

First edition, first printing: October 1995

5 4 3 2 1

ISBN 1-55583-285-7

ACKNOWLEDGMENTS

Alison Bechdel's "The Power of Prayer" originally appeared in *Gay Comics #19*, Summer 1993. Used by permission of the author.

Louise A. Blum's "Getting Out" appeared in a different form in *Love's Shadow*, edited by Amber Coverdale Sumrall, published by Crossing Press, 1993. Used by permission of the author.

Brenda Brooks's "Cerisy's Sphinx" appeared in a slightly different form in *Tide Lines: Stories of Change by Lesbians*, edited by Lee Fleming, published by gynergy books, Charlottetown, PEI, Canada, 1991. Used by permission of the author. "Little Girl" appeared in Brooks's *Blue Light in the Dash*, published by Polestar Book Publishers, Vancouver, BC, Canada, 1994. Used by permission of the author and the publisher.

Giovanna (Janet) Capone's "Stingrays" appeared in a slightly different form in *Common Lives/Lesbian Lives*, Fall 1983.

Dianne Reum's "Dear Grandma and Grandpa" originally appeared in *OH ...* #9 (November 1994), published by B Publications, Victoria, BC, Canada. "Happy Halloween" originally appeared in *Bluestocking*, October 1994. "New Year's Resolution" originally appeared in *Bluestocking*, January 1995. All three used by permission of the author.

Our thanks to Kiki Zeldes, for her friendship and unpaid labor, and to Michelle Benjamin and Kanani Kauka, for introducing us to the work of, respectively, Brenda Brooks and Dianne Reum. Karen also thanks Susan Reddy, because it's the thought that counts.

Contents

Photographs

Introduction

TOMBOY [f. Tom *sb.* + Boy *sb.*]
1. A rude, boisterous, or forward boy. *Obs.*
2. A bold or immodest woman. *Obs.*
3. A girl who behaves like a spirited or boisterous boy; a wild romping girl; a hoyden.
—THE CONCISE EDITION OF THE OXFORD ENGLISH DICTIONARY, Oxford University Press, 1971

The word *tomboy* first appeared in print in 1592.[1] From the start, it was not a compliment: "Of such short-haired Gentlewomen I find not one example either in Scripture or elsewhere. And what shall I say of such poled rigs, ramps and Tomboyes?" (a rig was "a wanton girl or woman"; a ramp, "a bold, vulgar, ill-behaved woman").[2]

By the late 1600s, the word was established enough to be included in dictionaries: "a girle or wench that leaps up and down like a boy," and "a ramping, frolicsome, rude girl." Rudeness seems to have remained linked to the concept for centuries: "He saw a great deal to find fault with in her rude, tomboy ways."[3]

For our favorite among the *OED*'s citations (especially in the context of this collection) we can thank a Mrs. Humphrey Ward:

1 For the really curious, *Tom* was of old a common generic name for any male (as in "Tom, Dick, and Harry"), including animals *(tomcat, tom-turkey* — even *tom-dog). Tom* was also featured in the names of several exceptionally large bells (balls?) and seemed to have been associated with phallic objects, as well — a Long Tom was a long trough in the mid-1800s, then the name of a naval gun.

2 Thomas Stoughton, *The Christians Sacrifice,* 1622. This and all of the examples that follow are taken from the *OED.*

3 Thomas Blount, *Glossographia, or a dictionary interpreting such hard words ... as are now used,* 1656; Nathan Bailey, *Dictionarium Britannicum: or a more compleat universal etymological English dictionary,* 1730, 1736; Mrs. Henry Wood, *The Master of Greylands,* 1873 or 1874.

"As a rough tomboy of fourteen, she had shown Catherine ... a good many uncouth signs of affection."[4]

This explication notwithstanding, *tomboy* seems to be so familiar a concept in contemporary North American culture that it needs no definition. We defined the term not at all in our calls for submissions, yet the hundreds of responses we received presented a virtually uniform picture of a girl who — by whatever standards society has dictated — acts like a boy. Despite this uniformity, the actual transgression of "boys' territory" takes many forms, of course. For some girls, it is excelling in — or even just playing — sports; for others, it's as simple an act as biking to the creek to catch frogs. Still other girls cross the gender line by preferring math to English, science to history, shop to home ec.

Here are the forms our own transgressions took.

FOR KAREN: People look at me now and say, *You* were a tomboy? I laugh and remember (in no particular order): crab apple fights, dirt bomb fights, and, of course, water balloon fights. An engineer's hat from my grandfather that I wore for years now hangs peacefully on my closet door, battered and worn, my printed name still visible in red marker under the bill. I remember playing with Hot Wheels, making roads and parking lots by dragging clothespins through the dirt, or sending the cars hurtling down a staircase on those ubiquitous orange tracks. My neighbors' chickens ate my pet toad. We played SPUD, kick the can, and running bases. Board games, too: Clue, Risk, Whodunit, and Life, with those little plastic cars with their pink and blue passengers.

Like miniature Evel Knievels, we rode our bikes through wet leaves, flying up ramps made from plywood propped on milk crates. Midnight wrestling on TV (before it turned "professional") prompted impromptu bouts on the front lawn, and Olympic years made track-and-field contenders of us all, competing in sprints, long-distance runs, even the high jump, with old mattresses to catch our falls. We fenced with yardsticks. We didn't do gymnastics, unless fence walking counts for the balance beam.

I remember backyard football, too: tackle, touch, flag. I suffered my first concussion diving for a pass and slamming my head against the frozen earth. (I suffered my second playing baseball, colliding with the catcher while going for home.) We played "kill the guy with the ball" — never smear the queer — on hard ground under an acorn tree. I took a few tennis lessons at the

4 *Robert Elsmere*, 1888.

public courts, but I had no backhand. I spent hours hitting the tennis ball against the back of the house, though, and developed quite a rhythm: crack a shingle, smash a screen, crack a shingle, smash a screen. Summers were filled with baseball, a term I use loosely: Wiffle ball, Nerf ball (even more fun when you soaked the ball), baseball with a tennis ball and plastic bat. I never played baseball with a real baseball. I played softball with a real ball, though, on the town's recreation league, my first time playing solely with girls. I played softball throughout high school, making the varsity team as a sophomore, only to be terrorized by the player whose position I "stole." That was the end of my tomboy passage, until now.

I recently visited my family down the shore. I felt like a kid again, eating Popsicles, making sand castles, and bodysurfing in the waves, and I realized that my tomboy never really went away. All she needs is a little encouragement to once again come out and play.

For Lynne: My parents were convinced that I was a boy when I was still in the womb, and my behavior out of the womb won me a boy's nickname all through childhood: Lynne-bo, the suffix *bo* being a Japanese signifier for "boy." In Oklahoma, I played for hours in the red dirt of the road in front of my house, until red ants found me and drove me running in, yelling for help. In Guam, I played in the jungle, climbed coconut trees, caught lizards, played army with the neighborhood boys (I always had to be the "dirty Jap"), and swung in the backyard, so high I made the swingset rock and nearly tipped it over. In Kansas, my mother, who sewed most of my sisters' and my clothes, got me to wear dresses by making me shirt dresses with matching ties. When I wasn't cutting up in school, I was playing marbles; learning Morse code or how to snap bottles from a lineup with a bullwhip in Todd's basement; fixing bicycles (my pal Peter and I charged ten cents per flat, twenty-five for a tuneup) or riding them (racing down the hill in front of my house and cutting between parked cars to hit the curb and fly, or hauling our bikes up the big slide to ride down it and up a ramp); skateboarding when that was a new invention; catching tadpoles and crawdads in the creek, even with a cast on my leg (from skateboarding); defending the little kids — and myself — against the neighborhood bully. In Germany, I continued playing with green plastic army men and Matchbox cars, then graduated to playing hot box and learning to fight with a knife. Back stateside, in high school, I played field hockey, maintained the family cars, and outdrank the boys. I didn't outgrow my tomboyhood even in my twenties, when I played semiprofessional football for a season in a women's league in the Midwest (a defensive linebacker, I earned the nickname Kamikaze, because, even at only five feet two, I'd hit anything). I went on to ride a motorcycle, fix cars, work sheet metal, and become a machinist in the Southwest. Living in Japan for a few years in my midtwenties, I was frequently mistaken for a boy, my body language all wrong for a Japanese woman. At twenty-nine, biking was a daily pleasure; at thirty, I learned to ski on snow and water, taught by my even more tomboyish partner. In my thirties, I finally stopped competing with men and came to glory in being a woman — a strong, capable, spirited, boisterous, romping woman. I still have a tool fetish and a knack for fixing things, and am still the one to rescue girls from mice and spiders and bats in the house. As injuries and age have caught up to me, I have taken to computers as my new playing field. And I continue to love the tomboy spirit in friends and lovers and myself — as much as I love the girl in all of us.

Such are the histories that brought us to this book and that we brought to its making.

In putting together this collection, we looked for work that, whatever its form, embodied the tomboy spirit in the telling as well as in the story told. You will find in these pages fiction, essays, reminiscences, poetry, photographs, and cartoons spanning six decades and the North American continent from the Pacific to the Atlantic to the Caribbean. What unites this multifarious mix is energy: vigorous, life-seeking energy.

Given the commonality of experience we discovered in the submissions, we had our work cut out for us in trying to deal with the overlap between stories. We wanted to include as many voices as we could, without making the collection redundant. One solution was to include short excerpts from submissions that had some special spark or captured some tomboy moment so aptly that we could not resist.

The commonality prevailed even across different ethnic backgrounds — at least in the work we received. We were admittedly disappointed in the limited response we got from women of color, despite our best efforts to include as great a range of voices as possible. Even so, in most of the work we've included by women of color, ethnicity is barely distinguishable. In fact, in the work of writers we know to be of a distinct ethnicity or cultural heritage — African-American, Asian, Pacific Islander, Native American, Hispanic, Jewish, Italian, Irish — the most visible groups are European. Perhaps the commonality is to be expected, since gender roles cut so broadly across cultural lines. We can't help but wonder, however, if the tomboy experience really is so similar across cultures, or if we simply failed to reach those with different experiences.

We also looked for work that shed light on how being a tomboy relates to a lesbian identity. Many perspectives are represented here. Among the less typical are contributions from a tomboy femme, a tomboy groupie, a late-blooming tomboy, and a tomboy-no-longer. For many of our contributors, being a tomboy was a source of strength that enabled them to survive queer-baiting, sexual abuse, prejudice, social disapprobation, familial dysfunction, and other assaults on selfhood.

The need to reconcile the concepts of girl and boy was a common theme. Some contributors wanted to be boys; some even thought they were boys; others emphatically did not want to be — as Jayne Relaford Brown put it, "How could I be the first girl on the New York Yankees if I was a stupid boy?" — they just wanted to do "boy" things. For most, whatever conflict arose came not from within but from outside, from societal limits on gender. The choice between boy and girl was rarely simple. For some, claiming the girl within was a long, painful process.

Tomboyhood has long been considered a phase, a condition that girls pass through on their way to becoming women. And this may be true for many women: some of our contributors describe losing tomboy friends — or temporarily losing their own tomboyness — as they entered adolescence. We ignorantly wonder if this may be more true for straight women than for lesbians. To judge from the submissions we received and the lesbian tomboys we know, including ourselves, tomboyhood is much more than a phase for many lesbians. As lesbians, we may look back on our childhood tomboy years with nostalgia, but we don't look back at them as if those years spent playing in the dirt were themselves dirty, or transitory, or merely cute. As tomboys, we were "other" then; as lesbians, we are "other" now. Though we were defined as tomboys by what we did, for many of us what we did turned out to be who we were and who we became, the behavior an expression of identity. Whatever ambivalence we may feel about our tomboy experience (and some of our contributors feel ambivalent, indeed), it seems to remain part of the foundation of who we are as adults. Should we be surprised? After all, as lesbians, we're still transgressing society's gender barriers, still not doing what "normal" women do.

Some of the stories here simply celebrate tomboyades.[5] Linda Bourke's "Button Nose" still makes us laugh out loud. A tomboy not to be tangled with is Patricia A. Gozemba, bloodier of noses. Rhomylly Forbes delivers a swashbuckling good time. Pat Pomerleau-Chávez and Franci McMahon pay homage to horses; others simply play HORSE. Giovanna Capone's steed was her Stingray, the Black Python. And there are cowboys, cowboys, cowboys, and baseball players galore.

And there are tributes to tomboys, mostly celebrations of friendship, such as Mia Levesque's "At Nine." Not to be missed is Brenda Brooks's "Cerisy's Sphinx," a lyrical, heartbreaking story of a friend lost to the world's evil.

A few stories hint touchingly at tomboy mothers and grandmothers. Stories like Tracy Alderman's "Easy Bake" and Marlene H. Lipinski's "Cowboy Heaven" may make some wistful for support they never had. And at least one story, "Marta's Magic," by Sally Sotomayor, reads like a fable we wish our mothers had read to us when we were girls.

We're pleased to be able to include photographs and a few cartoons. We had more trouble getting photographs than we expected. We had wanted to include a tomboy shot of each contributor, but many reported that they had none: their mothers wouldn't photograph them when they weren't in dresses — a sign of the times, perhaps. Three cartoons feature Dianne Reum's recurring tomboy character; a fourth is a baby Bechdel tale of "The Power of Prayer."

As feminists, we discovered many questions in the editing of this book: What makes a tomboy? Is there room for a girlhood in the concept? (There wasn't for at least one contributor.) Are we denigrating girls by celebrating tomboyhood? Will the label become obsolete as more and more activities become open to girls? Whatever answers each may come to, we're certain of one thing: whether the word survives or not, the tomboy spirit will live on. The simple reason? Girls just want to have fun.

---

5 *Tomboyade,* meaning "an escapade in the manner of a tomboy," was a nonce word coined for an 1886 *Blackwood's Edinburgh Magazine* article that referred to "Reminiscences of scrambles and tomboyades when they were girls together."

Little Girl

Brenda Brooks

Little girl,
I would know you
anywhere—

boot full of pond water,
hat full of fish,

you steal bees
by the jar
and free them by name
when the sun rises,

your fingers
seek the tick of the watch,
the quill in the grass,
the strum of the mushroom gill.

You are swift
off the trail
when the time comes,
training your horse
up the steep slope
where dragonflies whirr.

Little girl

singing the bees' names
in the tall corn,

stringing amber nuggets
on a blue thread
like the sun rising—

wear your hair
the way I know it everywhere:

a banner,

disheveled,
victorious,

flying.

Button Nose

Linda Bourke

In the fifties, art supplies made for kids were horrible. I wince at the memory of trying to make art with a brush that left behind a piece of itself with each stroke of lumpy poster paint on paper that was more like a wasp nest, ripping all the time because my technique was aggressive. I was insulted by the notion that these were "play" art supplies and the images I made were disposable. Even now, I'm both sad and angry that every single image from that period was thrown away.

I wanted real brushes. I knew about them from Mrs. Britton, who was the neighborhood craftaholic. She had a whole shelf of supplies that made me wild. I couldn't keep my eyes off the jars of brushes, the baskets of yarn and beads and glitter, the stacks of construction paper. Barbara Britton was two years younger than I, but I played with her occasionally anyway, just to get near that supply shelf, and once in a blue moon I got to make something. Mrs. Britton didn't do just ordinary crafts, either. I can still remember spray-painting my macaroni bows glued to a cardboard cone Christmas tree gold, boiling old 78 rpm records and bending them into flowerpots, and my favorite, frying marbles and dumping them into ice water so they'd crack. I thought the bracelets we were supposed to make with them were dumb, so I made a key chain and put my rabbit's foot on it, because I didn't have any keys.

And I didn't have any paintbrushes, so I spent a lot of time at home begging for them.

"Pleeease, Mumma! I *reeeally* need them," I'd moan.

My mother would first try to ignore me. But because I was relentless — in her words, "had a one-track mind" — she eventually broke down to at least answer me.

"Your sisters don't have brushes."

I would wait for the rest of the answer, but that was it.

Though we were lumped together as "the Bourke girls," my older sisters and I could not have been more different. Sharon, who was six, played with dolls all the time, and Bunnie, who was eight, liked to read. Why would they need brushes? I thought it was a cheap answer.

"But," my mother would say in a half-whisper, "I'll tell you what you *can* have." She would pause for effect, then announce, "You can have the cotton from the top of the vitamin pill jar." She made it sound special. Somehow it couldn't compete with frying marbles, but I really wanted to paint.

So most of my first marks were made with a huge wad of cotton rubber-banded to the end of a pencil. My mother would sit me in front of the heat register with a stack of newspapers or a Sears catalog, a bowl of colored water, and my new painting swab. I would stay there for hours painting clothes onto the women in the bra-and-girdle section, making art. Occasionally I would steal my mother's sable brown eyebrow pencil with the red plastic cap. It was soft and made chocolaty marks if I added just a little spit. The huge cotton swab was surprisingly fun to use, and soon I became a vitamin junkie, sneaking two or three a day, just to get a new hunk of cotton.

But I still wanted brushes.

One day, when we were only halfway through the jar of One-A-Days, I tried again: "It'll be a long time before we get new vitamins. Please buy me a brush." Any brush would have been okay at that point.

My mother wasn't answering.

Sharon and her best friend, Rhea Powers, were playing dolls in the next room. They started snickering at me and teasing me in high-pitched voices. "No, you can't have a brush," Sharon squeaked in a pretend mother voice, as if her doll were talking. "Go play while I watch my show," Rhea added. Mrs. Powers loved soap operas, and Rhea knew all the characters on *The Guiding Light*.

"M Y O B!" I yelled at them, then turned back to my mother. "C'mon, Mumma," I whined.

The look she gave me told me I had lost. There would be no brushes. Then she said what I was afraid she'd say: "Why can't you be a good girl and go play dolls? I'm sure your sister will let you join in."

I didn't do dolls. The one doll I had was unlike any other. It was a big pink baby doll. I had pulled its head off one day and lost it. Later I found a head from another doll that was much smaller and darker pink, but the neck hole was the same size, so I stuck it on. Its other unique feature was that, for some reason, this doll had no crack in her rear. She had one round lump. I called her Baby-No-Bum.

So just this once, I decided to try to play. I wrapped my jump rope around Baby-No-Bum, pretending it was a poisonous snake about to squeeze the life out of her. It had all the makings of a great jungle adventure, but Sharon and Rhea refused to play my version. They had a lot of different dolls, with boxes of accessories. Their idea of excitement was to dress them, do their hair, and make them eat fake food.

Sharon started taunting, "You don't even know how to play dolls. There are no snakes in dolls. You're a tomboy." This did not faze me. She started brushing her doll's hair. "Tomboy, tomboy!" she chanted. Now I was getting annoyed. Unlike most of her dolls, which had rubber heads with embossed colored ridges for hair, Rosemary, Sharon's biggest doll, had "real" hair. Little clusters of blonde hairs stuck out of holes in her head. The holes were neatly arranged in rows, like erosion-control sea grass planted on the side of a sand dune. It looked like a botched transplant operation. Sharon knew she was getting to me. "I have a brush...," she gloated as she stroked Rosemary's long hair with a little plastic toy brush. "I have a brush and you don't."

I snapped. I ran across the room, grabbed Rosemary, pulled a button off the back of her dress, and stuffed it up my nose ... It seemed like the right thing to do at the moment.

"Oh, *ick!*" Sharon yelled.

"She stuck it up her nose!" screamed Rhea, who had a flair for the dramatic. "Nose germs! Nobody touch it!"

Sharon wasn't sure she wanted it back, but it had a little flower on it, part of a matching set on Rosemary's most special outfit. "You better wash it five times!" she yelled. "Mommy! Linda stuck one of Rosemary's buttons up her nose!"

My mother bent my head back and looked. Sure enough. There it was. "Take that out!" she yelled.

I tried to get it out, but each time, I only pushed it up a little more. It was stuck. I tried blowing, but it wouldn't budge. When it became clear that the button was not coming out, and when I started to whistle from my right nostril, my mother panicked. She put me and Baby-No-Bum in the car and we rushed to the emergency room. It was exciting. I liked the attention, and the nose whistling made me giggle.

My mother was not amused. In the hospital, she filled out a lot of forms and we waited a long time. Several people were staring at me. Hadn't they ever seen a kid with a button up her nose before? Then I realized they were staring at Baby-No-Bum, who was still fighting off the poisonous rope snake.

Eventually I was strapped to a table and they X-rayed my head. Then a male doctor with bad breath came in and said in that voice that grown-ups use when they don't really want to talk to kids, "Well, it looks like we have a button up our nose."

It seemed like the right thing to do at the moment.

We? "I know I have one up *my* nose," I answered. "That's why I'm here."

A bit unnerved, he tried again. "And who is your little friend?"

"This is Baby-No-Bum, and here's why." I loosened the rope to show him her crackless bum. After that, the doctor talked only to my mother.

Several other doctors tried to loosen the button by pressing on the outside of my nose. They tried to block the left nostril and have me blow the button out, but nothing worked. Finally, they strapped me down again, told me, "This won't hurt," and proceeded to stick what looked like Captain Hook's hand up my nose to snag the button. It did hurt, and they didn't get it. So much for all the attention.

Finally, they told my mother to feed me crackers and bread. They had pushed the button in farther, and in a day or so it would make its way "out the other end." It all sounded gross to me, but I smiled a little when I thought about telling Sharon.

"Good thing you didn't put a button up *your* nose," I said to Baby-No-Bum.

What an ordeal. My mother was truly horrified. I'm sure she thought the hospital would have a no-muss, no-fuss button extractor, or at least magic sneezing powder. After all, we could have pushed it *in* ourselves.

The next day she presented me with a gift, because I didn't cry. *Now you're talking!* I thought. *This is the kind of attention I needed in the first place*. But when I opened the box, I couldn't believe my eyes. It was a *doll,* sort of like Rosemary, only smaller, with two stupid braids and snaps instead of buttons. I pretended to like it, but inside, dark feelings were rumbling. Why did everyone think dolls were so great?

I brought the present into my room and shut the door. I stripped off all her clothes. She had a bum crack. Then I found my blunt-edged scissors and hacked off one of her braids. I threw it across the room and it landed near a stack of my bra-and-girdle art. At that moment, a light clicked on in my head. Suddenly it wasn't the end of the world after all.

I stayed in my room for a long time. My mother came by and called in, "Are you playing with your new doll?"

"Yup," I answered. Technically it was true.

But really I was painting — with my two new paintbrushes, handmade from the hair of my new Baby-No-Braids.

Bloody Noses

Patricia A. Gozemba

In Somerville, Massachusetts, back in the 1940s, giving a bloody nose meant that you were tough. I gave them and I got them. The first one I gave made me the undisputed leader of the Sunset Road gang.

Joey Tartaglione, who was only eight himself, specialized in shocking the rest of us eight-year-olds. My gang — Carmen Tarantino, Tony and Sonny Laccarazza, Whitey Publicover, Francis White, Donnie Coombs, Jimmy Watts, Tommy Manning, before he got polio, and Philip Sousa, who was a little soft — used to dream all the time of getting even with Joey. He was no bigger than any of us, but he was crafty. He'd wander over from Chetwynd Road onto our street, Sunset Road, whenever he felt like it, looking for trouble. He was the first to put rocks in iceballs for snowball fights. He also came up with the idea of sledding down a hill and having one kid steer while the other fired rock-filled iceballs at anyone who happened to be in range.

It wasn't the iceballs that pushed us to a physical confrontation with Joey. We actually thought that iceballs were a great idea and immediately started making them ourselves. It was when Joey started cutting in on our bottle-collecting turf at Tufts College that Carmen and I finally had to face him down.

Back then, collecting bottles kept us in cash for the movies, candy, and bigger purchases, like jackknives and baseball gloves. Carmen Tarantino and I had staked out the two dorms on Tufts's Medford Hillside. Every day we combed the grounds for the big prize — five-cent bottles — and for two-cent bottles, which we liked, but didn't love. We used Carmen's Radio Flyer wagon to hold the bushel basket that we collected in. We actually had a very profitable business going and could usually make a buck apiece working just an hour after school. We liked the sureness of it.

Carmen and I could never understand why those college kids were so lazy as to not take their own bottles back. We figured they must be really rich to let those nickel bottles just slip through their fingers. Not literally, of course: they'd toss bottles out into the tall grass or just leave the empties on their dorm windowsills or fire escapes and Carmen and I would come by and scoop them. We had ethics, though. If a bottle had some Canada Dry ginger ale or some Coke still in it, we wouldn't touch it. We felt noble.

The day we found Joey Tartaglione collecting bottles on our route pushed us to the brink. It had never occurred to us that anyone would be so low as to infringe on our turf. It was an unspoken thing. Tufts seemed huge to us: there were plenty of other dorms besides our two and plenty of other bottles to be picked up. We weren't hogs. So what made Joey think that he could just move in on us?

We warned him in no uncertain terms that he was making a mistake. He snapped at us, "You don't own this place."

In a way, we did. Joey just didn't get it. We knew he was smart, though: we had felt the sting of those iceballs.

The next time we caught him at our dorms, Carmen and I grabbed his pillowcase full of bottles and told him to beat it. The two of us fought him off with some pushing and shoving. Joey warned us that we'd be sorry.

"We'll take our chances," we said, practically in unison, and hooked pinkie fingers to make a wish. Carmen and I had our lines down, though I did most of the talking.

When Joey left, Carmen and I looked at each other. “We could get killed,” Carmen said.

“Naw, just stay tough,” I told him. But I worried too, especially that night, as I thought about facing down Joey the next day. I figured that he wouldn’t be alone.

The next morning, Carmen and I met to talk about what the afternoon would bring. “You know, Carmen,” I said, “we’ve got to take him by surprise. If we wait until later on, he’ll be ready for us.” We decided to go over to his house and try to catch him off guard. We’d threaten him and see if that worked. We had nothing to lose.

Before we had a chance to worry about what might happen, we started for Joey’s house — just four minutes away, but in enemy territory. As we walked up Chetwynd Road, we saw him sitting on the third step in front of his house. He didn’t see us coming, because he was concentrating on untangling his rhinestone-studded Duncan yo-yo. I liked that yo-yo and had myself been thinking about putting out some of my bottle cash for a royal blue one.

He looked up and saw us. Then he casually looked away and began flipping his yo-yo, practicing his approach to an Around the World. Impressed, we just watched. He finally looked at us again. “Yeah, what do you want?”

“We want you to stay away from our area at Tufts,” I said.

“Oh, shut up, you tomboy. You just think you’re a boy.”

He was right: I did think I was a boy. I sort of knew that I was a girl — I had to go to the girls’ room in school, but I thought that was just school, a special kind of prison, because outside of school I went where all the boys went and I could do anything a boy could do.

He was right: I did think I was a boy.

The look on Joey’s face was smug. He had gotten to me and he knew it. I stepped onto the first step and stared at him as meanly as I could. “Yeah, I’m a tomboy and you’re a jerk.” Before I knew what was happening, I had taken a swing right at his face.

I don’t know who was more shocked — Joey or me — as the blood poured out of his nose. “I’m telling my mother,” Joey bawled. Carmen stood there in shock, but when I started to run, he followed. When we got back to my cellar door, Carmen got ahold of himself. "Why'd you do it, Patty?"

"Do what?"

"You know. Give him a bloody nose."

"I just swung at him. I didn't mean to give him a bloody nose."

"Well, you did. Now you're in big trouble."

Bloody nose. Bloody nose. The words kept echoing in my head like in some weird horror movie. Why had I gotten so pissed at Joey? Why did I haul off and give him a bloody nose? Carmen and I hadn't planned to get in a fistfight with Joey when we marched over to Chetwynd Road. We thought our big bluff was going to work.

Bloody nose
Bloody nose
Bloody nose
Bloody nose

"Ah, forget it, Carmen. It's over. Let's wait and see what happens." I didn't want to let on to Carmen that I really was worried. He was just like his father, bragging all the time about what he could do, would do. (My mother said all Italians were like that, and I had noticed that everyone in my Irish family was too, especially when they drank. Bragging helped make you feel better, gave you courage to do stupid things.) Plus, on Sunset Road, I was in charge, and everyone knew that no one could stay in charge who admitted to fearing anything. Being in charge meant that I got to decide what happened on the street. Everything, from when we switched from baseball to football, to when we had a carnival fund-raiser for the Jimmy Fund, to when and where we fought, was in my control. I got to be the big shot in our gang by being the best in sports, the toughest fighter, the kid whose father had the best tools in his cellar, and the one with the best ideas about where to go and what to do. Showing any weakness to Carmen would undermine my authority with him and all the other kids. I stayed tough and silent.

I was mostly afraid of what Joey's mother might do. Knowing what my Irish mother had in her repertoire of punishments, I shuddered to think what Joey's Italian mother might do. I didn't know Joey's mother, but I had heard Carmen's, screaming her head off at him and me when we started using my father's tools to build soapbox derby cars out of wheels and boards we picked from trash or scrounged from other kids' cellars. Mrs. Tarantino's voice rivaled the screech of my father's electric table saw, which Carmen and I both wanted to use but were afraid to. Even when we used nothing but handsaws, she'd screech, "Caaarrrmmmen, you'll cut your goddamned fingers off with that thing. I don't wanna see blood all over you." We knew the screech by heart. Sometimes we'd imitate it and laugh like crazy: "Caaarrrmmmen..."

True to family tradition, Carmen himself had a mouth like a torn pocket, always flapping in the breeze. He turned out to be a great public relations manager, telling all of the gang what trouble I was going to get in. The kids loved it, and we were smart enough not to let any mothers find out. I became a hero over that unintentional bloody nose, and I never had to pay for it. By skulking past Chetwynd Road for a couple of weeks, I managed to avoid Joey *and* Joey's mother.

When I did see Joey, about two weeks later, I was in the schoolyard practicing Walking the Dog with my unstudded Duncan yo-yo. Joey sauntered over. "Hey, want me to show you how to do it? Look, it's like this. It's easy." I watched and thought about my next move. He was showing off a bit in front of the other kids, but he wasn't challenging my status.

"Nice, Joey. You're good at that," I said, and flipped a perfect Around the World and walked away.

Maybe Joey never told his mother that a girl gave him a bloody nose. I knew from personal experience that it was a good policy not to let mothers get mixed up in kids' affairs.

Two years before, I'd kind of been in Joey's shoes — not over a real bloody nose, mind you, but over one that Cornelius Donovan *thought* he'd given me.

Cornelius had it in for me, because every time all the kids from Chetwynd, Sunset, and Upland Roads got together to play ball at the Tufts baseball diamond, he got humiliated. First, he never got to be a captain. That was a job you got by being mouthy enough to take over. I always took over being captain for one team.

Cornelius tried for the other side, but never made it. As if he could, with someone as good as Carmen around.

Worse for Cornelius was that those of us who were picking sides usually chose him close to last. He was bad. He couldn't catch, throw, or hit — though he, of course, thought he was God's gift to baseball. He was so Irish. Just like my uncle Tom Donnelly, who always talked about how great he was and, as far as I could tell, couldn't do anything except fix vacuum cleaners and get drunk and torture us.

This one day, Cornelius and I were monkeying around on our way home from school, and in the course of our usual pushing-and-shoving routine, he managed to get me off balance and shove me into a red barberry bush. I landed right in the middle of that old woody, prickly bush and got scratched up pretty good. As I struggled out of the thorns, I wiped my hand across my face and saw blood. "Ha, you've got a bloody nose," Cornelius snickered and took off running. He looked back once and laughed his stupid laugh.

Hoping that not too many kids had seen what happened, I poked around (taking care not to let anyone think that I was picking my nose) and discovered that my nose wasn't bleeding but I did have blood on my face, arms, and legs from the scratches.

When I got home and my mother saw me, she blew her stack. "What happened? How'd you get all that blood on your dress?" So concerned about the dress — typical.

"I fell into a barberry bush."

"What do you mean, you fell into a barberry bush? How does anyone fall into a barberry bush?"

"It happened on the way home from school. At the corner of Curtis and Raymond." I tried to throw her off with details.

Grabbing the front of my dress, she lifted me about two inches off the ground and interrogated me again. "How, at the corner of Curtis and Raymond, did you fall into a barberry bush?"

Dangling at the end of her grip, I strove once more to preserve my dignity. "I don't know. It just happened."

"'It just happened. It just happened.' That's no answer. What did you do?"

"Nothing."

She shoved me against the kitchen wall. "You tell me what happened or I'll let you have it."

It was hard to figure out who was tougher to deal with: my mother or any of the neighborhood kids. My friends and I called my mother "the Beak," because she had a long skinny nose with a ball on the end and because she beaked into everybody's business. I called her that in my head but didn't dare call her that to her face until I was twelve.

One belt to the face and I cracked.

"Cornelius Donovan did it. He shoved me into the bush."

"That little pip-squeak did that to you? Why did you let that happen?"

I shrugged, humiliated.

The next morning at breakfast, the Beak started in: "Don't let any punks push you in the barberry bushes today." As if the prospect of seeing Cornelius wasn't bad enough already. Still, when I set out for first grade that day, I thought that the little redheaded, freckle-faced jerk Cornelius was the worst I had to face.

At recess, his class didn't come out to the playground. When I went home for lunch, I walked fast to avoid bumping into him. My mother asked, "Did any pip-squeaks bother you today?" clearly hinting that I couldn't take care of myself. If she only knew that I hadn't been looking when Cornelius broadsided me and pushed me in the barberry, she'd respect me more. I knew from experience, however, that the best policy was to not give my mother any more information than necessary.

I called my mother "the Beak," because she had a long skinny nose with a ball on the end and because she beaked into everybody's business.

"No."

"'No.' That's it. Yesterday in the barberry and today 'No.'"

"Yeah. 'No.'"

"So what about that little redheaded weasel Cornelius? Did you see him?"

"No."

"Aren't you thinking about getting even with him? You can't let him get away with that."

I remained silent. I did want to get even with him, but on my schedule. I wanted to take him unawares, like he had me. I finished my grape-jelly-and-marshmallow-on-Wonder-bread sandwich and headed back to Cutler Elementary.

I spent the afternoon looking out of the window of our basement classroom at the ten-foot-high cement wall outside. From my seat, I could see, just above the wall, about two inches of the bottoms of lilac bushes. There were always candy wrappers, Creamsicle and Fudgsicle wrappers, and other trash stuck to the bushes, but never any bottles under them. I was planning how I would sneak my father's glove out of the house for our baseball game that afternoon and how I would get even with Cornelius. I fantasized doing something casual, like pitching him a beaner and then acting real innocent. He'd know, though. That's what counted. What ran through his mind now, I wondered. Did he dare think that he would get away with pushing me into the barberry bush?

When the bell rang at 3:30, I did my shot-out-of-a-cannon routine and headed for freedom and the glove in my father's closet.

My mother had other plans, though.

With all of the other kids in Miss Bunynski's class, I ran out the back door of the prison, across the tar playground, and past the swings. I made a right on Raymond Avenue. Curtis Street was in sight, just four houses away. I crossed Raymond and rounded the corner at Curtis only to see, standing right near the barberry bush, my mother, with my sister, Peggy, in a stroller. "Where's Cornelius?" my mother hollered at me. My heart started beating like crazy.

"I don't know."

"What do you mean, you don't know? Didn't he just get out too?"

"I guess so."

"You're one of the first ones here, so he must be coming."

Oh Jesus, I thought. Oh "Jesus wept," as my uncle Tom would say. What could possibly be worse than having your mother meet you after school?

"Let's go," I suggested.

"Not on your life. I want to see Cornelius."

"Why? He's a jerk."

"Jerk or no jerk, I want to see him."

I couldn't imagine what the Beak had in mind. Had I known, I would have run like crazy.

Cornelius finally rounded Curtis Street and practically bumped right into her. She looked down; he looked up. She looked at me and said, "Are you going to let him get away with it? Show him that you've got guts. Put your fists up — or do I need to show you how?"

Cornelius looked at me, half smirking, half terrorized. The smirk made my blood boil, and the Beak's goading made me want to punch both of them. I jumped at Cornelius and wrestled him to the sidewalk. We rolled onto the grass by the barberry bush. I held him down and he spit at me, getting me right in the face.

The Beak egged me on: "Get him. Get him." Cornelius spit at me again. I wanted to throw him in that big old barberry bush, but I didn't want to risk letting him up. "You're an idiot," I muttered, and I yanked one of his big, red, freckled ears. Then I slammed him on the ground a few times and got up and stepped on his right shin, waiting for him to get up so that I could slap his face. I almost forgot that the Beak was watching, till I heard her scream, "Make him apologize," and cringed. At that moment, Cornelius whirled on me, hissed, "Tomboy," and ran away.

"Why did you let him go?" the Beak screamed. By now, we were surrounded by kids, and my sister was wailing.

"Let's go," I said to the Beak, hoping to get away from the center of attention.

"Now I understand why that weasel got away with that. You don't have the guts to finish it off. 'Let's go' is right. Chicken."

I never really found a single great way to finish off Cornelius, not on that embarrassing day or any other day. Occasionally beaning him, socking him, or smirking when he got chosen last never quite did it. He had gotten me in front of the Beak and I never forgot that.

Three years later, however, when we all were nine, my revenge on him became almost weekly. By then, when the gang wanted to fight with someone, we'd meet them away from our houses, on Saturdays, at the Teele Square Theater, in the dark, down front at intermission. All of the ushers spent intermission by the candy counter, pretending to keep order as kids lined up to buy candy, but really checking out the older girls. So, with the ushers otherwise occupied, we had the wide center aisle and the space in front of the first row in which to rumble. Despite the gum and other gunk clogging the carpeting, that area was our favorite for fighting. The Sunset Road kids had their section of it; the Chetwynd Road kids had theirs — the turf was clear. Pretty much every Saturday, Cornelius irritated one of us and got socked a few times. He just had a personality that set off all of us. He'd pull our hair, give us wedgies, step on the back of someone's low-cut PF Flyers and pull them off, or pretend to bang into us and spill our popcorn. I can't remember if I hated red hair and freckles before I hated Cornelius or if he spoiled red hair and freckles for me.

Our victories at the theater earned Carmen and me quite a reputation, both in our gang and in the surrounding neighborhoods. In fact, it was after my cousin Tommy, from Winthrop, saw me in action at the theater during a visit to me that I got my first gig as a hired gun. Tommy and his friend Haggett, both seven, had been having some trouble with some big kids — nine-year-olds, like me — back in Winthrop.

Compared to Somerville, Winthrop had class. Everyone called downtown Winthrop "the Center." A doctor's house three blocks over from Tommy's had a big greenhouse attached to it, and best of all, there was a beach at the end of Tommy's street.

Tommy had been having trouble with some big kids— nine-year-olds, like me.

Everyone seemed rich. The kids played different, too. They didn't fight as much as we did in Somerville.

One school vacation after Tommy's visit to me, I got sprung from Sunset Road to spend a weekend with him. The weekend started well: that Friday afternoon at 4:45 on Winthrop's Montvue Avenue, I saw TV for the first time in someone's house — Marnie's. Marnie was the only girl Tommy knew in his neighborhood. She was a fruit. Not only did she have red hair like Cornelius Donovan, she wore dresses all the time and liked them. Tommy liked her, though, and she had the only television set on his block. He got to watch *Kukla, Fran and Ollie*, and *The Howdy Doody Show* over there. When I called her a "jerk" as we left her house, Tommy defended her. "Why don't you like girls?" he asked.

"I don't know any except for Tommy Manning's two stupid sisters, Virginia and Dorothy, and none of us will play with them. They're boring. They can't play any sports and their idea of fun is getting dolls to drink tea." The only time I had ever hung around with them was the year before, when Tommy had spent the summer in an iron lung in the Mannings' dining room. Even he told me that being trapped in the iron lung wasn't as bad as being trapped in the dining room all the time with his sisters. Girls never seemed interested in doing the kinds of things that the boys and I liked to do. Just a case of not meeting the right girls, I guess.

Because Tommy liked Marnie, I started to dislike her even more. The next morning, I told him about a new game that I had thought up, called Marnie. We'd go over to her house and ring the bell for her family's second-floor apartment. When she answered, we'd holler, "Can Marnie come out and play?" and then run like heck so that when she got down to the front door, nobody would be there. We did it three times inside of an hour and she never recognized my voice. Just like a girl. The game became a favorite, and Tommy and I used it to drive kids nuts in both our neighborhoods. We'd always ask for Marnie, even though no Marnie lived at any of the other houses we attacked. Who else would have a weirdo name like Marnie? Even my sister, Peggy, would laugh her head off with us when Tommy or I would say, "Can Marnie come out and play?" Marnie came to symbolize all the fruits we ever knew.

Anyway, that first Saturday in Winthrop, Tommy and his pal Haggett wanted to have a "get-even session" with the big kids who'd been picking on them every day after school. We'd decided to have it at intermission at the Winthrop Center Theater. (I picked the place: I liked floors with rugs.) John Wayne was starring in *She Wore a Yellow Ribbon,* and Tommy, Haggett, and I stuffed down Good 'n' Plenty, Tootsie Rolls, Necco Wafers, and a few Fireballs as we watched Wayne strut around in that great cavalry outfit.

At intermission, Tommy spotted the two bullies standing up in the first row of the balcony, winging popcorn boxes at the kids below. I sized up the situation and got a great idea: sneak behind them down the second row, jump over their seats, and push them against the brass railing. I thought we might be able to knock the wind out of them that way. I also figured that just scaring them might do the trick. They towered over us in height, being at least four feet tall, so we had to use our heads. Tommy and Haggett liked the idea and actually turned out to be pretty good little fighters, establishing a "rep" by their actions that day. What won the day for us was surprising the bullies. Once we had them bent over the brass railing, we twisted their arms and threatened to bring in more kids from Somerville: Kids who risked kids' lives by pushing them up against balcony rails. Kids who didn't believe that big kids should pick on little kids. Kids who knew no fear. They actually fell for our bluff, especially after we threatened to push them over the railing. We weren't interested in apologies. We made them say, "We give up," and, "We surrender," and then we let them go.

Having delivered our message, we ran like heck back to our seats. Tommy worried that they'd come after us, so we sat in the last row, where a five-foot wall protected our backs. At Haggett's suggestion, we cut out as soon as the second feature ended. We went over to torture Marnie one more time, this time using Haggett's voice as the decoy.

The Winthrop scene seemed great to me: good clean fighting, no bloody noses — until Sunday. Tommy had a great army hat with a visor and gold "scrambled egg" trim. He got it after our uncle Joe came back from World War II. I wanted it as much as I had ever wanted anything, even my first jackknife. I begged Tommy for it, but he wouldn't give it up. On Sunday, he let me wear it, though, and the more I wore it, the more I liked it. I remember sitting in his living room with the hat on, reading a Nancy Drew book and wondering how I could get a hat like it. Then Uncle Tom, with a few highballs under his belt and a cigarette hanging out of his mouth, said in his scratchy voice, "You look like a turkey in that hat, you little tomboy." I wanted to kill him. I thought I hated being called a turkey more than anything, but I realized that day that I hated more the tone in his voice as he called me a tomboy.

Tommy snickered when he saw my face. I wanted to strangle him, too. Uncle Tom was the one who looked like a turkey, with his bald head, little bits of red hair, red face, and scrawny red neck. Instead of swinging at anyone, though, I got up and took my book into the back bedroom to get away from them. Tommy followed me in and I whirled on him and threw him on the bed. We wrestled for a few seconds as he grabbed at the hat and tried to get it away from me. I barely know what happened next, but I landed on the floor between the bed and the wall and when I came up, my nose was bleeding. Tommy started to cry and I told him to shut up and go into the bathroom and get some toilet paper. When I got the bloody nose under control, I told him that he could keep his stupid old hat, I didn't want it.

"Girls don't wear them anyhow," he said. "Girls in the army wear those WAC hats. Maybe you can get one of them."

"Ah, shut up." I was sick and tired of hearing: "Girls don't do that." "Girls don't wear this." "Girls can't play football." *I* did "that," wore "this," and played football. It was slowly beginning to dawn on me that I probably *was* a tomboy, since all these jerks seemed to be calling me one. I didn't know any other girls like me. Nancy Drew did stuff that I liked, but she mostly wore skirts, and anyway, that was in a book. What was a tomboy, anyhow, but a girl who knew that fun was what the boys did? Tomboys were smarter than regular girls. But where were the other tomboys? Did the jerks actually know them? Could I ever meet any? Who could I ask? Who could I trust? Questions like these, I'd never ask. There seemed to be something nasty about the whole tomboy idea — at least, judging from the way people said the word. From then on, I got a big chip on my shoulder about being called a tomboy, though nothing changed in my routine.

There seemed to be something nasty about the whole tomboy idea — at least, judging from the way people said the word.

In the spring of 1952, when I was eleven and a half, my whole world changed. My mother and father decided that we had to leave Somerville because too many of "those people" — Italians — had moved into our neighborhood.

The first day in our new neighborhood in Waltham, I saw a girl walking up my new street, Warwick Avenue, with a baseball bat over her shoulder and a glove hanging from it. My eyes bugged out. Other than Babe Didrikson, whom I had seen once in a newsreel at the Teele Square Theater, I had never seen another girl with a glove and bat. I chased after her and asked, "Do you want to play catch?"

"Yeah, sure. But I'm going to meet up with some other kids and go over to the TB hospital for a game. Do you want to come?"

"Where's the TB hospital?" I asked.

"There." She pointed to a big brick building that sat on a hill just across the main road.

I ran into my house and grabbed my glove, a couple of bats, and my baseball taped with my special white tape. She nodded approvingly when I came running out with all of my stuff. "Great.

We need another ball; the cover just came off of mine," she said.

"What's your name?" I asked.

"Patty. Patty Corkery." I couldn't believe it: we had the same first name. Her red hair and freckles sent ghost-of-Cornelius-Donovan shivers through me, but I was too excited to worry about it.

"We've got this great field at the hospital. Nobody uses it but us. Timmy Kelly's father is a doctor at the TB hospital and the ball field is right next to his house."

"Who else plays with you?"

"Well, they're all boys. You'll be the only other girl." She paused. "My mother calls me a tomboy. Wait till I tell her there's another one."

"Tomboy" sounded different the way she said it. It didn't get me mad. I didn't want to throw a punch. She said it like she kind of accepted it. Didn't like it, maybe, but accepted it.

"Yeah, I've been called that too — 'tomboy.' Who cares? Usually it's jerks who say it. Oh god, I didn't mean to call your mother a jerk."

"She is one," Patty said.

"What do you mean?"

"She's a jerk. She thinks that everything my sister Bonnie does is just perfect, and she's always on my case."

I had never heard anyone call their mother a jerk. I had thought it about my mother a lot, of course, but I'd never said it out loud to anyone.

"Let's hit a few till the other kids come," she said.

"Your ups," I said with due respect and moved out past second base. I wanted to find out how good she was. We were both sizing each other up, our curiosity friendly. I put on a pretty good display of snagging the grounders that she drove at me. Then she popped a few to me, and just like my favorite outfielder with the Boston Braves, Sam Jethro, I moved under them and put them away. She was catching my throws back to the plate in her bare left hand and then smoothly tossing up the ball for the next hit. Amazing, I thought, another girl like me.

As the boys showed up, she told them where to go in the field and continued drilling us. Realizing that this was her turf, I couldn't help but smile.

"Okay, let's choose sides," she said, after the last expected kid got there. "This is Patty Curran, and she lives on Warwick Avenue, two doors down from the O'Malleys. I'll take her on my team. Go ahead, Timmy, your pick."

The great hits I got that day were almost as good as Patty's choosing me first. I began to feel that living in Glen Meadow East, our development, might not be so bad, and that being a tomboy wasn't so bad either.

On the way back to our houses that day, Patty asked me if I ever fought with other kids. I said, "Yeah, sure."

"Did you ever give anyone a bloody nose?" she asked.

Oh God, I thought, was she related to that redheaded jerk Cornelius? "Yeah, why?" I said, looking right at her.

"Nothing. Just asking. You look like someone who could."

T*omboy* is an odd word. Why not *tomgirl?* Because the word itself reserves certain freedoms for men only. A tomboy can be equal to a boy-boy only to a certain age.

The age at which it ended for me was in the sixth grade, when I lost my first fight. If things had been the way they are now, I could have pulled out a piece and history would have been different. As it was, I had just my fists and Stevie Tyler could hit harder.

It hadn't always been that way. I loved to fight. We used rotten oranges for weapons and dug foxholes in the orchards, camouflaged with weeds. We had escape routes over back fences and garage roofs, covering the whole block. We had tree houses and tire swings and vacant lots. When I was in the third grade, Dickie Smith's father told my father that I couldn't play with Dickie anymore because I was too rough. My father was kind of happy about that.

–Linda Niemann, from "Are You a Boy or a Girl?"

Evolution of a Tomboy

Hilary Mullins

In the beginning, it had nothing to do with liking girls. In fact, in the beginning, being a tomboy was not about whom I liked at all; it was about *what* I liked: climbing trees, building forts, playing any kind of game that involved throwing or hitting a ball. And in the beginning, for both me and my little sister, growing up in the Vermont countryside, being a tomboy meant putting on our boots and banging around together outside, walking through dark, rich spring mud or taking jumps on our bicycles, vaulting up boards propped on boxes. In winter it meant wading uphill through knee-deep snow, dragging the long wooden toboggan ourselves, leaping on at the top with a pounding, running start, and hurtling down, whooping in the whip-white blur of it, holding on with crusty mittens.

Of course there was pressure on me and my sister to conform, to rein our tomboy selves in and become more ladylike, but not as much as there could have been. My mother was, in her own way, more a woman than a lady, an artist who taught my sister and me that being different was actually good and freeing in a world where people so often settled for the dull and ordinary. Never mind that her mother back in Connecticut could not understand why her two granddaughters were not interested in shoes and party dresses. Besides, my sister and I did well in school, and our good grades and predilection for winning prizes no doubt soothed our parents, who emphasized academic achievement.

So though I knew perfectly well that I was not quite the girl I ought to be, I certainly never worried about being a lesbian. My little sister did, a fact I didn't learn until years later. That is another story, not mine to tell. My blissful ignorance on this count arose partly, I suppose, from innocence, partly because I was busy having crushes on older men, mostly teachers. For whatever reason, kids my own age simply did not stir in me that intense mixture of awe and need that adults did. But though I craved adults, their attention and approval, they were useless when it came to playing. Kids were the ones who knew how to have fun.

In my small, rural grade school class, all boys were required by unwritten edict to play ball every recess. What kind of ball had its strict seasons: fall was football — tackle when the teachers weren't looking — spring was softball. The requirement must have been fearsome for boys not inclined or suited to sports. But I didn't think about that then: I just wanted to play. Mostly, they let me. After all, I was the only girl who wanted to regularly, and I was good, up there with the two best players in our class: a fact all the boys knew, but never acknowledged, at least not to me.

Agile and energetic, I was the class tomboy — a girl, but different, my identity split. I liked that girls were mature, that they were more emotionally honest than boys. Girls were good to talk to, good for friends. But I scorned their exaggerated inability, the way they'd let a softball skip between their legs playing outfield, their silly shrieks when a kickoff sent a wobbling football and a swarm of boys their way. I knew I wasn't like that. But I knew I wasn't like the boys either, that I didn't want to be one, even though I liked to do the things they did. They accused me of it at times anyway, marking the boundaries of their male terrain like spraying tomcats.

One fall morning in sixth grade, some boys and I were playing a game that involved one kid clutching the football and running like hell until somebody could running-fly and take him down. Then, flat on his back on the dark, damp ground, the kid who had been tackled had to surrender the ball, propelling it high into the air so the next running fool could snatch it and dash off, the rest of us pelting after him, our sneakered feet cutting trails through the glimmer of dew on the grass. I loved that game, the fluid speed, slipping out from a tackle, the rush and tumble of bodies meeting when a few of us hit the ground rolling.

But that particular morning, an older boy playing with us while he waited for the high school bus took offense at my participation and warned me to clear out. When I tried to ignore him, hoping his hostility would blow over, he bullied me back behind Town Hall and pummeled me, saying as he left me lying tear-streaked in the dust, "That'll teach you to try to be a boy."

As I look back, this episode makes all the more chilling sense when I remember that we called that little game smear the queer. Ignorant as I was at the time of what that word really implied, I nonetheless paid the price for being queer myself. Not because I wanted to put my hands down other little girls' pants: the notion hadn't occurred to me. No, it was other parts of the male domain I had trespassed on. Sex wasn't the point: bending gender roles was.

And it just got worse as I got older. In eighth grade, the boss boy of our class took it into his head that I, being a girl after all, should not be playing boys' games. Barred from the field, I languished, but the teachers did not intervene. One noontime recess, knowing that the boss boy was home having lunch, I joined the rest of the boys in a softball game, gambling that they wouldn't have the nerve to say anything. I was right. But as soon as the boss boy returned, swinging back over the fence, he charged like an enraged bull right for me, hard little fists swinging, his face contorted with righteous male rage.

Surprised and scared, I went into automatic defense mode, trying to back off, shielding my face with my mitt. But worse than this one boy's attack

This episode makes all the more chilling sense when I remember that we called that little game smear the queer.

was the way that the rest of the boys circled packlike behind him for the kill, jeering and trying to get their own licks in from the side. I got away, but I was badly shook up, unnerved by the violence of the boys' reaction, the way they'd closed ranks as one.

Though I could not recognize it as such then, those incidents out in broad daylight were hardly the only time and place where I had to contend with boys closing ranks against me as a girl. One summer day when I was eight, my seventeen-year-old cousin took my twelve-year-old brother and me out back to the woods. The plan, our cousin said, was to build a lean-to. And for a while, that's what we did, breaking branches and lashing them together in a crude frame. But this industrious activity didn't last long, as our cousin turned his attention in a quite different direction: sexual abuse. First my cousin did it to me, then he got my brother to do it to me too, giving him lessons he thereafter repeated. Years later, my brother swore in a tearful rage that he never would have thought of abusing me on his own, but the damage was done and it gained momentum: soon my other brother was involved; then, sometimes, my brothers' friends too.

Not that they necessarily all enjoyed it. Looking back, it seems to me that the stakes were high for them, that those sex games were nearly as compulsory for these boys as ball games during recess were for the boys in my class. All of them had to prove their budding manhood to the other boys or else, and in this dirty little game, a female body was the field on which to demonstrate it. But how could a heady feeling of control not have been part of the twisted and intense sexual mix for some of them? For these were not scenes of mutual exploration between children of equal power. I didn't want to be sexual with these boys (or anyone else, for that matter), but once I'd been tricked into sex by my cousin, I felt implicated — as if it were my fault — and that trapped me in further abuse.

This was something I had not been prepared for, a kind of sexism neither my mother nor anyone else had told me anything about. Though I called boys who wouldn't let me play ball sexist pigs, when it came to these other kinds of games, I did not have my usual defenses. Indeed, in this arena, they had me pinned as a girl right where a girl was supposed to be, my back flat against a grimy old mattress as one by one they climbed on, grinding their little-boy penises into my opening that never seemed big enough.

From this, my tomboy spunk could not save me. I surrendered to the invasion and the degradation, to the treatment that persuaded me that I could not say no, that my needs and feelings weren't as important as my abusers'. Indeed, that is the primary lesson of oppression, the message scored into you over and over: that you are not entirely human, that you are a lesser-than being.

But it could have been worse: I could have dissolved entirely into my passive other self, and I didn't. To a large extent, that was the doing of my tomboy self, the part who knew what she liked, and what she didn't. Simultaneously the embodiment of my entitlement to joy and of my resistance to gender oppression, my tomboy still ran relatively free outside the strictures of "engendered" submission, riding her unregistered dirt bike on back roads and learning ice hockey in college at eighteen. As depressed as I was during many of those years, I still retained the ability to have fun.

From this, my tomboy spunk could not save me.

The crisis came in my early twenties. I had graduated from college and moved to the small, progressive city of Burlington, Vermont. Though I'd had a few flirtations with women, and even slept with a woman friend my junior year in college, I had been involved with older men since I was fourteen, when a teacher at my prep school had used my alienation and desperation to milk me of sex. After that, there were more teachers, even an alcoholic psychiatrist the summer after I graduated college. But I had gradually been getting disgusted with these men — their male arrogance and cynicism, their way of always assuming the upper hand in the relationship because of my youth and gender.

Sensing myself at an impasse, I took a break from everything but my job to read Simone de Beauvoir's *Second Sex*. I had bought my copy at fifteen and had read parts in my women's studies classes. Now I read it from cover to cover and came to the conclusion that — given the ways of the world — it was impossible for me to be who I was in a relationship with a man. There simply seemed to be no room for both the feisty intellectual tomboy I was and the man all those older guys seemed to feel they had to be.

That settled, I made the rational decision to become a lesbian. At this point, my sexual-abuse issues undealt with, my terror of sex still barely apprehended, I came to this decision by a primarily intellectual process. The way I went about it with all my studious thinking, you would have thought I had no body to consult in the matter. And in fact, years of avoiding my fear of and disgust about sex kept me from feeling much of anything when it came to matters of desire. It was need more than desire that propelled me in those years anyway, a desperately inchoate yearning for someplace, someone I could call home.

Looking back, I sense that another part of my dilemma was that I was coming of age still a tomboy. Nowhere did I see women my age or older like me. The only women I had ever seen who dressed the way I did were farming women, and that didn't really seem the same at all. I wanted to be a writer: I aspired to a culture of literature and leftist politics where grown-up tomboys seemed to not exist. I had nothing and nobody to show me who I could grow up to become.

These worries were not appeased when I scoped out the lesbian community. Every lesbian I saw in that mideighties East Coast town looked like a hippie to me. Unable to identify as a hippie, I was profoundly disappointed, naively assuming that if I did not look like the lesbians I saw, then I could not be one myself. And because I was too homophobic and intimidated to actually talk to any of these women, I next decided that I should try a young man. Maybe, I thought, they wouldn't be as sexist as the old guys. And knowing by then that power imbalance saturates age difference the way butter soaks into toast, I hoped that there might be more room for me as I was with a man my own age — perhaps one of those kind-looking carpenter types I saw buying organic rice in bulk at my food co-op.

It was a last-ditch experiment, the relationship I started later that year, necessary I suppose, considering what I had to work with, but doomed to failure. For one thing, marriage — which seemed to be the eventual goal of straight relationships — would have meant the end of me as I understood myself. Perhaps there are a few men out there who can tolerate, even enjoy, an adult tomboy, but this boy was not one of them. And even if I had found such a man, I understood that marriage was a good deal bigger than any individual and that I would have to be continually fighting to preserve my identity against its sheer, warping institutionalized mass. I was tired of fighting boys for the right to be myself, tired of fighting everybody about it. I was not interested in battling for transformation from within the institution. Furthermore, I was not interested in children, never had been. He was. And though I found my boyfriend pretty to look at, I wasn't attracted to him, systematically deflecting sex in a way that I was barely conscious of at the time. This man and I were not even spiritually kin.

All this boded ill for my last, great experiment with heterosexuality. But I think the event that sealed my decision occurred when I took my boyfriend home to my family and he allied himself with my brothers in their sly, sexist teasing of me. My brothers seemed to regard my femaleness as the one trump card they could always hold over me, and my boyfriend, looking for ammunition in some of our power struggles, jumped for it. In his eagerness, I saw a truth I could not tolerate: even in this so-called enlightened relationship, the old dynamic still held: no matter what, boys would always close ranks against a girl. Even though he knew that my brothers had sexually abused me, my boyfriend — the man I slept with — still chose to bolster his own position by aligning himself with their — and his — male prerogative. It was a bitter betrayal.

But on the flip side of this betrayal lies the fact that it was actually my boyfriend who first persuaded me to go into therapy for sexual abuse, which perhaps quite literally saved my life. Not that his motivation was all noble disinterest — he felt unjustly sex-starved — but there was genuine concern on his part for me too, making for a mixed gift.

It was a gift, nonetheless. For as I combed through the wreckage of my sex-scarred childhood, I began bit by bit to have the courage to live in my body in a way that, unsupported, I had not been able to brave before. It was an odd, difficult stage, filled with pain and wonder.

Without meaning to consciously, I began to take note of all the dykes at the same co-op where before I had noticed only granola boys. By happy circumstance, I was working as a substitute there, and I quickly came to realize that not all of the lesbians in town were hippies after all. In fact, women my age actually dressed more as I did. And as I began to inhabit my long-abandoned body, I started having strange, marvelous feelings. Not of attraction — I wasn't ready for those charged and troubled waters yet. But I would sit in my therapist's small, bright room with its big colorful pillows, and just feel — feel like a dyke, feel the essence of dykiness bubbling irrepressibly out of me. No definitions yet, just definite feelings. The tomboy was coming out.

There's a lot of renewed talk these days about homosexuality as predetermined. There is something comforting, after all, in the blameless notion that "we came this way." Goddess knows I needed some ammunition in the beginning to ward off all those assumptions that it was just my history of sexual abuse that made me want women. Without that trauma, the reasoning went, I would be "normal," would want what every woman wants: a man. Of course this is absurd heterosexist bias. But I don't believe the best way to counter heterosexism is to say we have always been lesbians if we don't remember always feeling like lesbians.

On the other hand, people who say that one's sexuality is chosen don't seem to have the bases covered either. The problem,

I think, is that the word *choice* does not begin to convey the way some of our decisions are really made. We really have no word for those unconscious workings that bring us willy-nilly into transformation. Even those experiences we call revelations or epiphanies are just reflected flashes of a larger evolution going on below the surface of what we think we know. Because my "choice" to become a lesbian resulted from a process that unfolded beneath the level of my consciousness, I did not, and still cannot, know what really happened. Still, it is worthwhile to attempt an informed hypothesis.

I was a tomboy from the very beginning — kicking and screaming at age three when my mother tried to get me into a dress for nursery school — but I was not a lesbian. I did not fall in love with the proverbial gym teacher, and looking back, I can think of only one grade school attachment to a girl that feels vaguely like a crush. No, for whatever reasons, I liked boys in the early days, most of them much older, but boys nonetheless. In fact, contrary to the usual assumption that a girl becomes a tomboy because she is really, underneath it all, a lesbian, I have come to believe that I became a lesbian because really, underneath it all, I was, and remain to this day, a tomboy.

I did not become a lesbian because I was "twisted" by sexual abuse. Sexual abuse certainly wounded me, but that was not the nature of its wounding, nor did coming out heal all injuries; I still have to contend with ongoing symptoms caused by those traumas: periods of intense anxiety and dissociation, difficulties with being sexual. But symptoms are different than lessons drawn. Sexual abuse taught me, young and hard, about the bad bargain between boys and girls, men and women. It wasn't just that they weren't going to let me play ball — the fixing of the game went deeper than that. In sexual abuse there was no pretense, just the stark bones of the arrangement designed to rob me of my integrity and personhood simply because I was a girl in a world where boys had to prove they were men or else. While parts of me bent under the force of that treatment, the tomboy never gave in. She was the piece of me who never accepted the arrangement, who kept me alive and later nudged all of me — not just my head, but my heart and body too — into that leap of faith called lesbianism.

In 1987, at the age of twenty-five, I left my boyfriend and came out as a lesbian. In 1990, also at the age of twenty-five, my sister came out too. When we go back home to the farm where we grew up, we still like nothing better than tying on our shit-kicking boots and walking around, hands in our pockets, faded shirts flapping loose over jeans. It's not about style, exactly: there's more to it, a certain kind of shared knowing, a connection between us and the land and the years we spent growing up on it. It's about our both always knowing that this was the kind of people we were, girls in big shirts who liked to use our hands.

Now, with both of us out as dykes, we still share that same feeling — something about the washed-out brown of fields in the spring, the chalkiness of the dirt road underfoot in the stretched, baking middle of summer. It's the heft in our hands when we lift the gate up and back to walk through, the furrowed roughness of old gray wood in the palm; something in the stride we hit heading up that hill we slid down in winter a hundred hundred times.

Tomboy has fit me since the day I was born.

I grew up in the 1930s on a farm in Texas. There were no girls living on any of the farms near us, so I had to play with the boys. I had two brothers who taught me to run, jump, and climb trees. We raced through grass burr patches just to see who had the toughest feet. We wrestled, swam in the river, hunted, and fished.

When we played games, I always wanted to be one of the male movie stars. The boys would try to get me to be the female star, but I would refuse, saying, "I don't want to be an ol' girl." The boys just wanted a girl to play house and pretend to cook. I wanted to pretend that I was the hero who rode in on the white horse to rescue the fair maiden.

I seemed to think and act like the boys. I was very angry when I found I couldn't urinate standing up the way they could. I improvised! If I positioned my fingers just right, I could pee standing up, though the fly of my jeans ended up with plenty of wet spots.

If I positioned my fingers just right, I could pee standing up

My mom tried to buy dresses and girl things for me, but I would hang them in the closet and wear coveralls or jeans. She would buy me dolls for Christmas, but I never remember playing with one. My sweet grandmother would buy me a gun and holster, which was what I really wanted. As I grew older, it was a BB gun and then a .22 rifle. I played tackle football and softball, and ran track on a field that was right behind our house.

I refused to do any of the things girls were supposed to do on a farm. I wouldn't cook, wash dishes, or clean the house. Mother never made me. Instead, she let me gather the eggs, pick the corn, water the animals, slop the pigs, cut the grass, and milk the cows.

I always felt wonderful, alive and happy, being outdoors. I'll always remember times when my mom and I would be driving to town and I would see a tractor plowing a field. I would plead with her to stop the car. When she did, I'd take off my shoes to run in the freshly plowed soil. It felt so soft, cool, and rich that I laughed out loud as I ran.

–Betty Moore, from "Tomboy, Woman, Lesbian"

I laughed out loud as I ran

The Importance of Horses

Pat Pomerleau-Chávez

When she told her parents that she had become a lesbian, that, indeed, she had at last discovered her true identity, her mother said, Oh! I always *knew* we shouldn't have let you have those horseback-riding lessons!

When I was a small child growing up in the era of Shirley Temple, my mother spent hours torturing my fine, straight blonde hair into long, bouncy ringlets. I tap-danced in little Mary Jane shoes but longed for a pair of cowboy boots. I hated Shirley's dimples and simpering smile. Above all, I hated her Goodness. Within my small and evil heart, I knew that it would not be my fate to travel aboard the Good Ship Lollipop.

I could hear hoofbeats on the road behind me.

Eventually, in an extraordinary and inexplicable move, my mother allowed me to discontinue the tap lessons after I complained that they were scheduled at exactly the same time that *The Lone Ranger* came on the air. My family had to struggle to survive during the Great Depression and perhaps the tap lessons had become too expensive to support, but whatever the reason, I was suddenly free to indulge my fantasy before the radio, which I sat watching, enraptured, as "Hi-yo, Silver" made the old wooden

Philco tremble and thrilled me to the bone. The Masked Man and his faithful sidekick, Tonto, thundered into the living room, ready to do their magnificent deeds — *on horseback!*

I longed to be Tonto's buddy and right-hand man. I was oblivious to the racism in the relationship between the Lone Ranger and Tonto: the cold, somewhat imperious Masked Man put me off for other reasons. And, anyway, my great-grandmother was a full-blooded Cree and I thought Tonto was a blood brother. I practiced toeing-in when I walked.

I loved tap dancing and, without benefit of lessons, I continued to tap freestyle, interspersing among my tap steps galloping motions. Half horse, half girl, I tapped and galloped down our dirt road, from the waist down a cross between a Tennessee walker and an Arabian, and from the waist up all cowboy in my Woolworth's Stetson, a nickel-plated Colt .45 whanging my hip. (I was a small cowboy, to be sure, but never, never a cowgirl. Cowgirls wore silly white boots and cumbersome skirts and had to be helped onto a horse. They and their ilk could go polish the brass of the Good Ship Lollipop for all I cared.)

Over the next few years, I learned some inaccurate, incomplete, and dangerously misleading information about male anatomy and human sexuality. I began to realize that even with a good horse and a full outfit, I still would never have the respect I longed for, nor would I gain true independence: I did not — alas! — have a *Thing!*

Nevertheless, when I was ten, I got the horse I had longed for. Riding her was impossible, however: she was quite young and not yet broken, given to flightiness, and dangerously unpredictable. She had great quality and her bloodlines were good, but she was headstrong and would need to be taken down a notch: training and a firm hand were all she needed, the men said. Eventually, I did ride her. I was the only one who did, as she was never fully broken.

When I was seventeen, the horse was sold to a neighboring rancher for his son's Christmas present. She and the boy didn't get along. Too much for the boy to handle, they said; a sassy horse! I began to know that having a penis didn't always bring love.

The horse was resold to someone who bred her to a good stallion, and she produced a fine colt.

I, too, was never fully broken, although at times I was subdued.

I was never bred.

I no longer wish for a Thing.

And I still hear hoofbeats on the road behind me.

Kisa, age 8
Santa Ana, California, 1950

I had two revolvers that took real cap bullets, a carbine, and a coonskin cap. And chaps that I tried to wear to Sunday school.

"God doesn't care if I wear my chaps," I screamed as they dragged me off to change into a dress. "A cowboy hat is still a hat."

My cowboy buddies weren't so subtle. Even if I could beat them up, I still couldn't have a buckskin horse. Or a white horse. Or a pinto.

"Why not?" I demanded, as we mounted up broomsticks behind the garage.

"Because you're a girl, and girls have to ride brown horses."

I thought back. It was true. In every cowboy movie, girls had to ride brown horses. Even Dale Evans, though her horse had a blaze. The little rats had me. Of course, I hadn't been thinking of myself as "the girl," but the details had tripped me up. Like the category of tomboy, my presence in the script was provisionary. At any moment I might be recalled to being a girl and demoted to a brown horse.

My girlfriends were much less likely to insist on gender casting. I could be the doctor, the gunfighter, the explorer — no problem. We tied each other up inside tree houses and had delicious orgasms on tire swings in the hot afternoons. On the roof of Alice's garage, we examined the naked women in my father's "photography" magazines and sets of racy Las Vegas playing cards confiscated from Alice's father's locked buffet. No one was there to point out that we would be those women. Or that we were looking at them with men's eyes.

—Linda Niemann, from "Are You a Boy or a Girl?"

At any moment I might be recalled to being a girl and demoted to a brown horse.

My presence in the script was provisionary.

One of the Girls

Susan Fox Rogers

The football was up and I sprinted out and left. Without breaking stride, I caught the ball and continued down the patchy field that served as soccer, softball, and football field. I could hear my teammates behind me yelling, "Go, run, go," and then, suddenly, "Look out." I sensed Jud hot behind me and knew I could not outrun him. A fourteen-year-old who had sprouted in all directions, he was six feet tall and weighed well over two hundred pounds. Sure enough, I felt Jud's hands at my waist, his fingers digging into my stomach as he took hold. He picked me up and sat me on the ground, effectively ending my run for six points.

Furious, I got up and slammed the football down. I started to walk off the field, leaving my four-man team one down in this pickup game.

"What's the matter?" Jud asked.

I continued to walk.

"I would have squashed you if I'd tackled you," Jud called.

"So?" I called back. I wanted to be squashed, tackled as Jud tackled all of the other kids, the other boys. I did not want to be treated differently, to be treated like a girl, because I was not a girl who played with boys, I was not a *garçon manqué,* as the French say, but a *garçon*. I was one of them.

The extent to which I thought I was one of them comes to me in one distant, embarrassing memory. We were playing an enthusiastic game of smear the queer (football without teams and the one with the ball was the queer — everyone wanted to be the queer) and I was tackled, five boys piled on top of me. Left flattened on the ground once we untangled our bodies, I reached between my legs, and called out, "Oh my balls," to the immediate hilarity of all of my teammates. They knew I was different. But I didn't.

"Oh my balls"

I was an odd sort of tomboy. I have stereotypical images of tomboys: short hair, baseball cap, scuffed-up knees, scrawny but strong. This was not me. I had long hair, though it was usually an uncombed mess, and never was I cool enough to contemplate wearing a baseball cap. I had few bumps and scratches and have never broken a bone, because though I have lived my life playing hard and close to the edge, I have always done so with control and care, as befits a good girl. It was my sister who in every way looked the tomboy, but people were too busy celebrating her brains to notice. She was the bookworm, the nerd, and nerd and tomboy were two identities that, in our world, did not overlap. Becky also happened to be an excellent runner and athlete, while I, despite my enthusiasm, was at best average at most sports.

So my tomboy status didn't come from my appearance or any jocklike ability but rather from the fact that I played and hung out with the boys. There was little intimacy between us, but what mattered was that I did what they did: biked freely around town, slid in the mud, stayed out past dark, smoked cigarettes on a dare. Fortunately, my parents were trusting, so they imposed few rules or restrictions in our house. Since I had the same freedom to move and do as the boys did, I didn't envy them anything — except that they were boys. I sensed that as much as I tried to be and was like them, the world would always remind me that I was a girl. And being a girl, everyone seemed to silently agree, was just not as good as being a boy.

The summer after fourth grade, however, the boys themselves let me know that I was not one of them. I remember playing freely, unselfconsciously, that hot summer of 1969, but during the course of our play, my sense of self changed.

That was the summer of rings. At some point, all of the boys I hung out with — Scott, Brett, Ricky, Tyler, and Jud — wanted to be my boyfriend. What that meant was quick kisses on the cheek as we untangled our bodies after a tackle or as we hid, wedged together in some small space playing flashlight tag. And it meant declaring their affection with plastic rings (a silver one from Tyler). I collected these rings in a box in the same way I collected the NFL stamps issued by the local gas station that summer. I wanted the rings as I wanted the kisses: as part of the game. I was game to play anything.

It was Ricky's aunt, sixteen years old and pregnant, who set us up to play strip poker at their house one lazy summer afternoon. She told us the rules of the game, then watched as we slowly became naked, removing our few clothes amid laughter and teasing, sitting on that double bed in the second-floor bedroom of their run-down house. The sole girl among three boys, I went along as I did with all of our other adventures: if they could do it, so could I. I didn't understand that, without me, this wouldn't be a game.

I remember not being able to really look at the boys, because I didn't want to see what they had that I did not. I remember exposing my white hairless body without shame. I remember Ricky, his feet playing with mine as we sat, legs outstretched, across from each other. It was a playful gesture, footsie in the nude — or so I thought, until he later told me that he was spreading my legs to get a better look.

Life shifted after that game, as we moved into fifth grade. I became aware of my body, its softness, its roundness, its possession of something more mysterious than balls. I felt vulnerable. When the boys ambushed me as I walked home from school, their tackles now involved a quick feel for my growing breasts, a pinch for my butt. I enlisted the help of my older sister to chase the boys away.

It was also in fifth grade that I met Donna and discovered that play with girls was a very different thing. In the back of the spacious closet of our science room, Donna and I would turn out the lights. There, we taught each other about kissing that was not a game.

not a game

I would like to think my lesbian history is that simple: that I was a tomboy, then discovered girls and devoted the rest of my life to women friends and lovers. But, of course, life is not so neat. I did spend junior high school mostly with the girls, but I didn't share their concerns and interests. They spent hours focusing on their dress and hair and how to get attention from the boys. And yet getting this attention didn't seem such a prize. I had to console Donna when her boyfriend got mad because she wouldn't let him finger her behind the bleachers. It was fine that Donna had a boyfriend, but that she might consider doing such things with him dismayed me. We parted ways. I had passionate relationships with Laurie, then Jo, then Allison, that involved passing clever notes in class, sleeping over on weekends, and discussing boys and how dumb they were. Then we would fight—break up, really—avoid each other in the halls, and write more heartfelt notes, about betrayal, love, friendship, and how much we cared for each other.

All this stuff of adolescence was infused with the energy and lessons of my tomboy days. What had those boys taught me? That girls were silly and boring. I believed them. With the boys I played, moved freely, had fun, and laughed. With the girls I ate M&M's, worried about my weight or pimples, and endlessly discussed relationships. Part of me still believes boys are fun — at least, what boys get to do is fun — and girls are not. So I was constantly drawn back to the boys, to doing and playing with them. By the end of high school I was back with the boys again.

not a game

It was the spring of my sophomore year in high school in central Pennsylvania and I was in a VW bug with my climbing buddy Munch, coasting down the far side of Pine Grove Mountain. He was grinning, his pale, freckled face spread so wide that his eyes were nearly shut.

"You have to do it," he said.

I nodded and smiled, sure I would.

"It" was a rock climb named Loose Woman, and what Munch was grinning at was the irony of me doing a climb with such a name. I was so far from loose, I was a sort of virgin warrior, keeping all of the boys at a good distance.

But I liked the name of the climb. It made me feel older, made me giggle and dream. I knew Munch was dreaming too, only, his dream was that I would become that loose woman and sleep with him. I was dreaming that I would become that loose woman and be free, be more interesting as a person, be normal.

At this point, there were only two options in my book: sex with boys, or no sex. So I chose no sex and felt like an oddball for not caring. In doing this climb I half believed I would get a taste of what people were talking about, and in some way be transformed. But it was only the climb I was willing to do.

All of my physical energy was being put into rock climbing. I had started climbing the fall before and had spent the winter fingering carabiners and hex nuts in the local outdoor shop. By spring I had fallen in love with climbing, and the sexy wild lifestyle of climbers in the late seventies. Climbing was freedom for this good girl, and when I entered the world of climbing, I was back in my tomboy mentality: if they could do it, so could I, and I was one of them.

When Munch and I pulled our car into the secluded green valley to climb, there were several cars parked at the side of the road. We recognized Dunk's white Chevy van, and when we got out we could hear voices up on the ridge. We guessed there was a top rope set up on one of the hardest climbs, Royal Delight, and the only people who could be working on that climb were Dunk, Mac, and Mac's girlfriend, Vicki. Vicki was the only other girl climbing in the area. She was older than me, a college student, and I felt we should be friends, or at least that I should respect her, but I knew I didn't. Tall, thin, with reddish blonde hair and round wire-rimmed glasses, she was cute, but overly talkative and enthusiastic. She was the kind of girl I did not want to be associated with.

Rumor had it that Loose Woman was named for Vicki. I was fascinated and slightly appalled by this possibility. The stories of Vicki's sexual ability, known throughout the climbing community, were greater than tales of her climbing talent. She was a good climber, but she had never done Loose Woman. And that made my desire to do it even greater.

Munch and I hiked up the short, steep hill to a low, overhanging section of the cliffs named the Salvation block. There were three routes on this block: Loose Woman, Damnation, and Salvation, all of which could be top-roped. Munch hiked around the side to the top to set up the ropes, while I put on my harness and stretched slowly against the warm rock, preparing to climb.

Munch called, "Rope," and it came flying down, landing heavily next to me. I reached for the gold-colored rope and tugged on it to make sure our top rope ran smoothly. Then I tied in with a bowline knot and waited for Munch to return to the base to belay me. I stared up at the route, imagining how I would feel climbing it: graceful, strong, focused.

I moved up the first ten feet of the climb, then got to the traverse that had stumped me in the past. I stopped and breathed and looked down at Munch.

"Do it," he said. No longer grinning, he was focused, intent.

"You got me?" I trusted Munch to catch me if I fell.

I reached over, slowly caressing the lumpy gray surface in search of a hold that matched my small, toughened hands. Slowly, I moved to the right, smearing my feet on the rock. Once I shifted my weight, I could lean against the ridge, pulling, nearly moving into a layback position. The hold began to feel solid, and my left hand joined my right as I moved my feet up. I reached for larger handholds, feeling slightly off balance but still good, my body moving in so close I could feel the solid roughness of the rock against my cheek. My feet danced and played with the small holds. I could feel the heat of my body as I began to sweat, and the heat of the rock reflecting the sun.

Soon I had solid horizontal holds and was balancing gently, my weight fully on my feet. I didn't linger long after the crux, because the rock continued steep. The holds were rounded but large, and I palmed them, pulling and dancing until I reached a wide ledge. I rolled onto the ledge, and lay breathing heavily.

"Nice work, loose woman," Munch called up.

Pleased with myself, I smiled, glowing inside. I wanted to just lie on that ledge, regain my breath and strength, and revel in my accomplishment, but I had to move on, complete the last few moves to the top.

LOOSE WOMAN

As Munch lowered me to the ground I could feel the blood rushing into my forearms, my body tingling with the effort.

I untied, then belayed, watching as Munch climbed, aggressively moving without hesitation. When he got to the top, I called up, "Good climbing." His words, "Nice work, loose woman," ran through my mind, and I knew I couldn't say those words to him. What he had done was climb well. What I had done was more complicated than a physical act. I had done "it," had taken the climb and made it a part of my body, incorporated it into my private history of desire and power.

As I lowered Munch to the ground, he had me stop, hold him at the crux.

"This is how you did it," he said, pointing out the holds I had used, the moves I had done. I didn't remember how I had done those moves, as my body had taken over, moved instinctively with the rock. And I didn't care to know, because as he said it, I could feel him, Ricky, and all the other boys spreading my legs, staring at me: yes, we were different, we climbed differently. I was a girl.

I expected to be changed by the route — to be no longer a virgin, really. And there was that morning-after feeling: my muscles ached in a pleasant way, and I felt slightly embarrassed, even awkward telling people I had done the route. When Dunk congratulated me, saying, "You're the first loose woman," I didn't meet his eye. And I didn't tell my parents, as if I actually had done something forbidden.

Beyond that, something did shift in me after that climb: I was still a virgin, but I was no longer an innocent who believed that my being a girl didn't matter. I hadn't done Loose Woman as Munch had, by conquering the climb, by moving through the route, but rather by moving with it. I had caressed the rock and seduced the holds. And that was how I moved through the world. That I was a girl meant everything. And I was beginning to know and like what that meant.

I came out to myself and the world quite a few years later, while in graduate school in New York City. And what sort of lesbian emerges from such a tomboy past? I'm athletic, at times androgynous, but I am very much a girl, who recently was taught by a considerate (butch) girlfriend how to put air in the tires of my pickup truck. I flirt with the girls as Vicki did with the boys, and I've had my moments of being a loose woman. That is about exploring and expressing desire, I've learned, and it does not make me bad or an airhead. Vicki is now a good friend.

I still climb and bike and ski with the boys, but I have finally taken in the message sent by Ricky, Munch, and many others: I am not a boy. Being with the boys is about doing, about movement and freedom, about, yes, having balls. Part of me will always be a tomboy, will always value what that allowed me: freedom to explore, move, and play. But I want more than that. Being with the girls is less direct, more mysterious, softer, seductive. I like being one of the girls.

I like being one of the girls.
I like being one of the girls.
I like being one of the girls.
I like being one of the girls.

"Are you a boy or a girl?" a friend of Alice demanded when she joined us in the backyard to play. I remember what I was wearing: jeans, cowboy boots, a red plaid flannel shirt. My short blonde hair was cut in a bowl. I wanted to sock her, because I knew the clock was ticking. We had to go to school the next year and girls wore dresses in school. There was a principal who paddled. Boys would look at your underpants when you hung by your knees on the bars. The playground had a boys' side and a girls' side. On the boys' side was basketball and softball; on the girls' side was jacks.

I was right about school: it was a version of church. I rebelled in small ways: wore black basketball high-tops with my dresses, played sports, took riding lessons, created a fantasy world where I was the hero of my own life.

—Linda Niemann, from "Are You a Boy or a Girl?"

TOMBOY
by DIANNE KEUM
©95

HAVE YOU MADE A NEW YEAR'S RESOLUTION?
THIS YEAR I'M GOING TO WIPE OUT CRIME.
My hero.

DON'T YOU THINK YOU SHOULD BE MORE REALISTIC?

WHY DOES THIS MORTAL REFUSE TO ACKNOWLEDGE MY POWER?
I'M HERE TO DO GOOD!

WHY DON'T YOU RESOLVE TO CHANGE SOMETHING ABOUT YOURSELF?
I THINK I'M BEIN' INSULTED HERE.
Is that a crack?!

ONE MORE INSULT, AND I'M GONNA FLY AWAY.

MAYBE YOU SHOULD RESOLVE TO BE MORE FEMININE...
...YOU ARE A LITTLE GIRL, YOU KNOW.

UP, UP, AND AWAY!
Ya think she'd appreciate a superhero in the house!
HAVE A SUPER NEW YEAR!

Easy Bake

Tracy Alderman

"How old is he?" asked a middle-aged woman wearing a yellow paisley dress. Her matching yellow beehive bounced on her head as she pointed her mood-ringed finger in my direction. Apparently, she was in a yellow mood.

My mother leaned against the picnic table and followed the woman's point to my returning stare. The GI Joes arranged in combat position between my knees were at a standstill, peace talks occurring as I waited for my mother to respond. This was not the first time, nor would it be the last. I always enjoyed the expression on the stranger's face when Mom would proudly announce that I was a she, her *daughter,* and definitely — without question — not a he. The stranger's face would contort with embarrassment and disgust. No longer was I a cute little blond kid kneeling on the park grass playing with my favorite toys. In their eyes, with the addition of one little *s* in front of a *he,* I had become a traitor, an embarrassment to little girls everywhere, a rebel threatening the existence of Betty Crocker Easy-Bake ovens across the world.

I watched as the yellow woman, lips pursed, strolled back to her table, where a young brunette in a plaid skirt was busy unpacking a white wicker picnic basket. Through my bangs, I watched as the yellow woman delivered the news that I was, in fact, a little girl. Though I could not actually hear the brunette's response, from past experience I could surmise that her red-painted lips formed words like "Shocking!" or "How dreadful!" or "Poor little girl." And even then, as a naive five-year-old, I realized that my preference for jeans, t-shirts, and war toys disturbed some people. At the same time, like most five-year-olds, I didn't care at all what strange women with towers of hair clinging to their heads might think. All I cared about at that moment was sitting on the soft grass in comfortable clothes and staging the biggest battle of all time, a battle that would leave no survivors.

"Mom!" I shouted through the mouthpiece of my police action megaphone. "Mom!" I sat on the pea green carpet in my room, waiting for a response to my calls. Nothing. I only wanted to know when we would be eating. I had fought hundreds of battles and several world wars since lunch and I was starving. "Mom!" Still no reply. Impatient, I stomped down the hall and followed the sound of my mother's voice to the kitchen.

Standing unnoticed just outside the kitchen doorway, I adopted my best GI Joe attitude and planned a commando attack on Mom. The plan was simple: I would ambush her, wrap myself around her legs, and hug her until she surrendered and served me dinner. Even my special combat-edition GI Joe with kung fu grip and live action sound could not have come up with a better strategy.

I gripped the gold shag rug of the hallway with my toes, silently awaiting the right moment to attack. I didn't want to interrupt Mom's telephone conversation — expert commandos are trained to be courteous, particularly during sneak attacks.

"Can you believe she just walked up to me and said that?" My mother's voice escaped the confines of the kitchen. "What could I say? I was in shock. The nerve of her telling me how to dress my own daughter!" Mom's words drifted through my mind, losing meaning as I concentrated on my mission. Anticipating a break in the flow of her speech, I simply maintained my position, eager for the pending attack.

"What are you saying? I can't believe that you agree with her! She's *five*. What difference does it make?" I listened to Mom softly mutter, "Uh-huh," a few times before I heard the sound I had been anxiously awaiting: the click of the receiver being placed in its cradle. Screaming as I stormed the room (all good soldiers scream when they attack), I wrapped myself around Mom's legs. Even Commando Joe would have been proud of this assault.

Mom rested her hand on my head and, with both exasperation and amusement, said, "Ready for dinner?"

Smiling, I looked up and nodded, eager to celebrate the success of my latest mission with a victory meal.

Tired from a day of world wars, peace talks, and the repeated resurrection of mortally wounded soldiers, I lay in bed wearing my favorite cowboy pajamas, hugging my favorite teddy bear, Barry, and waiting for Mom to tuck me in.

Mom came in bearing a package in her hand and a strange expression on her face. Throwing the covers aside, I bounced to the edge of the bed, anxious to discover the mystery in the corn-colored box, as well as the meaning behind my mother's softened, almost sad, blue eyes.

"What's this?" I asked, eagerly grabbing the gift from my mother's extended hands.

"It's for you," she replied.

"A present! What is it?" Excited, I forgot my commando training and tore open the package without waiting for a response. Inside the ochre package were two smaller, silver boxes. The first was the size of a shoe box, perhaps a bit smaller. My anticipation quickly turned to disappointment when I flipped open the mirror-like lid. Why was Mom giving this to me? Was it a mistake? Had it been meant as a gift for my cousin Betty? Trying to hide my disappointment, I pulled Hollywood Barbie from her coffinlike box and began to inspect her. She wore a silver evening gown covered with clear sequins, and draped around her neck was a wispy white boa. She had matching sequined shoes — high heels, of course — and a simple but elegant glittering silver purse, presumably for her makeup and other essential items.

I gently placed Barbie beside me on the bed and stared at my toes, pondering a response.

"Thanks, Mom," I whispered.

I peeled open the lid of the second silver box much more hesitantly than I had the first. A glaring sight greeted me: a dress, pink with white polka dots. I pulled the dress from the box and held it in front of me, as far away as possible. White lace strangled the neckline and gripped the hem. Hoping with all of my five-year-old might that it would at least be the wrong size, I checked the tag. No such luck: it was my size exactly. What was going on? Why was Mom giving me these things? Drained by confusion and disappointment, I gently laid the dress back in its box, sunk back on my bed, and clutched Barry to my chest.

Clueless as to what had just taken place and even more so as to how I was supposed to respond, I simply repeated myself. "Thank you, Mom."

"I thought it was time for you to have these. You're getting to be quite a young lady." My mother's voice was stern.

I did not understand any of this. I was only five; I didn't want to be a young lady. I wanted to be partners with GI Joe, great soldiers fighting for peace, justice, and fun. As confused as I was, I knew one thing for sure: soldiers did not wear dresses — especially pink ones.

"Why don't you try it on?"

I rolled on my side, away from Mom, trying to find cover from the incoming fire. I had been ambushed.

I had been ambushed

"C'mon, try it on." Mom patted my behind, urging me to sit up.

"I don't want to. I'm tired." I put a pillow over my head to try to buttress my fort.

My mother peeled the pillow from my head and sat me up. She held the dress against my chest and repeated herself, this time a bit more forcefully. "Try it on." She meant business.

I reluctantly stood up, dropping Barry to the floor in the process.

"I think you'll look very pretty in this." Mom's enthusiasm sounded forced.

I responded with a growl. Mom handed me the dress. Her impatience was becoming obvious. There would be no way out of this. I was going to have to try on that pink thing.

"Wait," I said, and handed her back the dress. "I need to fix something." I walked across the room and knelt on the floor. One by one, I picked up my GI Joes and turned them so that they faced the wall. I couldn't let them see me this way. They wouldn't understand. Soldiers don't ever wear dresses. If they saw me in this dress, I couldn't be a soldier anymore.

I ordered them to stay in position, to not turn around. Looking for guidance, I pulled the string on my special combat-edition GI Joe's chest. "We're being attacked. Get ready for battle," he declared.

I stood and faced my mom. This was a battle I knew I couldn't win.

"You looked very pretty." Mom gently kissed my forehead and tenderly tucked the soft blue blanket under my feet. She stooped to pick the crumpled dress from the floor, then walked to the closet and hung it up. It dangled tenuously between my jean jacket and my green sweatshirt.

"I didn't know this was in here," Mom said, more to herself than to me. She reached in and took something from the top shelf: her old baseball glove. She stood gently stroking the soft leather for a moment, then whispered good night and slipped out, taking the mitt with her.

I stared up into the darkness of my room. I felt as though I were being dragged by the ankles down a long dark hallway. I seemed to glimpse, through an open door, Barbie's sequined shoes dancing by their own volition, moved by some invisible source. A second door revealed a room of pink camouflage, in which a battalion of Barbies wearing white wedding gowns stood at attention, each cradling a hand grenade in white-gloved hands. In another room, two crew-cut Barbies clad in green jungle fatigues hugged each other, their faces dotted red with perfect lip-shaped marks. Across the hall stood several life-sized GI Joes wearing pink, polka-dotted dresses, machine guns slung like purses over their perfectly muscled shoulders. Slowly, I stumbled into sleep, my mind continuing to search open doors for a more soothing, more familiar scene.

"Get up, honey." Mom stood above me, her blue eyes glistening in the sunlight that streamed through the gap in my curtains.

Wiping sand from the corners of my eyes, I blinked rapidly, struggling to focus. "What time is it?"

"It's early."

I was awake enough now to see the silver cake pan cradled in my mother's left arm.

She smiled at my puzzled look. "Bakers always get up early. And today, we've got some baking to do."

I hesitantly rolled from my bed, wondering if I'd have to wear that hideous pink dress in order to bake. Following my mother down the hallway toward the kitchen, I noticed that her walk was free and full of life. It reminded me of the women I'd seen in television commercials mopping the floor or serving a meal to a happy family. Half expecting to see Betty Crocker herself standing by the stove, I entered the kitchen wide-eyed and anxious, dreading the endless possibilities of Mom's new interest in domesticity.

As Mom opened the enameled avocado door of the oven, its heat brushed my cheeks and I took a step back. Kneeling down next to me, Mom slung one arm over my shoulder and smiled, seemingly aware of my mounting confusion.

"I'm sorry," she said in a tone so genuine and so gentle that I wanted to cry. "I want you to have the honors." She reached up to the counter and magically produced the box containing both Barbie's casket and the spotted dress.

Joy and excitement replaced my confusion. Soon, the sound of our giggles flooded the room, drowning Barbie and her perpetually painted smile beneath waves of laughter.

Barbie lay in the nine-by-twelve silver pan, resting comfortably on her pyre of pink, polka-dotted cotton. She seemed content, almost thoughtful. Perhaps she was contemplating her upcoming prom, wondering which gown would best complement Ken's tuxedo. This is how I best remember Barbie, smiling in the four-hundred-degree heat, beads of moisture glistening on her brow, as serene as if this were just another day at the beach.

just another day at the beach

Forced to leave our house by the overwhelming — and possibly toxic — stench of the baking Barbie, Mom and I sat in a brown booth at Denny's, silently scanning the breakfast menu. We had worked up quite an appetite.

"And what will he be having?" asked the blonde, middle-aged waitress. She was wearing a dress remarkably similar to the one that lay back home, imprisoned in a pool of melted pink plastic.

Ignoring her question, my mom reached into her purse, pulled out my favorite toy, and placed it on the Formica table. Smiling, I grabbed the special combat-edition GI Joe (with kung fu grip and live action sound) from the table and held him in my lap. I pulled the string on his chest and out boomed his crackling voice: "We're being attacked. Get ready for battle."

The waitress smiled sourly. "I'll come back when you're ready."

Mom and I grinned at each other, knowing that the battle was over and that we had escaped, unharmed and victorious.

Balls and hoops and cutting the ice — for me, that's what tomboys were made of.

I became a tomboy at the ripe age of seven — in private school in upstate New York, playing speedball every afternoon on the athletic field. That was my first experience playing a team sport. And my teammates always included my two closest friends: Gerry and Zacky. We were a deadly threesome in any competition, on or off the playing field. We always won! I played center, Zacky played wing, and Gerry was the best halfback this side of the Hudson, with the kick to prove it. Interestingly, I never heard the word *tomboy* while attending private school, and certainly not in reference to us. We were, after all, the top athletes on a winning team. For us, the rough-and-tumble games we engaged in every day after school were simply natural. It was natural to boot a soccer ball as hard and as fast as we could to score a winning goal; to shoot an arrow from a bow and hit a bull's-eye; to swing from the limb of a tree or, on a swing, to swing as high as the crossbar so as to be able to flip over; to run baton races and sprints so fast that no one could keep up with us; to swim as quick as a fish; to peg a ball around the bases so fast that no runner could be called safe. And always faster, harder. Winning was our goal — being the best athlete; the most competitive; the toughest; and a good sport, win or lose. That's what being a tomboy was all about. Every tomboy that I grew up with thrived on that competitive edge. For us, the whole world rested on these tenets: Play ball! Play fair! And win!

At age nine, unfortunately, I had to leave the private school and my two closest friends, and go to live with family and relatives. It was my first experience out in the real world, and it was

difficult. Before, I had been rewarded for my speed, agility, and athletic skills. My peers esteemed me and liked me and I was always a top choice when we divided into teams. Now all of that changed. My family and relatives were not at all accepting of me and my tomboy ways. And among my new classmates, friends were few and far between. It was then that I first heard the word *tomboy,* and it was in reference to me.

At first, when others called me a tomboy, I liked it. I said my new name over and over in my head: *Tomboy ... Tom boy ... tomboy, tomboy, tomboy*. I thought it suited me just fine — until I discovered that people meant it in a negative way. I was terribly confused. I liked being called a tomboy. And I liked being a tomboy — why, I could almost fly! In everything I did, I felt such grace and agility and strength — and power. I felt so powerful mastering my body in space winging a fastball or finishing a race or beating all of the other kids — boys included — in every game that we played. What could anyone possibly conclude was wrong with my being a tomboy?

– TP. Catalano, from "Tomboy: The Original Gender-Bender"

A Player

Kate Stoll

There I was, PF Flyers laced, ready to race out the back door and straddle my new glistening gold 1971 Schwinn with the high chrome sissy bar, baseball glove dangling from the handlebars. I was anticipating a great game today and the clock was keeping me from it, ticking off the last five minutes of the half hour way too slowly. Though it was summer and the day had begun hours earlier, I wasn't allowed out of the house to commit juvenile havoc in the neighborhood until 8:30 a.m. This rule was put into effect because I had a habit of bolting out of the house at 7:00 a.m. and waking up all my friends' parents by banging on their doors, looking for someone to play with. My three older siblings never had this rule, lacking as they did any sense of adventure or fun.

I lived on the middle of the three blocks that constituted Arlington Avenue. No one worth any playing value lived at the north end of the street, on either side. The only fun lay to the south. Running out my back door as the minute hand reached six, I hopped on my bike, yelled bye to my mom, and pedaled standing up to Glenn's house, three doors south, my first stop on the potential-playmate route.

Glenn was eleven, a year older than I, and, some said, the better athlete. Rather than being a cause of jealousy between us, though, our mutual athleticism bound us, made us best friends. In the summer I would spend the night at his house twice a week and we would stay up until the morning hours, playing with our Hot Wheels, sorting our baseball cards, or watching television. It didn't matter to his parents that we left the house at 7:00 a.m. Glenn rarely spent the night at my house: we had to turn the television off when the news came on, and the lights out soon after. Sometimes, I didn't want to spend the night at my house, either.

Glenn, who knew about my 8:30 rule, was usually at his back door waiting for me, but not today. I rapped on the aluminum door three times with my knuckles. That woke the south and the north ends of the street, not to mention Glenn's teenage sister, who came to the door blinking dazedly and yawning, retainer in mouth, and declared, "Glenn is at work with Dad."

I decided to quietly move out of her sight. If I was lucky, she might think my waking her was a dream.

Now I had to go knocking on the Hickmans' door all by myself. Shoot, I had already woken Glenn's sister — why not go for broke? The Hickmans' house had six kids to wake up.

I hopped onto my bike and sped out of Glenn's driveway, popping a wheelie at the first tar mark in the road and holding it twenty-five feet, until the next tar mark, breaking my record from the day before. Narrowly dodging stereophonic honks, I darted through the intersection and turned sharply into the Hickmans' driveway. No signs of activity.

I came to an abrupt stop with a short, sharp squeal that left little rubber. An all-star skid. Mr. Hickman would have lost more hair if he saw any trace of my tire tracks on his long clean driveway. As it was, the squeal probably gave him back spasms as he lay in bed.

I opened the gate to the Hickmans' backyard slowly and deliberately. I had learned not to knock immediately, but instead would peer through the screen door into the kitchen to see if anyone was awake before arousing the entire household. Today, my peering was rewarded: Doug was scooping the last spoonful of Cap'n

Crunch into his open mouth. All right! Someone to play catch with.

A skinny boy with bright red hair, freckles, and eyes big and white, Doug smiled as he glimpsed me through the door. Despite being two years younger than I, he was fun most of the time, full of energy and usually full of himself. He tried desperately to keep up with Glenn and me, always willing to do anything we asked of him. He enjoyed hanging out with us more than he did his own birthday. We slammed the gate shut and sped off on our bikes.

The next stop on the baseball tour was a quick ride: Brian and Steve Stuart, who were three and four years younger than I, lived next door to Doug and were just getting onto their bikes, baseball gloves and bats in hand. Success: I had now collected enough baseball players for a game, using criteria little less rigorous than a scout for the Chicago Cubs might use.

A game of hardball down at Lincoln Elementary School was what I had dreamt of the night before. Quickly, we pedaled to the field for a game of two on two. Pushing down our kickstands and setting our bikes on the warm blacktop, we stood looking over the cement playing field. This was the short field, where we usually played when the Stuarts were playing, because they were younger. Here I could hit the ball over the fence many times, whereas in the long field, I could hit, maybe, two or three a day. This is where Glenn had me beat. He could always pop the ball over the fence and into the street on either field.

Ten home runs later, with a win for Steve and me, we stopped and went to wet our whistles with Pepsis from the fire barn. Just a dime for sixteen whole chugable ounces of sweet carbonation.

The pop machine was located inside the fire barn, next to the recreation area for the firemen. To our pride, we knew some of them by name. Sometimes they would watch us play ball from across the street and impersonate Jack Brickhouse, the television announcer for the Cubs. Other times they would be off saving cats or putting out fires, leaving the fire barn vacant. Then it was our duty to protect the large red brick structure while they were out.

The sun was pushing up the mercury today. I downed two pops. After a few burps from the gang, we cruised to our respective homes to eat. After my bologna sandwich, I went back to Glenn's house, where he was now waiting for me. Hopping onto the back of my bike, he held on dearly to my sissy bar, for he knew I was Evel Knievel on a Schwinn. We soared over the curb and off to the second half of our double-header.

Spotting Pete Jensen in his backyard, we stopped to recruit him. The Stuart boys couldn't play with us in the afternoon, so Pete would round out our team.

A year younger than I, Pete was a nice boy with a great laugh. He was playing with his older sister Ruth, with whom I was also friends. She was Glenn's age. Glenn and I cruised up their driveway, and pretty soon Julie from across the street came over. Glenn asked Pete if he wanted to play ball with us and Doug. Before Pete could answer, Ruth shouted, "I want to play too."

"No!" Glenn barked. Usually no one messed with him.

Knowing he had Glenn's support, Pete talked back to his sister. "You can't play with us."

"We can play every bit as good as you guys can," said Julie, glaring into my eyes.

They could, too. I spoke up: "If Ruth and Julie don't play, neither do I."

Glenn and Pete looked stunned. The girls looked at me happily. Knowing he couldn't disagree with me, Glenn suggested that we play pickle instead. Pickle it was. The girls decided they didn't want to play after all. Glenn turned his smirk in my direction as he claimed his small victory over the girls and me.

After a few rounds of pickle, Glenn and Pete took off their shirts and suggested we get a drink at Doug's while we rustled him up to play more baseball. Taking off my sweaty Cubs shirt and tucking a wad of it in my back pocket, I sprinted over the sidewalk and into Doug's yard, neck and neck with Glenn, who touched the Hickmans' gate barely ahead of me. He happily chided me for not being as fast as he was. I just smiled at my friend as he opened the gate for me. Pete came in a distant third, laughing, and shut the gate behind him.

While Doug finished his lunch, we drank from his hose and rested before the next game. Sweat trickled down my sides and back as, baseball cap soaked with sweat and dusted with dirt, I stretched out in the shade of the Hickmans' oak tree and drifted off into a fantasy while the guys talked about the upcoming game. There I was: standing in the on-deck circle at Wrigley Field, waiting in my pinstripes for my turn at bat behind Ernie Banks. I *was* a professional baseball player. Then *bang!* Just as I was hitting in the winning run, the Hickmans' screen door slammed, jolting me out of my fantasy.

I looked up to see a stern Mrs. Hickman, hands on hips, taking a good look at us three bare-chested youngsters. She hesitated for a long time, collecting her thoughts. What was she going to say? Were we in trouble? Was I in trouble for waking Mr. Hickman? Suddenly her sharp voice rang out: "Laura, put your shirt back on. You are not a boy. What would your mother say? Girls don't play baseball."

I was stunned. Not a boy! Who said I was? I was just a hot and thirsty baseball player taking a break between innings. I had to act different because I was a girl? I thought I was just a kid, having a good time with friends and dreaming about playing in the big leagues.

The rest of the day was ruined for me. Too embarrassed to play with the boys anymore, I sadly pedaled home and changed into a clean red t-shirt, contemplating my existence as a girl. From the moment Mrs. Hickman stopped shouting at me, I knew things were going to be a lot different than I had ever imagined.

I was just a hot and thirsty baseball player taking a break between innings.

Girl

Catherine Houser

We all live in suspense, from day to day, from hour to hour; in other words, we are the hero of our own story.
—Mary McCarthy

I ripped the head off of the first and only doll I ever had. The arms and legs became projectiles aimed at the green plastic army men my brothers had lined up behind mounds of dirt. I wiped out whole platoons with the pudgy plastic arms and legs. I was two, and already I knew the lives my parents had created for my brothers, lives filled with baseball gloves, footballs, basketballs, and even little army guys, were far more fascinating than the "doll" life they were constructing for me.

girl, girl, girl ... you will never be enough...

At six, I started playing softball — only because it was 1962 and baseball was closed to me. I'd learned how to throw by throwing a baseball, not a softball, and how to hit by swinging at a ball half a softball's size coming at me twice as fast. But girls, no matter how good they were, were not allowed in baseball. By day, I played hardball with my brothers in the backyard, but evenings, I had to stretch my glove wide to take in a bigger, softer ball in games played on a crude field without lights behind the lighted diamond where my brothers were playing baseball. On our field of dreams, we had no Sandy Koufax or Mickey Mantle as a role model: all we had was each other.

At school, girls were required to wear dresses, which doomed us to games of jacks and hopscotch at lunchtime. By second grade, I'd figured out that if I wore a skirt and took a pair of shorts with me to school, at lunchtime I could slip on the shorts and whip off the skirt, freeing me to play football on the playground with the boys. At first, I was the only girl playing, but it didn't take long for the best athletes among us to catch on to the freedom that the skirt trick allowed us.

When I was eight, my mother sent me to the Wendy Ward Charm School to learn how to "walk like a girl."

girl ... you will never be enough...

Nights, I left my girl body frozen in terror in a sweaty bed. Mornings, I'd head out of the house, hungry, in search of my own power. I'd found salvation in hitting and throwing things. Survival instinct took me to the track field. At ten, I began throwing javelin and discus as a member of the Amateur Athletic Union. I carried a discus with me everywhere, molding my fingers around its edge, making its heavy weight mine. And the javelin, my spear, cut through the sky every afternoon. Then the night terror stopped, and, suddenly, at thirteen, I stopped too. I didn't quit: I just stopped. My obsession for throwing deadly objects receded, softballs notwithstanding. It wasn't until I was in my thirties that I understood the divine wisdom of my girl body: I couldn't throw the weight off of me at night, the weight that smothered and raped me, but for hours every afternoon I could heave it through the air, again and again, and even win medals and trophies for it.

girl ... never enough...

At eighteen, I was still playing fast-pitch softball, getting scouted for college scholarships. I bragged about it at a family dinner, how

I was still a contender while my brothers had gone to seed. My older brother threw me up against the wall in my mother's dining room, pinned me there, and said, "You think you're so strong and tough — what would you do if someone grabbed you like this, huh?" I struggled with my arms, but his hands slammed them back against the wall. Still not strong enough. But my legs, the legs that had carried me out of that house every morning onto fields of competition, came alive, and I laid him out with a knee in the balls. "I'd do that," I said. And that was the last time he touched me.

girl...

At twenty, I quit playing ball. I said out loud that it was because I needed to work two jobs through the summer to help pay for college, but inside I knew I had lost my heart for it. I had taken a pitch in the side that had cracked two ribs. I had come to like my face and I'd seen too many girls, including my sister, scarred for life by hard-hit grounders that had taken bad bounces and sliced open their young, pristine cheeks. I no longer had the courage to face a fastball and I'd begun pulling my head in at every pitch. At six, I was called Speedy Houser; at twelve, Grace. When, at twenty, my teammates started calling me Turtle for ducking pitches, I knew it was time to quit.

At twenty-one, a car wreck prompted my first knee surgery, and I got a glimpse of my future as a former tomboy lost in stories of my glory days. I began running as hard and as fast in the other direction as I could. As soon as I could, I got fitted with a heavy metal brace to help secure my knee, then took to the racquetball court and to water skis, feeding off of that tomboy power and strength I had developed as a girl.

...never enough...

By my midtwenties, I had begun running, and nothing short of serious illness could stop me. I'd competed in several 10K runs, a couple of biathlons, and a marathon before doctors discovered the

you will never be enough...

tumors silently growing in my neck. With a diagnosis and drugs, I felt that my body, so adept at fighting *against,* had begun to fight itself. Tumors crowded my larynx, and body memories from the incest tormented me. There were days I couldn't walk, nights I lost feeling in my arms. Feeling betrayed by my body, I betrayed it by becoming silent physically. Years passed with barely a bike ride or a ski trip interrupting the alienation campaign I was waging against my body.

From before I knew how to spell the word, I had identified myself as an athlete. Now, after years of dismissing as "childish" the power I'd found in that identity, I had come to feel, for the first time in my life, physically vulnerable. Night, on a Boston back street, all I could feel in my body was "victim": cancer — incest — victim.

girl ... never...

At thirty-eight, I found my voice and body in the same place I'd discovered them originally — on the ball field. With the first throw, I began to find my way back home, to the best of home, a home where I was free to feel secure and powerful. It has not been an easy journey. For the first time in my life, I am not the star of the team. I sit the bench at times, I bat low in the lineup, I constantly learn new lessons in humility. But I am there, shoulder to shoulder with girls who know what it is to feel strong and confident in the power of their bodies. We are girls again, fed by our own competence.

girl, girl, girl...

Recently, I sat in the bleachers watching my little sister (now thirty-six) play third base on a coed softball team. They have special rules, these coed teams: the batting lineup has to go boy, girl, boy, girl; the infield has to be divided equally between boys and girls; and if you walk a boy, the girl up next gets an automatic walk. I sit there watching the boys step in front of the girls to grab flies and infield grounders. Between innings I ask my sister, whose knees and face bear the scars of a lifetime's worth of snagging hard-hit balls, what's up with these screwy rules. She says, "It's 'cause we're girls." At the top of the next inning, a one-hop hit comes straight at my sister, and as she readies herself to grab it and go for the long throw to first, the boy playing shortstop cuts in front of her and takes it himself. She drops her head, stares at the ground, says nothing. When the inning is over, she comes running by me on her way to the bathroom. I follow her. She bends over and throws up until all that's left is bile.

...enough...

simply because she is a girl

The girl is tough. She has brothers and wants to be treated like them. She wants their independence and self-determination. Dresses and tights cannot bind her to a chair. She peels them from her body like layers of dead skin. At ten, she has her legs wrapped around a boy and has him pinned to the ground. He is suffering the worst humiliation, simply because she is a girl. Like her brothers, she wants acceptance and glory when she hits a home run or steals third base. Instead, she is forcibly dragged from center field, simply because she is a girl. She is the fastest, strongest, most athletic girl in the neighborhood. The kids admire her prowess and call her tomboy. The adults admit, "She'd show promise for a career in sports, if she were a boy." She is constantly proving herself, being tested, simply because she is a girl.

—Diana Le Blanc, from "Squeezing Ponytails into a Football Helmet"

Boy

Chaia Heller

At eleven,
I run with hair full of mud,
play war in the woods,
my P.O.W. bracelet
blazing on my wrist
like a medal. I am a boy
of the worst kind, small, skinny,
hard and hated, with softball
breasts pushing up
under striped button-downs.
And in their peace and love
t-shirts, real boys spit dirt,
sharpened whispers, and once,
an airplane, arcing crisp
white wings over rows of chairs,
nabs my back. Unfolded
it reads, *Lezzie, lezzie, thinks she's*
a boy, and I stare
hard at my P.O.W. bracelet,
think of the boy lost
in woods faraway, no mother
or friends, ducking bombs
and airplanes, how very hard it is
to be a boy.

Throwing Like a Girl

Chaia Heller

I want to tell you about throwing,
what it is, to be in sixth grade
on the blacktop behind school,
playing bombardment
with that big red ball,
when a boy shouts, *You think you're a tomboy*
but you throw like a girl.
I get him after school,
dig my work boots
right in his shins; I learn how
to make an impression.

Throwing like a girl
is underhanded.
Throwing like a girl is
where I belong.
Don't tell me
I throw like a girl:
I already know.

Throwing like a girl can be serious:
in high school, on my knees
before that hoop of pearl,
I whittle myself down

to the width of a line, hunger
a skill I master like geometry.
I am almost beautiful, all angle and proof,
clocking ten-minute miles
in my ten-year-old sister's shorts.
I throw my weight
around, it boomerangs back,
girls are never good at math
but we sure can subtract.

At eighteen,
straining muscles that shouldn't exist,
I pitch a brick
through the window
of my parents' living room.
Only, it's no brick:
just a sheet of yellow paper,
plain and wholesome
as elementary school.
That only a few words,
I am a lesbian,
could shatter a picture window,
shake the house down
to its very foundations.

That's what throwing like a girl
can do.

My father built this house,
pouring and shaping cement,
carving my mother's initials
into one slick gray block
with his finger. There is a picture
of the two of them standing
by the foundation, my father's foot
planted squarely on one tiny wall,

arm around my mother,
who is pregnant with me,
all curve and possibility.

My parents will have to build again.
They move like ghosts
through the rubble of their house,
questions of construction
carving deep lines across their foreheads.
I didn't mean to throw that brick,
to write that letter. In fact,
none of us do. That's what it is,
to throw like a girl: it comes so unnaturally,
we don't even know we have it in us.

You are throwing your life away,
my mother tells me
once a year, just for
good measure. And I say, yes,
I am throwing away my life,
like a pair of shoes too tight
for real dancing, like a pitcher's mitt
with no catch. I am throwing away my life,
tossing tiny stones into a dark pond at night.
I cannot see where I throw, but I know
there are ripples, eagerness, perfect
gliding rings that widen
with each toss. I know
I have made my watery mark.

Throwing like a girl is
what I do best. Throwing like a girl
is what I do. Yes, I know
I throw underhanded:
my aim may be bad
but it's true.

Getting Out

Louise A. Blum

My mother hits the brakes and pulls over. The side of the road is wide, gravel; the fields loom around us like a wasteland, no one in sight.

"Get out," she says.

I am seven years old. The field outside my car door is like hell, the Hades that my father talks about when he quotes the Old Testament. I look at her. Her eyes glitter at me, Nazi blue. "Get out," she says again.

The gravel from the shoulder whips into my face, flung from the tires as she speeds off. I watch her fade away. Around me, the field hums, caught in its solace. The sun beats down on my head. I think that I could grow to like it, this sanctuary that has been forced on me.

An hour later, she comes back. I am still there, eating grass. "Get in," she says, and I comply.

We drive in silence for a while, the fields rolling by.

"Well," she says. "Have you learned your lesson?"

I look out the window. The telephone poles flash by. Here and there, birds roost on the wires. Grasshoppers sing, frying in the sun where they sit, vigorously sawing. I imagine myself running alongside the car, effortlessly, full of breath, tireless, while the sun buoys me up like an inner tube. Beside me, my mother keeps her eyes on the road. Have I learned my lesson? Yes.

I glance over at her. Her profile in the sunlight is sharp, full of edges that sparkle in the light. Her hands are loose on the wheel. She has it together. She keeps the car on the road with a touch of her fingertips. "Pull over," I say. "Let me back out."

She keeps driving, her gaze steady on the road, but her knuckles are white. I sit back in my seat, eyes on the fields that flash past my window, satisfaction a small round presence in my stomach.

My mother runs a comb through my hair, parting the snarls as if they were jungle brush. She sighs, shakes her head. "So many wisps," she says. She pulls my hair back from my forehead with the teeth of the comb and examines my face in the mirror. My face is small and round and dark; small caverns dent my cheeks; the hair around my forehead is dark and wild, unruly. My mother sighs again, her lips pursing together in the mirror above my head like a too-tight stitch. "If I were you," she says, her voice tragic, resigned, "I'd have electrolysis done when I get older."

I am still seven years old. It's taking a long time, this growing up, and somewhere outside the window that field waits for me, its gentle curves stretching on forever.

My mother tells me I will never have a boyfriend. She is sitting on the side of my bed, putting me to sleep. "You'll be just like me," she says, rubbing my back beneath my shirt. "It's better to have small breasts. Really."

I do not ask why, just continue to lie with my face in the pillow, concentrating on breathing evenly, in and out, like the bellows that my father sometimes pumps the fire with. Her hand rubs my back in smooth, even circles till she gets distracted; then it rests on my body like an anvil, growing heavier by the second.

"You're so thin," she says. I can hear the distraction in her voice, like she's about to float up and bump against the ceiling. "Men don't like their women thin."

I breathe as slowly as I can, in and out, in and out, take breaths only when they're absolutely necessary. I pretend they cost money. Protect them, save them, dole them out only on occasion. Perhaps she'll think I'm dead, draw the sheet slowly up across my face, leave the room, leave me in peace. I go limp in the darkness of the room, as slack as the corpses I have seen on television.

But she has recommenced with the rubbing. There is no escape. This is our together time, hers and mine. Necessary time, like a jail sentence. Someday I'll get out, break loose and float off into the sky like a helium balloon, drift over an ocean and spiral gently down into the waves.

Her hand pauses; her fingers scrape my skin. I tense despite myself. "Your skin has little balls on it," she says, shaking them from her fingers in distaste. "I don't know what's wrong with you."

I lie in the darkness after she has left, close my eyes and think about my distant field, salted with dandelions, circled by hawks, dotted here and there with trees whose trunks when I embrace them are so thick my fingers do not meet.

My mother tells me I'll never have a boyfriend, but when I see Johnny Martin across the playground at the beginning of third grade I know that he's the one. I don't even say anything to him, just start running, picking up speed all the way across the rock-hard pavement. When I get to him, I leap and grab him around his waist. My momentum carries us both into the chain-link fence that holds us in; the clang brings the other kids running. They surround us as I straddle him, hold him tight between my thighs and press my mouth to his, ignoring the blood that is dripping from the scrapes on my elbows, just holding him to the ground and kissing him the way I've seen on TV. The kids around us chant and cheer, but I ignore them, just go on kissing Johnny. He kisses back.

They make us dissect frogs in seventh grade. Sherry's frog is pregnant: black eggs spill like caviar across the wax paper spread along the tables. Sherry has to leave the room. I feel sick, but I cannot take my eyes away. The teacher lets me stay after school to dissect the leftover frogs. I line their organs up, use their eyes to magnify a line of print. I feel things coming together, making sense. The scalpel in my hand feels like it belongs there. I tell my mother with a sense of confidence, a sense of wonder. "I want to be a doctor," I say. "I know that I can do it. I know that it is what I want to do."

She is kneading bread on the kitchen counter; she has flour on her arms, across her face. She is concentrating: fold, push, turn, fold, push, turn. Her hair is pulled back from her face. The flesh on her upper arms is loose, flaps away from the bone that stands out all over her beneath the skin. She doesn't look at me, just keeps on kneading. Her concentration blocks me out. "I always thought you'd make a good secretary," she says, flouring her dough, pinning it to the counter with the heels of her hands. "With your grades," she says.

I choose auto mechanics instead. I like the cars: I like to lift their hoods and peer into their engines, touch my fingers to their grease, feel it like acid on my tongue when I lick my lips by accident, listen to their hum, diagnose their illnesses.

I go out with Johnny Martin all the way through high school. We wear leather jackets and smoke cigarettes under the pine trees out behind the vocational school, smoke joints in his room at night under his black light, surrounded by Dead posters. He has long black hair and half-shut eyes. When he touches me, his fingers flow like lines of poetry. I think I have made him this way. I think he is lucky I chose him, kicked his legs out from under him one afternoon in elementary school, straddled him, and taught him how to love me while the wind whipped around us like a flag.

Senior year, Johnny breaks up with me for a while, starts seeing someone else, a slender girl with a long neck and a doe's eyes and light brown hair that falls down her back like a tapestry. Dawn's a junkie who wears leather miniskirts and a choke collar, but her eyes are full of fear, her face open, breaking, like her name. Her lips are raw from the pull of her teeth. When I look at her, something stirs in my gut. I have no name for it. I go over to her house one night when I know that Johnny is out with his buddies, racing their motorbikes in some dark part of town. It's a guy thing: he never took me, either. Dawn takes me up to her room; we sit on the bed and share a bowl, listen to the Moody Blues with the door shut and her parents downstairs with the television on, Archie Bunker's voice a whining rasp through the floor. She doesn't protest when I touch her face, doesn't say a word when I pull her toward me across the bed, touch her slender thighs with my fingers, push her skirt up toward her waist.

She's the best thing that has ever happened to me. She is light and dark and every color in between. She is like a rainbow between my hands; her face when I make her come is the face of an angel, lifted in transport, poised in prayer. She stretches her hands to the sides of the bed, arches her back, and hangs on. Her tongue touches the corner of her mouth and she closes her eyes, her lashes velvet on her cheeks. We do not have to talk. Her need is naked, enormous. It hangs between us, fills the air. It is all I have to know of her.

We spend hours together; she's always stoned, but she's pliable. Johnny's pissed, but so it goes. It's the parents that make the real scene. We keep it a secret for a while, make muffled love with the door closed and the radio on. But one night I have my head between her legs, probing her cunt with my tongue. Dawn is lying on her back, her legs spread wide, and when I look up at her, she has her arm between her teeth, to keep herself quiet. This only excites me more: I run my tongue along her clitoris, plunge three fingers deep inside her. I come with her hand nowhere near me, I come in a long and shuddering rush that makes me gasp, makes the room revolve around me while with my fingers I work her orgasm like I'm tuning up an engine valve. None of it seems real; we're not even on the planet anymore. I watch as, as if in slow motion, Dawn bites down too hard on her arm and nearly breaks the skin, jerks it away from her mouth, and screams as if her soul were leaving her body, a series of screams that spill out of her like heartbeats and reverberate against the walls, fill the room, overflow and echo down the stairs, swelling through the house, bursting its seams, and we can hear the footsteps running toward us but we cannot stop, my fingers have taken on a life of their own, I keep pumping, pumping, pumping, and Dawn is gasping, moaning, her body moving like the beat of a song. It's out of our control: her left arm sweeps across her nightstand and knocks off everything on it — her clock, her birth control pills, her books, her junk — all crashing to the floor as she reaches for the bedpost and squeezes it till it seems that it will break, the teeth marks stark in her flesh like a brand, while in one sudden movement the door is flung open and I bury my head in her cunt, hoping I will disappear, hoping it will take me in, suck me deep inside where I really want to go, swallow me forever.

It's a compromising position.

"Jesus Christ," her father says. Dawn opens her eyes, sees him frozen in the doorway like an ice sculpture, and kicks me in the teeth without thinking, pushing herself to a sitting position. "Get out of here," her father says to me. I back away from the bed, checking to see if my jaw is still intact, wait for Dawn to say something, but she only brings her knees up to her chest and hides her face in her hands, covers herself with her hair, silver in the half-light coming in from the hall.

It's a compromising position.

"Listen," I say, but her father cuts me off, orders me out of the house.

"Get out," he says. "You pervert." I make myself as tall as I can as I go past him out the door, summon all my body to me, but he does not look at me. His eyes are on his daughter, sobbing into her hands as if her heart will break. She doesn't look at me either; no one says another word. I walk down the stairs with this silence like blue light all around me; the house seems to be filling with it, slowly, freezing out the breath, obscuring everything from view. I open the front door and let myself out, walk down the driveway to my truck, and open the door with fingers that shake, still wet with her come, fingers that can barely fit themselves around the key that will get me out of here, get me away. I feel a gun at my back. I don't breathe again until I'm on the road.

My mother is hanging up the phone when I walk into the kitchen. A fresh loaf of bread lies cooling on a wire rack on the counter. A warm breeze ripples the curtains at the window above the sink. My mother turns to face me, her hand still on the receiver; her breathing is hard and fast. Her eyes hold me at knifepoint. "You," she says, spitting it out like bad milk. "You disgust me."

I walk to the counter, making myself breathe evenly, take up the bread knife and cut myself a piece of bread with hands still shaking, don't look at her as I take the butter from the refrigerator door. "Incidentally," I say, smoothing butter on the warm bread I hold in the palm of my hand, "you're right. I'll never have a boyfriend." I take a bite, force myself to chew with even bites. It's like trying to eat a matchbook, but I keep chewing anyway; when I swallow, I feel my tonsils, rigid as bouncers standing there with folded arms, protecting my esophagus. I wear my nonchalance like butter: I am greased with it. "Never again, at least," I say. I make myself look at her: she is standing perfectly still by the phone, her face tight as a wire. Her cheeks look as if they will break. I look straight at her, straight at the blue-ice eyes. "No man will ever be enough again."

My mother slaps my face, but I slap her back, leave the imprint of my hand white on her flushed cheek. Slapping her feels like God. It feels bigger than I am. It feels like everything I live for, everything I am inside.

She throws me out of the house, and I throw my bag in the truck I bought from Johnny's dad. "Don't come back," she says.

"Don't worry," I say, "I'm out of here." I turn the key in the ignition; the engine fires like the answer to a prayer, the gearshift in my hand moving smooth as salvation. I pull out of her driveway so fast I burn rubber turning onto the road. I drive first to Dawn's house, but her parents don't let me in. It pisses me off, but she doesn't exactly come running out to greet me. I stand in the yard and yell up to her window, but the blinds are drawn and the curtains are still. I think her parents might have killed her, but just before I leave, I glance in the rearview mirror. Her window is open, just a little: she is watching me go. I touch the horn, wave out the window, leave her in her bedroom, where I imagine she is shooting up. We all do what we have to.

I go to Johnny's and we drive out to the river, sit there and smoke some hash his brother brought back from Vietnam. The smoke hits my brain like a machete cutting a swath through a jungle. We lean back on the bank and touch hands in the grass. All around us the trees are waving like regretful generals; the river sings its solace from the shadows. We take a map from my glove compartment, close our eyes, and touch down with a finger. Johnny brushes the hair back out of my eyes, kisses my mouth. He gives me the rest of the hash and all the money he has.

I make good choices.

I squeeze his hand before I leave, fill up the bowl and lay the pipe on the seat beside me, take off slow down the road with the radio on low and the sun setting behind me. I don't look back at him. I keep my eyes on the road: there's a field in the distance. I know I'll get to it.

I make good choices.

Mom tries to control me by controlling my reading. I like to curl up in the armchair in the corner of the living room by the fireplace and read. I get lost in stories. *Jane Eyre, Little Women, Little Men, Anne of Green Gables* — these are my favorites. I also like animal stories. The library is just a block away. I go there almost every day, because Mom doesn't like to see me reading after school — when, she says, I should be playing with other girls — and has limited me to checking out only two books at a time. She gave the librarians a note. Words on paper are powerful. Planted next to the library is a jacaranda tree. It blooms with purple blossoms every year. It is the most beautiful thing I know.

–Henri Bensussen

She preferred the freedom of the outdoors. When the league diamonds were occupied with teams, she would pedal her purple Schwinn far away, feeling the dusty hot wind on her face and a gratifying, pleasant ache in her calf muscles. She hated sitting inside the house on hot summer afternoons. Even reading a Nancy Drew mystery was more enjoyable when she was perched in her favorite black cherry tree in a fork high above the ground.

—Susan M. Hafner, from "Not the Only One"

In Some Shining Moments

Kris A. Billhardt

My rage was blind and immediate. It arose in my gut and swiftly dispatched corpuscular messengers, drunk with adrenaline, to all battle stations. Heeding the call, I lunged at my sister with the fury of an injured beast: I had been shot again with her most powerful weapon, her twelve-gauge taunt, and, as usual, she would pay dearly.

Quickly, Lisa backed toward the twin bed that was her fortress, scrambling to assume what she felt was her best defensive position. Diving between her wildly kicking legs, I clutched the front of her red turtleneck sweater. She answered by frantically clawing my bare arms with pink-polished, treacherous talons. Straddling her, I pinned her arms with my knees, rendering her deadly fingernails useless, and raised my fist in warning above her terrified eleven-year-old freckled face. I had her now, and I savored the sweet intoxicant of my victory, righteously prolonging her captivity. But, suddenly, inspired or desperate, she realized that her best weapon was still at her disposal, and she fired with savage relish:

"You're a girl! You're a girl!"

"Girl! Girl!"

"Shut up! Shut up!" I roared back at her, clamping my hand over her mouth to silence this blasphemous outpouring. Ever willing to violate the code of honor, however, she bit my hand, forcing me to release her odious mouth. Thus freed, she screamed with all the air left in her defiant lungs, *"Mo-om!"*

Which, of course, was the beginning of the end of my vengeance, though I managed to get the last word in before our mother entered the fray:

"Chicken! You big fat scaredy-cat chicken!"

I was nine, and though physically stronger than my big sister, I lacked the intellectual prowess to convince my mother that my sister did, indeed, deserve to die for her offenses: Lisa is alive today thanks only to my mother's infuriating beneficence.

It was the 1960s, in the newly developing New Jersey suburbs. I had no language with which to describe the difference I felt, but, clearly, I was different from most of the girls I knew. I knew that, anatomically, I was not a boy. But when I looked around me at the neighborhood kids, my schoolmates, and my three sisters, my being a girl didn't quite compute. I was more like my brother than like those strange creatures whose interests bored me to tears. If I had to be one or the other, why, I'd have to be crazy to be a girl!

Years later, when I read of "penis envy," I chuckled, remembering a time when I demanded that my family see me as a boy— or at least pretend to. I did not want a penis. I did want short hair, never to wear another dress, all the latest *Man from U.N.C.L.E.* paraphernalia, and Emma Peel. And though my stubbornly evolving dyke self suffered occasional indignities, I managed to get much of what I needed, including broad leeway in how my identity was allowed to form and manifest. Luckily for me, my immediate family developed a kind of noncondemning (if not exactly jubilant) understanding toward this daughter. That she wore pajamas, never nightgowns. That her Saturday chore would be mowing the lawn rather than vacuuming and ironing. And that, if she didn't come when called for dinner, she could be found at a neighborhood baseball game, not a Barbie doll conclave.

In retrospect, I also recognize that essential to my survival was a quiet, private, inner knowing that many of my aspirations could be fulfilled, but that such fulfillment must be deferred for now. I know little about where this wisdom came from, for I certainly never had discernible guidance or coaching. Maybe it came from an occasional role model (my muscled junior high gym teacher, my forever-unmarried ninth-grade English teacher) or perhaps from my observations that, even in my small part of the world, there were others like me, tomboys: girls who built forts in the woods, did daredevil stunts on their bikes, and rejoiced when the school board decided that we could wear pants to school. Wherever this abiding comfort came from, I did not despair often: I knew that there was a place for me, and that I would one day find it.

Meanwhile, however, Old Farm Road held no shortage of its own brand of suburban jungle adventure. Sometimes, particularly on long, boring, hot, sticky summer vacation days, I had to seek it out, create it. And I did — in the skeletal beginnings of a new housing development, where we found and smoked cigarette butts left by the construction workers. Or in the unlocked twelve-passenger plane that sat for one glorious week on the runway of the local airport: I biked there every day that week with my cousin Tami and played at being a spy, Ilya Kuryakan to Tami's Napoleon Solo.

Sometimes, though, adventure found me, dared me, with one beckoning finger, to find in myself the resources to meet its challenge. Such adventures doubled as rites of passage in my development of a butch lesbian identity, serving as signposts pointing the way to that place where I knew, one day, I would live.

The Cedarbrook Gang was a tightly knit, martially minded group of older boys who lived on Cedarbrook Road, the nearest cross street to my own. By today's standards, the word *gang* would hardly apply, but in our day, those six or seven kids were trouble from the word *duh* (bright they were not). Too old to "play" anymore, and too young to be working or dating, they were bored and restless, and they collectively discovered that there was considerable entertainment value in terrorizing the younger kids in the neighborhood.

To us, they were enormous, hulking, ancient. Their preadolescent presence introduced caution and watchfulness to the innocence of our full-tilt play: they were bullies. They ridiculed and taunted us, and they were known to physically hurt those they could catch. We respected this fact of life: we avoided them, left if they showed up, hoping to ensure our safety by never crossing their path. But sometimes they left us no choice but to take our chances against them...

They were bullies

It was Halloween. The night was to order: dark, spooky. I was walking home, full of a sense of mystery fueled by imagination and exaggerated by an absolute lack of vision inside the sweaty dime-store plastic mask I had been wearing for three hours. My little sister Bonnie walked distractedly beside me as she rifled through her trick-or-treat bag, blissfully examining her loot. We were exhausted, but we had an enormous haul. Bonnie had come with me because I was the best and fastest in the family, as proven by the candy count we did each year. We had thoroughly scoured the neighborhood.

Suddenly, I saw a half dozen figures coming toward us, and I realized we were on Cedarbrook Road. I quickened the pace. We were so close to home; soon we'd be safe in the warmth of our living room, making ourselves happily nauseated eating "just one more, Mom!" I listened to my instincts and moved to the other side of the road, but so did the gang. I inched closer to Bonnie, whispering, "Shhh!" trying not to scare her but wanting to be ready to signal her to run. The boys were only feet away now, and they were laughing at our costumes, guffawing wickedly, coming menacingly close. We walked straight ahead, eyes fixed on the road, hearts pounding. Just at the moment we were finally, safely past them, unharmed, gulping air in relief, one of them turned and grabbed Bonnie's bag!

enormous
hulking
ancient

She instantly started crying. Hearing her whimper, I resolved to split my candy with her: I would make it all better, if we could just get out of here alive! Resigned to defeat by a force greater than myself, I led the way home. But with each step, I felt a flame licking at the inside of my belly, and then it crept up my spine, and I turned back and faced the creeps who had ruined my little sister's Halloween.

It was the oldest boy, Johnny Fletcher, who had snatched Bonnie's bag and begun distributing its contents to his buddies. He was the Big Man, their leader. I stared at him: I had right on my side.

"Give it back!" I heard someone say, someone who sounded like me. Had I really drawn my little six-gun against their half dozen rifles? Did I hear the townspeople gasp as I stood up against Injustice itself?

Johnny stared back; the gang quieted in preparation. I was shaking inside, and for seemingly interminable seconds, I pondered my fate. What was I doing? How would my poor mother cope with my loss? As I wrestled with fear to keep my gaze steady, Johnny must have experienced a brief flash of something like compassion, or perhaps a moment of respect for a little kid's guts. Because, miraculously, after perfunctorily pillaging a few more Hershey bars and smashing a candy apple on the pavement just inches from my Keds, Johnny shoved the bag into my hands. Unbelieving, but with all of the cool and dignity that I could gather, I turned to the scared little Bugs Bunny frozen in her tracks at my side, grabbed her paw, and broke the previous New Jersey land speed record running home.

I had triumphed, but I had also marked myself. For after our standoff, the neighborhood scuttlebutt that Johnny Fletcher had backed down *to a girl* spread like mold on a month-old slice of Wonder bread. He was compelled, in the interests of his wobbly-legged young manhood, to turn the tide of public opinion, to regain his stature as invincible and fearless. His mission: to make my life a living hell.

Johnny's menacing prepubescent shadow intruded in all aspects of my life. Walking to school, I watched my back. At the neighborhood pond, I skated far from the older boys' hockey game to avoid a close encounter with the ice. I weathered his taunting, walked away from his sneering challenges, and endured his ridicule. I held my head high throughout: my breaking down would have given him even more pleasure than his pounding me would.

He grew increasingly impatient to penetrate my outward calm, and after many errant attempts, he somehow hit the bull's-eye: he began to torment my family. Our home became the target, and we, the sport, for the gang and a number of younger confederates who, seduced by the intrigue, were drafted for the cause. Johnny and his crafty cronies executed a series of elaborately clever misdeeds. We found rotten pumpkins stuffed into our mailbox. One night a dozen eggs were thrown into our attic vents. My youngest sister's sandbox was dumped out and hung upside down on our clothesline.

I was not alone in being incensed at the nerve of the architect of this diabolical conspiracy. My mother, who, after all, was most directly affected by these ingenious (and often smelly) acts of vengeance, was first amused, then mystified, and finally quite annoyed. On each occurrence, she systematically called the mothers of all the suspected perpetrators. Once, when she caught Johnny peeking in our windows, my mother ran screaming into the night, chasing him twice around the house (at a pretty good clip!), until he finally sprinted to safety.

By the time spring arrived, the foundation of sensible restraint that I had painstakingly built up over the long, hard winter began to crumble. I was tired of rising above: I dreamed of swift and lasting retribution. And when the day finally came, I was readier than an overblown wad of Bazooka to explode all over Johnny Fletcher.

On a sunny day in May, Bobby Farrelli and I stood in his backyard, proudly surveying the four-foot-deep hole we had just dug together. Having a foxhole to jump into had seemed like a good idea that day,

I dreamed of swift and lasting retribution

so we took turns with my father's shovel, grunting and sweating until the little cavern reached impressive proportions. As we worked, a crowd had gathered. Some had appointed themselves our advisors ("You'd better stop digging that hole ... your mother's going to be *so* mad!"); others stood simply to document the event: it was a slow news day on Old Farm Road.

Johnny Fletcher's low voice cut through our proud industriousness.

"Your mother's crazy, Billhardt. There's something wrong with her. Everybody thinks so; everybody laughs at her all the time. I feel sorry for you ... I'd hate it if she were my mother."

Now, it was true that my mother had developed somewhat of a reputation, willing as she was to call other parents to task for their children's behavior — not a popular course of action among the kids. And she *had* been witnessed chasing Johnny around our house, and I believe she was wearing her pink plastic rollers at the time: this scene also made quite an impression. Nonetheless, as mortified as I myself had been at her behavior, Johnny's public diagnosis was definitely over the line.

I glared at him. He laughed and pushed me. I pushed him back harder. We escalated to wrestling, and the crowd formed a ring around us. I know there was shouting, but I heard none of it clearly: adrenaline had concentrated my focus to but one object. With all my might, I shoved Johnny Fletcher again, and this time he lost his balance, falling right into the freshly dug foxhole. The crowd roared. Johnny looked up from below, humiliated. My sister Lisa, usually my archenemy, suddenly became my biggest fan, laughing and jeering as though she'd had money on me and my victory had just made her a rich woman. Suddenly, Johnny rose out of the dirt. With a wild, psychotic growl, he grabbed Lisa by the hood of her blue fleece sweatshirt and dragged her, caveman style, across the yard.

Lisa had a gift for changing her tune to suit any circumstance, and she screamed for mercy. The neighborhood kids stood gaping. Johnny was clearly a madman, and someone had to stop him.

If I had thought about what I did next, I might have reconsidered. He was three years older than I and much bigger, and, besides, a room to myself would have been kind of nice. But family was family, and this was not right. So I ran up to Johnny Fletcher, balled up my fist, and sunk it as deeply into his solar plexus as I possibly could.

He cringed. He cried. He dropped Lisa and hightailed it home. And when he returned later that day, accompanied by his mother, he would not meet my gaze as he uttered his very solicited apology. Somehow, the truth had prevailed.

Something shifted for me that day. Something that I had always felt, something that I had known about myself but almost always carried inside, quietly, privately, had lived outside in the daylight, for one bright moment. It was something big, and full and complete and perfect. It was — me.

Childhood rolled on. Sadly, Mrs. Peel failed to ever present herself at my front door as my loving, and limber, companion. As for my calling Johnny Fletcher to account in defense of my mother's name (and my sister's life), today some spoilsports would call me a rescuer. And yes, thank you very much, I can rescue, in true nineties fashion, as well as any lesbian. But in my tomboy youth, ah, then, I was a hero.

I never thought much of the role models that society had to offer me: Donna Reed and June Cleaver were not my type of woman. The only saving grace was Diana Rigg as Emma Peel on *The Avengers*. British TV broadcasters may never know how many budding young dykes they saved from psychological suicide with that character. Seemed like the women on TV didn't do much more than sit and wait for the guys to finish the adventure part, with a hot meal ready on the table. Except for Mrs. Peel, of course, who managed to do her fair share of rescuing and kicking ass. She also had a higher IQ than her partner, John Steed. Yes, she was my kind of role model, indeed.

—Anna Van Evera, from "Segue Sonata"

The Other Kind

Kanani L. Kauka

Look at me. I'm no jock. Never was. Hated team sports. Hated being forced to play games where everyone except me seemed to know the rules. Hated playing those stupid "boys against girls" kickball-dodgeball-basketball-whatever games those merciless gym teachers thought up. I'm not one of those dykes who gets misty-eyed at the thought of her first softball mitt, her first home run, touchdown, or layup.

Okay, so we've established I'm not a jock. I like to watch (some) sports—especially women's basketball. The players make it look so easy, like anyone in the world could get on a court and pick up a ball and handle it like a goddess, float down the court like an angel. The beauty and grace and blood in a good game is almost overwhelming, and I watch to get that feeling. But I'm not a jock.

What I was and what I am is a tomboy. Not, as I've said, a sports-playing tomboy. The other kind. The exploring kind. More solitary. I was the tree-climber, the stream-wader, frog-catcher, fearless baby butch. Recently, while taking a walk near my apartment on a road that runs along a shallow, pebbly stream, I stopped to watch two eight- or nine-year-old girls upending rocks and logs in search of crawfish. One was braver, reaching into holes under the bank she couldn't see into, telling her friend to stand by with the net. That was me at that age, wading knee-deep in the stream across the street from our apartment, leaving my girlfriends on the bank as I replenished my supply of guppies and threw rocks at the mongoose, pretending to be a solitary explorer in the Amazon.

In all my games of imagination and make-believe, there were always boy characters and I was always the boy. One game we played was called interview. In that game, my friends Judy and Dory were Vietnamese women whose village had been bombed, and I was Dan Rather, interviewing them, asking them how it felt to be homeless, how it felt to have lost their families. Other times, I was the young American soldier who had bombed the village. It was 1974, and I was eight, watching the Vietnam War on the six o'clock news, gleaning new stories every day for us to act out. Not all were stories about the war: some involved Wonder Woman or the Bionic Woman or sometimes Jane Goodall, studying chimps in the jungle.

stream-wader

By the time I was eleven, my best friend Fiona and I were making up elaborate, never-ending plays in which we were archaeologists, scientists, Indians, explorers. I don't remember if our characters were gendered, but we took for granted that any character we created had absolute freedom to run, shoot, fight, climb trees, ford rivers, rescue people. In real life, the school we attended did not allow girls to wear pants, and I was miserable. Skirts meant no playing on the jungle gym, because boys would tease you about your underwear. Skirts also meant no running.

Tomboy. Tomboy, I was called. It was meant as an insult, but I wore it like a medal. Tomboy was almost being a boy, which I thought was the best thing you could be. In some ways, though, tomboy was even better, because real boys were expected to like team sports. As far as I was concerned, the only real disadvantage to being a tomboy was that, in the end, you were still a girl, and therefore forbidden from falling in love with other girls. Boys could have crushes on girls; boys could marry them. Girls couldn't. Tomboys couldn't. I couldn't.

Sixteen. Can you still be a tomboy at sixteen? I was. By then, most of my girlfriends were interested in boys. I wasn't. I had lost the desire to be a boy, but the longing to be with one had not replaced it.

One early entry in the journal I had started keeping at thirteen read simply, "I think I might be a lesbian." Later, when I was a junior in college, I would say yes when a friend asked me if I thought I was a lesbian. But at sixteen, I had happily buried the knowledge recorded in that journal entry, reveling instead in knowing that while my other tomboy friends were running on soccer fields or basketball courts, I was alone, on my bicycle, riding for myself only, with no coaches or teammates or rules.

Riding down to the Esplanade in Boston one day, peddling lazily, dodging the runners and dog-walkers, I looked up and saw a young woman cycling on a parallel path. She smiled at me and, with a nod, indicated that we should race.

Standing on the pedals, feeling the muscles in my legs and shoulders pop and burn, I pump until the two parallel paths suddenly converge and the woman and I are side by side, pushing ourselves and each other, neither of us gaining much on the other for long. I can feel her, inches from me, breathing as hard as I am, pumping hard, glancing at me, telling me somehow that she and I are alike, that I am not alone. She is pushing herself but I'm being shoved, and I know we are riding against ourselves, not each other. I look up and see the boathouse, my destination, just to my left. I pull to a stop with a grateful shout, answer her over-the-shoulder wave, stagger inside, and collapse, ready to throw up but laughing instead.

My friend Gary brought me ice, and when I caught my breath and my legs stopped trembling, I told him what had happened. He looked at me and said, "You're not like any girl I ever knew before."

So, no, I wasn't a jock or a team player. But I'm proof that there's more to being a tomboy than that: tomboy was how I was identified when I was growing up and tomboy is how I continue to identify. I was comfortable in my body growing up: I knew I could make it do almost anything I asked. I spent one summer at camp, playing stealthy hide-and-seek games in the dark, running sure and confident in the woods at night, trusting my eyes to keep me from crashing into trees. I climbed the biggest, scariest elm at the camp, leaping from branch to branch without fear. Even when I broke my arm, showing off with some stupid stunt, I didn't blame the log I was standing on for rolling, or my body for losing its balance. I blamed the sudden foolish panic that made me stretch my arm out as I fell, instead of curling it close to my body so that I would tumble but not break. I hit the ground with a profound snap, breaking both bones in my right forearm, with only a flash of pain before I slid quietly into shock.

What is it that makes a tomboy?

My only other major injury came five years later, when I fell off my bike while speeding along a slick, narrow road. I looked up to see that the rider in front of me had fallen, jammed on my brakes, and, in slow motion, sailed gracefully over the handlebars. Sliding palm-first across the asphalt, I felt a sharp jolt in one knee, then lay gaping like a fish, no air left in my lungs. My palms were fine, and the road rash was minimal, but my knee — oh, it swelled to the size of a cantaloupe. Even so, as long as I put no pressure on it (I didn't wear long pants for six weeks), it worked well enough for me to continue to ride. As the swelling gradually went down, it turned every color of the rainbow, until finally it was a faint yellowy green that could be seen only if you were looking for it. But the damage I had done to both knees from undertraining and overuse has stayed with me ever since. I had finally asked too much of my body.

So is that enough? What is it that makes a tomboy? Have I broken enough bones, do I have enough scars, to be in the club? My friend Kathy could hit a ball farther and run faster than her older brother Peter — did that make her a tomboy or him a sissy? My identity as a tomboy was defined less by how I acted than by how I didn't act. I wasn't interested in playing house. I didn't experiment with my mother's makeup or play dress-up. I never decorated my school notebooks with stickers of hearts or teddy bears or unicorns. My Barbies languished, neglected, while I built houses for them out of discarded cardboard boxes and balsa wood. I spent my girlhood and early adolescence dreaming of glory as a jockey, or maybe a marine biologist or paleontologist. It never occurred to me to want to be a nurse or a wife or a kindergarten teacher or any occupation so stereotypically "female." I felt different, but not really alone. I thought I was a late bloomer, and that the day would come when I would stop falling in love with my girlfriends and start falling love with boyfriends.

Since my interest in team sports was nonexistent, I escaped the dyke-baiting and name-calling that seemed to follow my friends who did play, especially against boys. I lived my tomboy life internally, in a land of fantasies and make-believe. When teachers or relatives called me a tomboy, the label was offered gently, almost condescendingly: I never strayed so far beyond the gender boundaries that teachers worried about me. I'm sure they thought that I was just going through a phase, that someday I would learn to love feminine clothes — at least I wasn't on the field competing against the boys.

The weirdest thing about being this living-in-my-head kind of tomboy was that few could see it. When I was winning the Kentucky Derby or performing dangerous feats, the only ones who knew were me and maybe one or two close girlfriends who played the roles I assigned. As I got older, I came to recognize in my younger tomboy self a particular kind of subversiveness, though at the time, of course, it was completely subconscious. Outwardly, my only major trespass was an almost categorical refusal to wear dresses, and during the 1970s, this was rarely a major issue, especially for my feminist mother. I saw sports-playing tomboys punished, though, when they got too good, or when they insisted on playing baseball instead of softball. In my internally driven tomboyhood, I could do what I wanted, go anywhere, be anything. *Can't catch me,* I thought. *Can't catch me.*

Can't.

Winning

Lynne Yamaguchi

Front tire patched, wheel straddled,
handlebars trued with a twist;
the last trace of Turtle wax
rubbed out with an old shoe rag,
chipped paint polished hard as lapis.
Test time, the road too,
sloping past my house away from town,
trucks out all morning laying tar,
and gravel pale as Peter's grandmother's hair.
Steamrolled flat, there's not a spot on it,
not an oil drip or skid mark and not a father
due home for hours.
Wheel nudging the line next to mine, Peter
is thin as a blond monkey
and faster. His bike's bigger.
He thinks he can win.
Right foot on the ready pedal,
One, two, go, and I'm off.
My head's leading, elbows up, shoulders
planed like wings. Never faster,
these legs locomotives,
Southern Pacific, westbound, Wichita.
Dogs stand back. Houses
pull their shades and blow without waving.

Then, at the foot, instead of the dip
that's supposed to hurl me home free,
gravel, a swollen sea of it.
I slam back on the pedals and hold,
ride through on my left face,
the rock biting hard as army ants
and I can't bite back.
I was winning, I tell the arms that collect me.
I don't hear an answer.
The rest of the summer I stoopsit in pajamas,
star pupil in my sister's playschool,
wearing a scab like a birthmark
I'd have been drowned for back when.

Late Bloomer

S. Jayne Melton

Wandering through the garden section of a do-it-yourself store one day, I stopped to flip through seed packets. Dianthus, marigold, primrose ... Some little lavender blossoming thing caught my eye: "Blooms May to June. Plant one inch apart, thin when seedlings." I began wondering: if I were a plant, what would my seed packet say? Hmmm, let's see ... "Variety: Thomus Boyus. Late flowering. Plant in December. Modest blossoms of variegated color, thirty-odd years later. Warning: If not watered and tended, will go dormant."

I am a tomboy of a late-blooming variety. Some of my species bloom into surprisingly prim and proper little misses; some of us grow into tree-climbing, bat-swinging, rough-housing tomboys; and some of us are stunted. Me, I was never your traditional tree-climbing type. You could call me a flower or call me a weed depending on which side of the mainstream fence you lean on. Like a perennial, I kept coming back, even though society kept trying to cut back the natural course of my character. It took me from age six to thirty-six to adapt to the way society views women who prefer power tools to needlepoint. I didn't know at the time that this was what I was doing. All I knew was that, like a flower, I just kept growing toward the light.

You wouldn't have known the tomboy seeds were there, to see a photo of me at six years old. But they were. They were just quietly germinating in the greenhouse at the time. My mother had the first crack at tending and cultivating the garden. The family photo album bears testament to her annual efforts to force my blooms. Each Easter, Mom would dress me up in pastel-colored finery and patent leather shoes, turning me out in lace and bows with my long hair flounced into cotton candy puffs tamed by ribbons.

Here is my gap-toothed grin captured on film at age six: Poodle curls frame my face like puffs of shaving cream. Satin bows of robin's egg blue perch jauntily on top, perfect matches for my dress, which itself is a cascade of poofy crinoline broken at the bodice by waves of white lace. My hands extend to each side, shoulder high, palms up, like the dancers found painted on the sides of ancient Egyptian vases. In one outstretched palm is an Easter egg. From the wrist of the other hand a patent leather pocketbook dangles by its strap. Under the influence of dear old Mom, I appeared destined to traipse down the path to forever femme. Hardly the makings of a tomboy on the outside. Inside was another story.

I suppose you could call me a mental tomboy. Exploring things was adventure to me. I had not yet discovered trees or swings made of old tires. Instead, I had an insatiable curiosity and imagination and was forever taking things apart to examine them. One such item was my grandfather's pocket watch. I remember prying open the back case when I was seven or eight and discovering a myriad of whirring, moving parts. The delicately balanced, fine-tuned inner workings were fairylike to me. Mesmerized, I slowly pried each layer of fine metal apart from its hinges and sprockets until every single part of the watch lay on the chair I had been kneeling beside. By the time my mother discovered the reason for my intense silence, it was too late. She shrieked at me for ruining his gift and I blithely told her, "It's all right. I can put it back together." Alas, my young mind hadn't quite grasped the enormity of such a task. My mother was quite disgruntled as she swept

The tomboy seeds were germinating in the greenhouse

the contents of the watch from the seat of the chair into a dustpan.

My mother tried her best to win me over to the land of femme. Once, she even made doughnuts from scratch. I was captivated by the smell of warm dough and cinnamon and amazed at the way the little orbs of dough expanded as they hit the hot oil. Still, it never crossed my mind to don an apron and help her make the next batch. Instead, I grabbed a few that were still warm and headed downstairs to the basement. Both she and I were learning about me: that I'd rather be pounding nails than kneading dough; that I'd rather make the bread board than the bread.

The gadgets and tools in my father's basement workshop won my heart over the frills, ribbons, and perfume of my mother's turf. It was a full basement with unfinished gray concrete walls that leached dampness from the earth outside. Dark and dank, but warm and welcoming to me, the basement proved fertile ground for me to explore and develop my creativity.

In one corner of the basement was a train set. Dad had constructed an entire village and countryside on a plywood platform. The platform had a square hole cut out in the middle so that he could scoot under and up and twiddle with the scenery that lined the miniature railways. Bright green grass covered the plywood board, and tiny fake trees with bristly green branches and brown plastic trunks decorated the landscape. Dad and I had made papier-mâché mountains with passageways cut for the train to pass through. I would watch, rapt with wonder, as the train engine blew real steam. I remember to this day my fascination with the miniature workmen as they pumped their little painted arms up and down to "propel" the flatbed handcar around the track.

At the other end of the basement was the workshop. Dad often headed downstairs after work, and I remember rushing through my kitchen chores to join him. I loved the high-pitched whine of the table saw and would watch in amazement as the blade seared through a chunk of two-by-four, sending wood chips and shavings across the floor. I made comparisons in my mind between the seeds Mom and Dad had each sown, now beginning to germinate. Patent leather shoes: drill set. Lace socks: cap guns. Ribbons and bows: bows and arrows. Frilly hair and frilly dresses: train set, Tinkertoys, erector sets. Guess which took root.

When I was a little older, and Dad was satisfied that my interest in the basement and woodworking was sincere, he bought me a working set of tools, sized to fit my small fingers. I had my own hammer and a hand drill that really bored holes in wood. I also had a wood planer and, soon, my own wood scraps, which I nailed into odd shapes, crude chairs, benches, and tables. "Respect the tools and learn how to use them and they won't hurt you," Dad told me once, seeing me quiver as I watched him send a two-by-four through the table saw. Sometimes he would let me push a big chunk through until I lost my nerve and let him finish. I could tell he was proud of me for trying.

I felt content and happy in the basement, banging out my creations alongside my father. I'd often ask him childish questions, interrupting him in his work. He always took the time to answer. In the basement, sunshine reached me even through the smoky, half-sized windows. Then, in seventh grade, life sprayed a pesticide.

It was called home economics.

Home ec. class and apron making withered me in one fell swoop. For an hour every Tuesday and Thursday, I was prisoner to a soft-spoken, malignantly misguided home economics teacher. She was a product of her time, fertilizing our young female minds with her perceptions of what we needed to learn to become successful young women. Her ideas had nothing to do with hammers or sawdust, and she and I eyed each other warily from the start.

We were expected to make an apron from scratch by the end of the term. I procrastinated and made every excuse I could to delay the inevitable. Finally, my mother, learning that I had less than a week to complete the project, held me hostage and drove me to the piece goods shop to pick out my materials. It took me two days to cut the materials and another three to sew the fabric into submission.

"I'm finished," I yelled to my mother, who was in the kitchen. She had instructed me to remain in the bedroom with the sewing machine until I came up with an apron. I had previously escaped with thin excuses. She had caught on after the third or fourth time I claimed to not have the right color thread or buttons or snaps.

Stuffing my apron into my bookbag, I sighed deeply, relieved that the torture was over. I thought I had done a decent job, all considered, and was about to pat myself on the back and escape to the backyard to ride my bike when my mother's face told me otherwise. She strained to hide her dismay as she suggested that I might iron some of the wrinkles out before taking it in to class, but even she, with a load of starch and a hot iron, couldn't get the thing to lie down and cooperate. I had sewn in the wrinkles. When my mother gently suggested that I make another, I cheekily reminded her that it was due the next day. I had no time. I would just go to class with what I had: me and my ugly apron.

I had sewn in the wrinkles.

Mrs. Duffy was not as kind as my mother had been. She chastised me for my pathetic effort in a Sunday school voice that cut through me like a sharp pair of scissors. She made no effort to lower her voice and all the other girls in the class heard her as she failed to understand how I had submitted such a hopeless specimen.

"All girls should be able to sew and cook," she said.

Her accusing eyes and caustic tone said that I had committed blasphemy, deliberately creating this horror. She took her wrinkled brown finger and poked its sharply manicured nail along the bright red rickrack I had used for trim. That wicked finger found all the big loopy gaps in the stitching, but Mrs. Duffy didn't stop there. She picked up another student's work and held it up next to mine.

"Now, Carla took her project seriously, unlike some of us."

Carla had chosen tasteful quiet pastels, with tasteful contrasting rickrack for the trim and her name neatly stitched across the pocket. Her apron ties were nice and flat. Mine had turned out like pasta spirals. Carla could hardly hide her smirk.

I just had my first lesson in inferiority. It was a bitter poison and I could feel myself wither in front of everybody.

It was tradition for the class to display their work in the hallway. Mine was easy to spot. It resembled a sheet of notebook paper that had been wadded and uncrumpled. The warm colors I had chosen — bright yellow with red trim — had once made me feel happy. Now, every time I had to walk by the display case that held my ugly apron, I cringed to see its bright colors screaming for attention like a drunken reveler at a New Orleans Mardi Gras.

Then, at recess, I saw my friend Chucky carrying a brand-new baseball bat. He was stroking the finish proudly.

"Where'd you get that?" I asked.

"Made it," he said proudly.

"Where?" Where could you make something so neat and useful in school?

"Shop class." He threw the words back over his shoulder as he went to show off his bat to the unlucky boys who had to wait until next semester to take shop class.

I didn't have a clue as to what shop class was. It hadn't occurred to me that while I being forced to make horrid aprons, the boys were somewhere else having fun. The discovery opened my eyes to the difference in society's expectations of boys and of girls. But I had ideas of my own. After all, I had played in the basement for as long I could remember. I was familiar with the powerful whine of the table saw. I knew how to use a handsaw and pound nails into boards fairly straight. That evening after dinner I brought the subject up with my father.

"Dad, I want to make a bat. How come Chucky can make a bat at school and I can't?"

"I dunno."

"Can I make one downstairs then?"

"I suppose you could, but I don't have a lathe."

He impatiently folded his paper, thought better of his answer, and looked at me.

"You can always make something else."

The boys moved on to metalworking. The girls moved on to making Jell-O. I was miserable. All I wanted to make was a bat — no Jell-O or cakes, and no more aprons. And I won't even tell you the disastrous story of the red denim jumpsuit with the zipper down the front. Suffice it to say that it resembled a straightjacket. I suffered through the rest of home economics with a child's silent dignity, unable to voice my unhappiness, feeling, and rightfully so, that it wouldn't matter if I did. The bloom was off the rose, as they say. I could feel myself curling up inside as a part of me withered away.

In the ninth grade, I thought I'd found relief from mandatory home ec. This was the year the school administration decided to let girls and boys choose for themselves whether to take shop or home ec. I chose shop. But the shop teacher was none too thrilled to have girls in his class. On the first day of class, I saw the lathe in the corner and just knew I'd finally get to make that baseball bat I'd been longing for. Soon I'd be able to take a rectangular block of wood and carve away the pieces until something smooth and curved appeared. We started leather tooling first, then metalworking. Two months later, one of us got brave enough to ask when we'd get to do woodworking. The answer from this mustachioed man who must have not agreed with the policy of liberation was short and gruff: "No, too dangerous."

I was beginning to figure it out. I remember thinking, *But then how come the boys do it?* But I remained silent. For me, the strength to speak out against the oppression of women would be years coming. Besides, he was an adult, and I had been taught to respect and not contradict adults' opinions. So I silently noted the difference and kept my mouth shut...

...and made an aluminum tray for my dad to keep on top of his bureau. Etched with acid on the top surface was the face of a Scottish terrier. For emphasis, I had punched an outline with an awl and hammer. I had learned a valuable lesson that year: shop class was a facade and sometimes you have to bide your time. Like a daffodil frost-damaged after a false spring, I went dormant. Waiting. Silently. For the light, for the thaw.

Meanwhile, my inner tomboy was being threatened by my gangly adolescent body. The transition from child to adolescent was an awkward one for me. I blinked and suddenly found myself left in the dust by all my peers. The girls went on to excel in softball, volleyball, basketball. I went on to drop balls, flub plays, and stumble. I plodded my way to obscurity. My body betrayed me at every turn. I could not get my arms and legs to move in the same direction to retrieve any moving object. I felt like a giant flailing windmill.

My arms and legs were growing like kudzu, long, lean, and gawky. In a matter of weeks I went from being friends with my body to feeling weedy and tangled. There was no point in shopping in the girls' or the women's department.

By the time I had reached the eleventh grade, I thought my athletic fate was sealed. I would be forever branded Four-Eyes, Nerd, Wimp, Klutz. I was convinced that despite my wanting to excel, any athletic endeavor was impossible for me. The accolades always went to those who picked up the skills quickly. The gym teachers took great pride in coaching the quick kids, not the ones who needed the extra time — like me.

I was becoming more and more of an outsider, unable to find where I belonged. I wasn't a part of the gaggle of girls who hung out at the 7-Eleven after school, slurping frozen ice drinks as they thumbed through *Teen Beat* and ogled pictures of David Cassidy and Michael Jackson. The boys didn't want to play with me anymore, and I wasn't invited to hang out with them on the stoop between classes. The thought of kissing one did not cross even the most remote corner of my mind. A stranger to myself and to everyone around me, I had more in common with scarecrows, with my bony wrists sticking out of too-short sleeves. Unable to find approval and acceptance and self-confidence in sports, I retreated to the safety of books. I read my dad's *Popular Science* magazines and Cousin Willie's *Boy's Life*.

In college, the thick snow keeping me dormant began to melt, and the ground began to thaw. After years of feeling awkward and inhibited, my first chance to believe in myself came as a fluke, but the incident slowly changed my life. One day in a mandatory gym class in my freshman or sophomore year, I served seven volleyballs in a row to a big burly fellow who couldn't return a single one of them. It was the first sign of physical ability I'd seen in myself in years. On my own, I learned that I wasn't inept: I was physically "dyslexic." Like a kid with reading problems, I learned physical skills in a different way and at a different rate than my schoolmates. Later on, I tried my hand at fencing and might have made the team had I not graduated the next year. A couple of years later, I picked up golf. A coach who worked with a prominent college team encouraged me, saying I had promise and a natural swing.

Today, I'm working hard to make up for lost time, holding fast to the new athletic parts of me. I've been running from pumps-and-pantyhose jobs, searching out the jobs involving tools and jeans and work boots. I look for jobs that allow me to use my own judgment. They're hard to find. Whether I don the execu-drag or jeans and work boots, I keep encountering unaccepting attitudes. "Suits" notice my tomboyishness and disapprove of me for not falling into the office-clone coalition, and working-class men still have trouble accepting that a woman can lift, haul, and use power tools. I have had men take my own tools out of my hand to work on something I'm working on or physically push in my way when I am already holding my own.

I am finally blossoming. Despite the lack of water and warmth and light and tending, something inside me has persisted like a genetic code. Now, at age thirty-seven, I am more physically fit than I ever was at twenty-one. I have learned to play golf, and to sail. I learned to swim at thirty-two and began a relationship with the water that I had long longed for. Now kayaking is my new-found love, a perfect sport for long arms. I used to be afraid to dunk my head in the deep end of the pool. Now I have learned to Eskimo roll and love every minute of getting wet. In the course of all my learning, I have watched my self-esteem improve and my social skills grow.

My partner and I often compete with each other to do the tomboy chores around the house, dispelling the old lesbian myth that a couple must comprise one butch and one femme. She does most of the cooking, but beats me to the outdoor chores if I don't keep an eye out. I do the cleaning and dishes but hold my own where the power tools are concerned. We both love tool shopping and going to the do-it-yourself shops for cement mortar. I knew I loved her when she told me she had a Black and Decker power drill. And my heart pounded and my legs quivered when I watched her use it. We recently relandscaped the back garden and I think we secretly battled over who would get to the tools first.

I am still cultivating my own renegade spirit. I still require water and weeding. Occasionally, slugs invade and nibble at my enthusiasm. But the sense of freedom and satisfaction I feel paddling a kayak along a coastline rich with wildlife or hitting a golf ball well serve as nutrients to remind me: It doesn't matter when you come into your own. Just never give up until you do.

At Nine

Mia Levesque

At nine, I knew the world: all the streets and houses, their driveways and backyards (especially those with dogs or cantankerous owners), the lines of the beach, the paths through the woods. Every day I explored the universe of my neighborhood, waking up early, as innocent children do, before the stresses of life make sleeping in so desirable. My days were simple, filled with decisions about what games to play and which fields to traipse through. And I did plenty of traipsing.

I was no girlie-girlie. I prided myself on my ability to withstand daring amounts of pain without crying, at least not in front of anyone. Despite dramatic falls from trees and frightful scrapes on pavement, I refused to shed a tear, more afraid to let my guard down than to ride out any physical discomfort. I wore my bruises and scabs with honor, a true tomboy. And with my long, brown hair touching my waist, I somehow felt more brazen because of my unmistakable girlness. I never wanted to be a boy and didn't have to be. I would stand up to the toughest of them, even when I couldn't possibly win more than a verbal confrontation.

This was me at nine, before I had ever read about Scout or Idgie. In 1975, not even the Bionic Woman had jumped or run (in slow-motion, of course) into my life yet. Role models for baby dykes were few and far between. Good thing I had Sardine.

There were so many things I loved about Sardine. She wasn't only my best friend; she was the essence of all I wanted to be and of all I wanted to be with. Wiry and stubborn though I was, I could not match Sardine. Rough and rugged, she appeared fearless of everything, whether it was the terrain or boys or rules. And she convinced me that I, too, did not have to be afraid — or at least she tried. She could always jump a little higher, run a bit faster — or figure out a way to justify cheating, coming up with reasons such as "I had to start before you 'cause I just ate three [always exaggerating] sardine san'wishes for lunch." I admired her butchness, her androgyny, though I had no name for these traits.

The day we met, I was riding around on my purple bicycle with the white banana seat when I spotted her sitting on a minibike in the driveway of the house on the corner that had been for sale. Her hair, scruffy, straight, and black, hung in front of her deep brown eyes. Though she stood at least two inches shorter than I, she seemed tall — maybe it was just her presence that took up space. She looked tough, and many couldn't have pegged her as a girl or a boy. But I knew right away. Even now, I retain an unfaltering image of the six-inch scab, partially picked, that ran vertically up her left shin. It was awesome, a true badge of tomboy honor in my mind. But, for all the stains on her shirt, I think I had still more, which satisfied me immensely. After all, I claimed this neighborhood as my own: head tomboy, unknowing baby dyke, protected by a slew of older sisters and brothers and their friends.

"Is that yours?" I asked, tough but timid.

"Yeah. My stepbrother said I could have it 'cause now he's got a real big bike."

"Why would he give you a minibike for a bicycle?"

"No, stupid, a motorcycle, not a bicycle." She paused. "Want a sardine san'wish? They're my favorite."

And so began our illustrious summer, filled with missions and games, mischief and childish intrigue.

Much of what I loved about Sardine I also hated. She spoke her mind with little, if any, thought about the consequences of her bluntness. Many times this trait led to afternoons of spontaneous adventure. Other times, it was like a slap in the face from an ice-cold hand. I remember both, the fun and the misery, the adventures and the slaps.

Still, I wanted desperately to emulate her every characteristic. I had always been inclined to stand up for myself or for the underdog, whatever the circumstances. Now, in attempts to impress her, I often found myself in difficult situations: challenging some boy to a tree-climbing contest in which the winner would have to not only climb the highest but also cling to the skinny treetop the longest, or yelling at a group of older kids for hanging out too close to our spot at the cove. Unfortunately, I had never been taught how to fight, unlike Sardine, who knew how to fight not "like a girl" (that is, like someone who was never taught how) but like someone who could take on the best of them.

One afternoon that summer, I remember, Steven, this very average boy, called Tyler a fairy. Now, Tyler, like Sardine and me, didn't always fit society's requirements for his gender. He was also my best *boy* friend, and so, when Steven kept teasing him, I, of course, stepped in. We sparred in a circle, neither of us wanting to make the first move. When Steven eventually punched me in the stomach, doubling me over, knocking the wind out of me, what was I supposed to do? With each punch, I realized how ineffectual I was: weak jabs, poor aim, hesitant blows. I wanted to hit back with force and confidence, but no one had ever taught me how. As a girl, I had to learn on my own, now, by doing. I tried to ignore the wrenching pain in my gut, refusing to retreat, give up, accept defeat; convincing myself that if I held on, eventually I would regain the wind that he'd knocked out of me. I didn't. I was thankful that at least Sardine had wandered home for lunch and, therefore, wasn't witness to my ineptitude. Her vicious taunting always cut through even my thickest layers of self-protection, and I was in no mood to listen to her gloat about how well *she* could fight. I knew her nasty streak all too well.

Until I was ten or eleven, I had a seemingly incurable fear of the dark and of nighttime in general. This phobia kept me from any overnight activities that required my being away from my family, but I, of course, kept this a secret. So when Sardine asked me again and again to sleep over, I eventually ran out of excuses — the truth not being an option. Digging deep, to the core of my young butchness, I convinced myself that I could overcome my anxiety.

I packed my light cotton, summer pajamas (tiny, lavender-polka-dotted boxer shorts with a matching button-down shirt), grabbed my toothbrush and one very special stuffed bear named Winston, and set off, duffel bag in hand, cutting through familiar backyards. Sardine had promised to take me for a ride on her minibike if I got there early enough. It was still daylight when I arrived. I spotted the minibike leaned up against the front of the garage, where it always was, still out of commission, essential parts removed for repair. I had started to think that it would stay there forever, as Sardine's brother rode around the field on his new Honda dirt bike. But I didn't care: I had enough to worry about just by sleeping over. Distracted by chasing the Good Humor truck and playing kick the can, I forgot, for a while anyway, that I wouldn't be going home. I remember little else about the evening until after we'd brushed our teeth and retired to her bedroom.

That's when I saw it — a cot, neatly set up, parallel to her single bed. Panic set in. Somewhere in the back of my nine-year-old mind, I had assumed that we would share the same bed, and this thought had enabled me to confront my fear of night. The cot stared back at me as solitude and isolation loomed. Why couldn't Sardine and I just sleep together? We were both small, both girls. It seemed the natural thing to me. But, "You sleep there," Sardine said, pointing to the jail-like cot. I wanted to ask why we couldn't cuddle and giggle together in the bed, let our stuffed animals lie on the stiff cot. I said nothing. Proud baby dyke, I lay down with Winston clutched under my arm.

I tried to envision riding on the back of Sardine's minibike — imagining it was fixed, of course. Every time I shut my eyes, however, visions of clowns or other horrid images appeared. And the stomach pains started: rolling waves of cramps, accompanied by panicky gasping. When I started moaning and groaning, my eyes swollen with tears that refused to drop, Sardine went to get her stepmother, who with pursed lips and skeptical eyes, phoned my parents. Ashamed and humiliated, I sat in the back of Sardine's parents' Chevy station wagon, clutching my knees, no longer knowing if the pains were real.

A few nights later, I saw Sardine walking past my house with Kelly, a wimpy girl who lived three streets down from me. When I yelled hello from the window, Sardine replied, "Going to sleep now, Chloe? It must be past your bedtime." They both laughed. I was heartbroken. Of course, nine-year-old hearts often mend quickly. I never could stay angry at Sardine.

All summer, Sardine and Tyler and I played down by South Cove, barely noticing the heat that all the grown-ups constantly complained about. Our activities kept us occupied and amused for days at a time: so many paths to explore, ditches to crawl through, rocks to skip. One day we might find a shipwreck (an old garbage heap), and we would dig for treasure, usually old plates and cups or a rusty tool. Sometimes we would find a toad or a snake and have a pet for the day. Occasionally, in our journeys along the twisted line of the water's edge, we would come upon a duck blind, designed to hide the unfair advantages of shotguns and imitation quacking behind deceptively neat rows of marsh grass and reeds. Recognizing the inequality of the hunt, I always felt obliged to tear the blinds down. I loved ripping through each layer of camouflage, pulling down the facade until all that stood was the shaky wooden frame. I took great pleasure in then smashing the remaining shabby boards to the ground, never noticing my cuts and splinters until much later. The destruction of the duck blinds became a ritual.

At the edge of the water, we found one perfect spot where the mud was mixed with enough sand so that we would sink only a couple of inches. (In most places, the slime would pull a person down a good foot.) That spot, adorned with large rocks split with crevasses, bordered by marsh grass under a canopy of trees, became the site of our "town." There, we would set up and act out different roles, creating and pretending freely.

Sardine was always the "construction worker," setting up and building "homes" or "offices" for Tyler and me. I always ended up being the "town doctor." My nurturing side already prominent, I bandaged cut knees with giant fresh leaves or wrapped jammed fingers against homemade wooden splints. Tyler ran the "town store," because he had access to the tea that we used as tobacco. About once a week, we would sneak into his older sister's room and grab handfuls of jasmine, Earl Grey, or Darjeeling from her many tiny tins. I, in turn, would snatch a clump of clay from my brother's stash in our basement. After molding small bowls, we would collect the driest, hardiest reeds we could find and construct our own pipes. When we ran short of matches, as we often did, Sardine would disappear for a half hour before returning with a new supply. I still don't know where she would go. Sometimes, Kelly would join us. She always wanted to pretend that she was Tyler's wife, though, which didn't go over well with the rest of us. Most often, it was just the three of us: Tyler, Sardine, and me, inventing our own world.

On the day Sardine told me she was moving back to her biological mother's house somewhere in Vermont, we planned our last childhood adventure together. For the next month, we diligently developed our town. Combing the trails through the woods that touched the edge of the cove, we found many seemingly useless items: old plates, spoons, bicycle parts, car tires, broken tea cups. We found a use for everything. One day, along one of the paths through the plush green foliage, I found a pile of discarded Styrofoam, which I lugged back to our site. Though Tyler and Sardine argued over its possible uses, I figured that we could use it to make a raft. Then we'd be able to float out to a mammoth gray rock that loomed about twenty feet from shore. Since the water was too disgusting to swim in, we had tried floating to the rock on logs and boards, but nothing worked. The rock appeared flat from a distance, and I always imagined Sardine and me lying together on it in the August heat, dangling our feet in the water, scooping drops of wetness from the surrounding pool. I wanted so much to be close to her — physically, her disheveled hair resting on my dirty shirt; emotionally, through whispered words blown past her ear. I had thought we would always be together, or, rather, I'd never considered any other possibility. Subconsciously, in the deep-rooted romance of my child heart, there existed a future for us — even when she bullied and tormented me. That rock in the middle of South Cove had somehow come to represent our future: distant but attainable. The raft became all the more important, therefore, once I learned that Sardine would be leaving.

As with everything, we debated how to best build a raft. I personally thought that we could construct a wooden frame from driftwood and salvaged rusty nails, and I tried to persuade Tyler to agree. Always in the middle, virtually opinionless, he was inevitably the deciding vote in our very democratic decision making, since Sardine and I disagreed on almost everything. In this case, too, she had another plan, which, in retrospect, I admit was the better. She had discovered a construction site not far from her house that was left unattended on the weekends. It was a virtual hardware store: hammers, nails, wood. We set a time to meet the following day, deciding that we could survive one Saturday morning without cartoons and *Schoolhouse Rock*. Excited, I arrived early. By the time Sardine rode up on her bike, I had already seen the stack of skids and guessed her plan. Sitting on a mound of sawdust, I hollered to her, but she just smiled and walked down the cement steps into the soon-to-be basement. I knew to follow. I watched as she moved toward the back corner. Slowly, she pulled two bottles from behind a cinderblock and slipped the beer into a paper bag. Heading together to grab a pallet, we discussed how we should carry it back to "town." We sat, knees touching, mapping out a route in the dry dirt. After what seemed an hour (kid time), Tyler appeared on his red bike and stayed just long enough to tell us that his overbearing mother wouldn't let him out of the yard for more than fifteen minutes because she found his plans for the day "too vague." That meant I'd have Sardine to myself for the whole day! Unable to explain my sudden delight, I kept it to myself.

Struggling, Sardine and I pulled the pallet down the path through the woods, adrenaline pumping, glass bottles rattling with each step. When we reached the cove, we ignored our fatigue, our splinters and scrapes, and immediately shoved the Styrofoam into the skid. Splashing into the water, Sardine climbed on first, with me right behind her, until my weight started tilting and sinking the raft.

"Get off! Get off, Chloe!" Sardine yelled.

I found myself up to my knees in stagnant water. Even stuffed with all the Styrofoam, the raft would support only one person at a time. How were Sardine and I going to be together? I had to find a solution.

"I have a plan. Wait here."

Running the most familiar trail, I tripped over rocks and roots, sticks and stumps. But nothing mattered. Determined to share the sun with Sardine on the monstrous boulder, I continued jogging even with a stitch in my side. When I finally returned with the rope slung over my shoulder, Sardine was already floating around on the raft, pushing herself along with a large stick, like Huck Finn, only better, because she was a girl. I stood on the shore yelling, holding up the coil, and eventually, she brought the raft in. After I tied one end of the rope to the raft and the other to a thick tree trunk, she made her way out. As soon as she climbed onto the rock, I pulled the raft back. Eagerly, I scrambled onto our newly made raft.

"Chloe, get the you-know-what," Sardine yelled.

I didn't "know what" at first, then realized she wanted the beer. I jumped off, grabbed the bag, and stopped at our hidden stash of English Breakfast before hopping back on. As I pushed out with the stick, Sardine was jumping up and down, screaming for me to hurry. When I reached the rock, she grabbed my hand, wrapped her even-smaller fingers around mine, and braced me as I leapt across. I'd never known such happiness. We lay together, oblivious to other worlds, spilling more beer than we drank. By the time we noticed that the raft had drifted back to shore, the sun had numbed our senses, dulled any fear. We looked at each other and giggled, clinging to each other, till I stood up and did a cannonball into the murky cove. At that point, I couldn't have cared less about the gooey, grimy water coating my skinny body: I had had my day with Sardine.

The world made more sense to me at nine than it would when I became a teenager. At nine, girls stuck with girls; boys, with other boys. For the most part, girls and boys seemed to detest each other, and this was accepted, even encouraged, as the norm. In many ways, Sardine, Tyler, and I were already breaking the rules simply by hanging together. *Fairy, lezzie, gay, fag, queer.* These words were undefinable then, merely ammunition for name-calling. It never occurred to me back then that what I felt for Sardine would someday gain definition, hinder and haunt me. Back then I was tagged a tomboy, a fairly acceptable label for a girl, since tomboys supposedly strove to be boys. That's not how I looked at it then or how I perceive it now. When Sardine left in early September, I moped for a few days; then I started fourth grade. I didn't see her again until I was fifteen, when the world was filled with questions lacking answers, and things no longer made sense. It was at that same time that I started to understand what I really felt for Sardine, when the world changed forever.

My dad built me a fort out of bamboo. When we moved to another house, he built me one out of plywood. When we moved again, I built my own tree house while my parents were away. They were dismayed to discover that I had taken Dad's electric circular saw up into the tree house to trim off excess plywood: I could have cut off my arm, they said.

My forts and tree houses symbolized for me a world apart, where I could unabashedly be myself. I decorated them with objects from this separate world. I put my astronomy books, star charts, my comic book collection, and a large poster of Farrah Fawcett in there. (When I did go in the house, it was to watch *Charlie's Angels* on TV.) Sometimes I took a kerosene lantern out to my fort to stay in it at night. The little circle of light illuminating my space heightened my sense that I had my own perfect world.

–Lauren Renée Corder, from "Forts and Farrah Fawcett"

The Long Road Back to Ten OR Reclaiming My Inner Tomboy

Jayne Relaford Brown

I nearly lost that part of me — my tomboy girl — along the way. I remember her as a spitfire, remember feeling cool and strong riding my bike with no hands down the steep curve on Madrid Way. I'd hook my thumbs in my pockets or let my arms float out like wings, controlling the bike with a slow lean and a press of the thighs. I remember the smack of a hard line drive snagged in my glove's well-oiled and pounded pocket; the tingle in my hands as my Louisville Slugger made contact, sailing the ball through the hole between second and first (I'm a lefty) for a stand-up double.

Girls wore skirts to school then, but I was the one hiding rolled-up cutoffs underneath who dumped my skirt in the dirt by the classroom door when the bell for recess rang; the one who played football with the noon duty guard, going out for long ones instead of practicing Chinese jump rope or double Dutch or hanging from my knees on the monkey bars. I was the one who challenged Jeff, the creepy kid who was always in my face, to meet me after school and duke it out. I marked a box in the dirt with the heel of my tennis shoe, daring him to see who could stay inside the longest, no holds barred. When he broke open my nose, I didn't cry and run like he thought I would; I just knocked him to the dirt and punched him until he rolled away from me across the line.

I loved feeling strong and agile, mouthy, scrappy. Even having someone hate my guts felt good. It meant I was alive, was having an impact. What made me give that up? What made me begin to crave approval more than anything? My friend Liz describes the years around ten as "the time when everyone really goes to work on you" to turn you into a girl. One way they did that was by saying "tomboy" like it was a dirty word. It sounded like "problem child" or "going through a phase" coming from my mother's mouth; like "cooties," from the girlie girls'.

Dirt didn't seem stick to the girlie girls, and the dirt that stuck to me was part of what marked me as a tomboy. We all had recess on the same gravel lot, but these girls seemed to walk above the dirt. They made it clear that they thought they walked above me, too: pointing out my dirty fingernails, muddy socks, dusty shins; telling the teacher if I'd had my feet up on their seats; smoothing their skirts away from mine if they had to sit by me.

Wearing "boys' clothes" marked me too — pants, t-shirts, baseball caps. I threw overhand and hard, not "like a girl." I wasn't scared to catch a dodgeball in the gut. It meant something to me to be able to catch. Once, I went up for a fly, hit my ankle on a low rock wall, and rolled backwards down a steep embankment spiked with tumbleweeds. Flat on my back at the bottom of the hill, I raised my glove to show the kids peering down at me the baseball still inside. The game we had been playing didn't count, but, for me, hanging onto that fly did, in a way that learning all the patty-cake to "sailor went to sea-sea-sea" or all the cat's cradle permutations never would. Sometimes people asked me if I

How could I be the first girl on the

wanted to be a boy. *Of course not,* I thought. *How could I be the first girl on the New York Yankees if I was a stupid boy?*

And yet, "I gave away my bike, and fell asleep what seems a hundred years." I wrote these words, about the years before my coming out, in a reverse-Cinderella poem, a poem about a woman put to sleep by the prince and awakened by the witch. And, indeed, I think of my coming out as a coming to, a waking from a long bad dream. Not until aroused from my "heterosexual swoon" could I let my tomboy girl emerge again.

I remember Fred, the noon duty guard, watching me play two-square with Alan, my sixth-grade boyfriend. Fred knew I could throw a mean spiral pass and would fling my body across the gravel lot to catch one thrown too wide. Yet here I was, playing tea parties with a boy, bouncing the ball gently so I wouldn't show him up, and Fred was smiling his approval. Aww, she's growing up, that smile said. To me, that smile stands for all the carrots and cattle prods that led me down the path toward the way I was supposed to be.

And when Alan's father was sent to prison for embezzlement, I took that boy under a pepper tree whose branches brushed the ground and, welling tenderness, put my arms around him and held him while he cried. I remember really falling for this so-nice image of myself, thinking, *So this is what it means to be a woman.*

I also remember this: walking home from seventh grade with my friend Vicki, arguing all the way to the spot where our roads diverged. It was photo day, and I had curled my hair into a flip, shaved my legs, and put some lipstick on. "You look stupid," Vicki said. "Why are you doing this stupid stuff like everybody else?"

"Obviously, you're not mature enough to understand," I told her. "Anyway, who cares what you think?" I remember trying to figure out what her problem was, wondering why she was making such a big deal out of this, acting as though I'd betrayed her. Now I recognize her "problem" as the loneliness of the long-distance lesbian whose friends are all leaving her, selling out for the approval of the crowd.

New York Yankees if I was a stupid boy?

That was pretty much the end of our friendship. I usually walked home with Vicki after school, but that day I took a right and walked up the hill to my house by myself. After that, if we saw each other on Campo Road or Ramona Drive, we took opposite sides of the street and didn't speak. In my sanctimonious seventh-grade mind-set, I saw our parting of the ways as me leaving her behind. I was growing up, and she was not.

The next time Vicki and I walked on the "same side of the street" was at our twentieth high school reunion. The organizing committee had refused my request to publicize a gay and lesbian alumni get-together, so another friend and I brought a poster of our own to the opening event. Vicki, who had flown in from Colorado, stood with us and helped us put the poster back every time a former football player took it down or turned it backward. The three of us had coffee the next day with two other alumni, and Vicki and I parted with a hug.

I interpret our earlier parting of the ways differently now. I was at the beginning of a long, long detour from myself, and it would be twenty years before I found my way home. But even during those wandering years, my tomboy girl never disappeared completely. Though I walked in my sleep, she occasionally leapt out: sassy, bold, and sure of herself, giving not a shit what anybody thought. I didn't know how to bring her out for my own defense, but she was a fierce Amazon advocate when someone crossed one of my friends. When my other friend from the reunion got branded a dyke in high school (which, of course, she was), I walked shotgun through the halls with her, glaring at anyone who stared or snickered. When a football player tried to interrupt our first-ever anti-war rally in the high school quad by making wise-ass cracks while my friend was trying to sing, I asked him once, nicely, to please shut up, then punched him in the nose when he failed to listen.

I tried hard, with moderate success, to do the heterosexual thing, but I realized even then that I felt like myself only when I was out with a carload of girls at the drive-in or emptying gold plastic carafes of sour coffee and packs of cigarettes with my girlfriends at the 24-hour coffee shop. It's no coincidence that most of that clique has since come out. In the midst of my detour then, I was the one they considered successful with the boys. One night when we were out driving down the boulevard, a carload of guys pulled alongside, hollering and making kissy-mouths. "They're doing that at you," said my branded-a-lesbian friend, who was driving. "You're the kind they like." I wasn't sure she meant it as a compliment, and I was even less sure I wanted to be the recipient of that attention.

I knew having a boyfriend was supposed to be a good thing. Having one in front of my friends felt good, but having to be alone with one felt too much like hand-to-hand combat with a creature from a different planet.

If I had to be with a guy, I felt much better when I had a girlfriend around. My friend Monica and I double-dated for a while with two college guys. When they threatened to stop giving us joints because we talked and giggled with each other instead of putting out for them, we broke up with them.

On prom night, instead of going to the dance, Monica and I took our dates (different guys) down to the beach. I remember leaving my date, whose name and face I can't remember, on the sand while I swam naked through the surf with Monica. We swam out toward the moon, then floated awhile, rising and falling together as we talked in the swells out past the waves. The guys on the beach thought our nakedness was for their benefit and were stunned when we ran up to the blanket, put our clothes back on, and told them to take us out to breakfast.

Yet I also veiled myself in white, dressed myself up as Juliet (who kills herself for the love of a boy), and let myself be handed off from my father to my husband. I remember thinking, *This marks the moment from which I'll never do anything bad again: I'm settling down now*. Settling. As in a Sunday school verse that always stuck with me, I thought I was putting away a "childish thing": that rebellious part of me, my tomboy girl.

After I married, I tried so hard to be perfect. I ground my own baby food from organic vegetables, I baked bread, and every time my husband quit a job, I smiled and said, "It will all work out; something better will come along." People used to compliment me by calling me a saint. I believed I should wait until all the babies were in school before I went back to school myself, but I could feel my ability to think, to say (or even know) what I thought, slipping away, and I was terrified. I thought of "the woman behind the man" as a prescription, and believed I could make everything work if I just kept a positive attitude. Small wonder that I found myself growing deeply depressed, cycling between bouts of insomnia and a literal inability to wake and dress myself and my kids. Small wonder that the "childish thing" I'd put away, which turned out to be such a fundamental part of myself, began to shout and pummel me inside with an insistence that could not be stopped.

Feeling dangerous, like a failure, and deeply afraid, I literally put myself away. I was blessed to share the ward with a kind gay man who wove me a necklace of seaweed and shells and with a blue-eyed butch who recognized my need. On a field trip to a miniature golf course, she asked permission to use the rest room, and I asked if I could, too. When I followed her inside, the blue-eyed butch held her boot against the door, took me in her arms, and held me in a kiss.

I swooned again, but this swoon marked the beginning of an awakening. Coming out has in so many ways brought me back to that tomboy girl of ten. Being a lesbian has meant once again being disobedient, defiant, inappropriate; once again letting my cutoff jeans hang below my dress, running out to recess and leaving the skirt in the dirt by the classroom door. It's opened the way back to my courage, my sassy self. I'm not afraid to fight again. Most of my fights don't involve fists anymore, but I take tai chi and self-defense just in case. Now the fights are about standing up for myself, for my kids, or for other women who have lost their tomboy girls. I work a hotline; I read "out" poetry in public every chance I get; friends and I are suing the

disobedient

defiant

sassy

church and the minister who abused us when we were girls. I applaud my daughter for being strong and independent, for having a great service ace and killer ground strokes, for telling off a guy who was pressuring her for sex. The best birthday present I ever got was having the chance to save a woman who was being attacked. Driving through Florida Canyon on our way to my party, my friend Robin and I saw a woman on the roadside and a car stopped near her with its lights off. She told us later that she had hitchhiked and the guy who picked her up had taken her down there and pulled a knife. We pulled over, bundled her in, and took her home, watching in the rearview mirror as the car slowly skulked out of the canyon in the opposite direction.

Reunited with my tomboy girl, I once again feel balanced, agile, strong: sufficient unto myself. I celebrated my most recent birthday, my forty-second, by buying myself some boots and hiking up a mountain. My lover took a picture of me at the summit. I stand there waving, face red but grinning, as the city spreads behind me, hazy in the fog I've risen above.

It was a long detour for me, and it's good to be home.

The Year I Was Ten

Ann L. McClintock

I am exhausted and ecstatic and filthy. Sherrie and I have spent this hot spring day out in her father's fields chasing over the just-plowed soil after his truck, plucking rocks from the dirt and lobbing them into the truckbed. Most were easy, ranging in size from an egg to a softball. Some were two-handers though, that didn't always make it to the truckbed on the first heave. It is a zen activity before I know what zen is. I know only the joy of working hard out under a clear Montana sky.

On other days, Sherrie and I ride her pony, Babe, out through the gully to the sandstone mesa beyond. We ride bareback and sometimes practice one of those fancy TV mounts — like leaping on from behind after a running start like a gymnast mounting a pommel horse. We ride like we imagine Indians would, galloping furiously at times, meandering at others, shouting and whooping at the top of our lungs whenever we choose. There is no one else around, even far beyond what the eye can see — and from the top of the mesa, we can see far indeed: open prairie and farmers' fields, cut only by dirt roads that are little more than tracks.

The old farmhouse on Sherrie's family's land, little more than a shack now, also fuels our imaginations. We are miners staking a claim, trappers after furs, gunslingers on the run, farmers claiming a homestead on this land when it was even less settled than the sparseness we know. An iron bed occupies one corner, and a rustic pine table, another. Water comes from the pump outside; light, from oil lamps. The very air seems desiccated, as if from a time long passed.

10

The swish of the basketball through the net makes me grin. I've been working on this shot for weeks, and today, I make it every time. I have it cold. Alone in my neighbor's driveway, I jump and dribble and shoot my way through whole games. I'm not always alone here, but Sunday mornings when my neighbors go to mass is my time to master my game. Visions of Olympic medals, of an NBA championship game, of playing for the glory of my school and proudly wearing my letter fuel my endless practice.

The early-evening darkness transforms my little town into whatever I want it to be. I duck behind a tree to escape the headlights of a passing car, then dash across the street to take cover behind a bush. I crouch low to blend with the brick wall enclosing the yard on the corner and run, down the alley, then down the street. I am a spy. I am a criminal, a burglar casing a house. I am a detective tailing a suspect. I am innumerable TV and movie characters. And then I am at the Girl Scout House and back to being myself.

The troop leader suggests we work on one of the homemaker badges as a troop, and my best friends, Barb and Deb, and I roll our eyes heavenward and groan. We openly disdain those badges, avoiding them whenever possible, choosing instead to work on the nature and outdoor skills badges. Together, we have learned to tie knots, make a lean-to shelter, read a compass and topographical map, and do first aid.

Barb snaps her fingers. "We just won't do any of the stuff. She doesn't give us the badge, no big deal. If she does, okay." Deb and I look at each other and grin. We know we won't display the badge on our sashes anyway. But no amount of moaning and groaning gets us out of learning how to iron and sew.

I sit on the edge of the bridge over the Milk River watching some dogs play in the water upstream. The sun is hot on my back, but a cool breeze sweeps up from the water and the trees on the bank. Often I ride out to the bridge and watch as the setting sun saturates the blades of grass and leaves and water with color and heightens their shapes with dramatic shadows. Little traffic crosses this bridge, well beyond the outskirts of town, and I can be alone to dream and sing and think, and feel free of the constraints of other's ideas and perceptions of me.

To my delight, "I'm going out for a bike ride" seems to satisfy my mother's need to know where I'm going, what I'm doing. I can go almost anywhere on my bike, see anyone. My friends and I need only jump on our trusty wheels to be off to adventure in the far corners of our little domain.

10

My Levi's are soft and worn, finally, and I feel as tough and rugged as the ranchers I see wearing them every day. I wear sneakers that actually have soles with traction, not the silly Keds that all the girls wear. But, come winter, my mother draws the line at Pak's, the greatest of all outdoor snow boots. Barb has a pair, handed down from her big brother, and all the boys I know have them. But, even though I am out running around in the snow like the boys, my mother refuses, and all winter, I am stuck in wussy girls' snow boots. Someday...

I run the three blocks to my grandmother's house. She is just where I expect her to be on this hot midsummer afternoon: on her tree-shaded, screened-in front porch. Her book set aside before I reach the door, she immediately pulls me close for a hug. "How was camp?"

I bounce with excitement as I tell her of the cattail roots and wild strawberries we ate, of the early-morning walks in the creek by myself, of learning to shoot a bow and arrow. She gazes in admiration as I flex my new muscles for her, muscles grown from hiking and swimming and running around for two weeks.

I know already that my grandmother is fiercely proud and independent, gracious and compassionate. An adventurous spirit whose mind still ventures out through books, she feeds my spirit with grand tales of her many rail and steamship journeys. She values fitness and physical activity, honors integrity of mind and spirit, believes in a supreme being and shows it in her actions, cherishes the great wide world around us, and fosters community, particularly among women. She nurtures me, this tomboy, without reservation.

In the years that follow ten, I become less free with my friends and my body, as the adult world begins to enforce its rules about feminine behavior and dress through parental and peer pressure. My friends begin to take more interest in dating rituals than in adventures. As even my boy pals' conversations become dominated by sexual concerns, I, by virtue of time and gender, become "other."

I forget about the year I was ten until one day I find a pair of black cowboy boots just like the ones I wore riding Babe. I grow a garden and remember the smell of the soil and the joy of physical toil under the hot sun. I have to tie a knot while out backpacking and my memory provides me with the right one. I go riding on my bike and watch the sun create a light-and-shadow show in the trees and grass of Golden Gate Park.

At ten, I had a vision of the person I wanted to grow up to be. Along the way, some pieces of that vision got lost, and others were buried under social expectations. As I recover them, I find that I am rediscovering my Self, still heart and soul a tomboy.

Dear Grandma and Grandpa,

← This is a very good picture of me and Darrel and Tumbles, huh? (Darrel don't think so). I'm sending you this picture so you can remember what I REALLY look like. (Mom is making me send you a picture where I look like someone else).

Oh. That reminds me. Remember when you said I should come visit you more? I'm thinking about coming to your house to **live.** (I know you'd like that).

1.) How is the weather there?
2.) How do you feel about dresses?
3.) Who would you rather have with you for protection, Superman or Barbie?

I'm also considering Eygpt, to live in a pyramid. (plus pyramids). Me and Tumbles like sand, too.

Write me soon.

(Don't forget to answer the questions) (If there's too many of them, just answer 2). and 3).).

Love,
Dianne Reum
(your granddaughter)
XXXOOOXXXOOO

P.S. I might want a camel for Christmas.

Our little Miss Di

Skirmishes in the Tomboy Wars

Barb Netter

My first real memory in life is of waking up from a nap, still in my crib, wearing some frilly Sunday dress and wailing. Did I hate my clothes even that young? My mother always had her way on Sundays. She would dress my sister and me in matching dresses and silly hats (the boys got to wear white shirts and ties) and march us all off to church. When we got home, it was a contest to see who could change clothes fastest. I nearly always won.

Clothes were guaranteed flashpoints in the tomboy wars that made up my childhood.

When I was four, I fell in love with Dale Evans. She was smart, she was strong, she could ride a horse, and I thought she was beautiful. (Okay, maybe not beautiful, but my only TV choices at the time were Dale and Lucy, and even at four, I knew Lucy was way too much of a ditz.) I wanted to dress like Roy Rogers. I begged Mom for months for a real cowboy outfit: boots, hat, black vest, black pants. On Christmas morning, I opened a package to find my mother's compromise: a beautiful black-and-red shirt with white piping and pearl buttons, and a white skirt with leather

fringe. I wore the skirt the first day (because it was Sunday) and never wore it again. I wore the shirt every day my mother would let me until I outgrew it.

Clothes weren't the only point of contention between Mom and me, however. She wasn't thrilled by my physical activities, either.

At six, I fell in love with the girl next door. Linda was big, and mean, and two years older than I. She loved to tease young girls, and I was so smitten, I would do anything she dared me to. She convinced me to climb a huge oak tree in her front yard, to ride my bike with no hands down hills, and, once, to jump off the top of the slide at the school playground. For months afterward, my mother would introduce me to friends as her "tomboy daughter" while I smiled at them, proudly toothless. Linda tired of me when she realized she couldn't make me cry.

That December I wrote a solemn letter to Santa Claus, explaining why I needed a hockey stick. Christmas morning, I looked everywhere for a tall, thin package. Santa, however, had decided I needed a doll crib.

When I was nine, I fell in love with baseball. All the boys in the neighborhood played, and they wouldn't let girls play, but after plenty of begging I was finally allowed to be the foul-ball chaser. I would put on my brother's old glove — on the wrong hand, because I was left-handed — and wait for the chance to splash into the creek behind our house to retrieve balls. I didn't learn to bat until I was twelve.

The only game the girls were allowed to play was running bases. Two boys would throw the ball back and forth and try to tag out the kids running between them. (Girls were never allowed to throw the ball.) During one particularly fearless slide, my face collided with the knee of one of the throwers. I was so amazed by my two black eyes that I didn't care that my mother was now calling me "accident-prone," having realized that I heard "tomboy" as a compliment.

That Christmas I asked for a bow and arrows. I got an Easy-Bake oven.

At eleven, I fell in love with Susie. She was soft and sweet, a year older than I, and the only "good girl" in a wild family. Her goal in life was to be the first of her siblings to finish high school without being expelled. We spent that summer swimming in her backyard pool and dancing to Motown in her room. In the fall, her brothers taught me how to play basketball and break into cars. That winter, I taught Susie how to smoke and whistle with her fingers. She taught me what sex was. Explicitly. Neither of us knew yet what lesbians were. I don't think my mom did, either; I certainly didn't ask her.

On Christmas, as my sister played with her new Barbie Dream House, I shoveled the driveway so I could try out my new basketball. Mom had finally given in on sports.

She didn't give in quite as easily on clothes, though. When I was fourteen, she ended an argument with "When you pay for your own clothes, you can choose your own clothes. Until then, you'll wear what I buy." I got a job. I spent my first paycheck on bell-bottom Levi's and never wore a dress to school again.

High school was a blur of anger and discovery: Realizing there was something different about me when undressing in the locker room with fifty other girls, and being very careful not to get caught looking around. Finding myself in writing and photography. Dating a boy and wondering why. Being ostracized for liking gym class and shop, and refusing to take home ec. Developing an intense friendship with a teacher who abruptly needed to end it. Being called "queer" for the first time and spending the next day in the library, looking up "homosexual." Going to summer school to get out of high school as soon as possible. Fighting with my mother only occasionally over flannel shirts and blue jeans.

I always feel somewhat guilty looking back at how my mother treated my older sister. At some point, Mom figured out that all the pleading and complaining in the world was not going to make me wear dresses, or play with dolls, or take even remote interest in makeup or proms. This realization strengthened her efforts to "feminize" my older sister. Karen was subjected to Avon parties, to forced eyebrow plucking, to ballet lessons, to constant pressure to do whatever it took to be popular with boys. Luckily, Karen has recovered fully, and her own daughter is free to explore her sexuality on her own. Right now, at three, that daughter is married to two imaginary friends, one male and one female. Karen hasn't told Mom about them yet.

As for me, some of that tomboy quality has never left. At thirty-three, after a long series of girlfriends, I fell in love with a wonderful woman who enjoys many of the things I do: we camp, play softball, shoot pool. We are happy.

This Christmas I gave her a dress. She gave me a black-and-red shirt with white piping and pearl buttons.

Diane F. Germain, age 8 or 9
Colchester Avenue, Burlington, Vermont, early 1950s

A Day in the Life of the King's Musketeers

Rhomylly B. Forbes

I was called Ponzo in the old days, back when I was young and handsome and one of the King's finest Musketeers. France was my home; Paris, my playground; intrigue, my specialty. I had a nose for it, you could say, a sixth sense that procured me more adventures than it saved me from. Let me tell you about one of those adventures, so you can understand what it was like to be a man of the sword and a man of honor in such dangerous and dishonorable times.

On this particular morning in late summer, I rose early, an uncommon occurrence, as I had been at my favorite tavern, drinking and enjoying the company of a pretty wench, until very late the night before. But I had to report for duty with the captain of the Musketeers, Monsieur de Treville, at ten o'clock, so I reluctantly washed, then brushed and oiled my black, shoulder-length curls and short mustache (about which, I must admit, I was rather vain). I carefully dressed in the standard Musketeer's uniform: blue doublet with the gold cross and fleur-de-lis emblazoned on the front over the standard black knickers and white linen shirt, all under a black coat. Then soft, worn thigh-high brown leather boots folded down at the knee, a black hat with a large white plume, and my father's sword strapped to my waist.

After a quick breakfast of hard bread and soft cheese (washed down with warm wine), I left my rooms to collect my partner and companion, Montego, who lived some houses away. Together, we made our way through the familiar streets of Paris to Monsieur de Treville's.

Actually, I was called Becky in the old days, back when I was eleven years old and living in a small college town in Kentucky. At a time when other girls my age were indulging in more socially acceptable interests (boys, record albums, slumber parties), my best friend, Katie — whom I called Montego in private — and I played at being the King's Musketeers, dreaming of the day when we would be the finest swordsmen in all of France, performing heroic deeds for the honor of King and country. The fact that we wanted to join an incredibly sexist organization that hadn't existed for at least two centuries hindered our games not at all. We created endless adventures, rescued countless damsels in distress, and proved ourselves swashbucklers of the finest caliber, demonstrating beyond doubt that the line between dreams and reality is only as fine or as thick as you choose to make it.

HONOR

ADVENTURE

On this particular morning in late summer, I rose early and packed a few essentials for an overnight stay at Katie's farm. It was too early to leave, so I washed, then brushed my annoyingly blonde hair into two perky pigtails. What I would have given for thick, curly black hair like that of my alter ego, Ponzo! I carefully dressed in what was nearly a uniform for Katie and myself: blue cutoff shorts concealed by a way-too-large t-shirt that ended near my knees, striped tube socks, and sneakers.

INTRIGUE

After a quick breakfast of Cheerios (washed down with cold milk), my mother drove me to Katie's farm.

"Be good," she called as Katie ran out to meet me. "I love you. Don't give Mrs. Hanson any trouble. See you tomorrow."

"Bye, Mom," I called back. "I love you too."

"I will not be assigning you to King or palace today," said Monsieur de Treville. "However, there is a rumor circulating at court that the Duke of Buckingham has taken an unofficial leave of absence from London and is here in Paris. I have also heard that our good 'friend' Cardinal Richelieu would love for his Guardsmen to find the Duke and assassinate him. So go. Find out if the rumors are false, and find the Duke and get him safely out of Paris if they are not. The King will be most pleased if you do."

Montego and I smiled broadly at each other. Intrigue, our favorite game!

"No, I don't have any chores for you today," said Katie's mom when we asked her. "So go play outside. It's too beautiful a day to stay indoors."

Katie and I grinned at each other, then went to her room and finished donning our Musketeer uniforms. Our somewhat confused but loving mothers had made us "real" doublets out of blue denim, each with a gold felt cross and fleur-de-lis glued onto the front. These we pulled quickly over our heads, capping them off with huge, white-plumed black cavalier hats: a floppy brown denim hippie hat for me and an old straw gardening hat for Katie (both adorned with spiky chicken feathers). After grabbing the bamboo sticks we used for swords, Katie (excuse me, *Montego)* and I headed for the barn and the pastures beyond, two loony tomboys looking for adventure and intrigue in hot tunics and ugly hats.

Summer is Paris's least romantic season. The streets are filled with a thousand pleasant and not-so-pleasant smells that, enriched by the sweltering heat, make the eyes water and the nose cringe. The streets are also more crowded in the summer season. Every thoroughfare and alleyway seemed one giant marketplace that day as merchants displayed their wares in the open air, each stall groaning under the weight of the goods for sale. Buyers jostled one another with a great clashing of baskets and sacks as they made their purchases and deftly avoided the thieves and cutpurses in their midst.

"I do so love this time of year," said Montego, twirling the end of his brilliant red mustache at a comely damsel in a blue frock.

"You do?" I found summer in Paris smelly, sweltering, and smelly.

"But of course I do." He chuckled blithely as another pretty girl wilted under his passing gaze. "There are ever so many more lovely country blossoms in full bloom and ready for plucking!"

Women. Always Montego and women. And since every imaginable rumor was being passed along the marketplace except the one we most wanted to hear, I decided I was hot and hungry. We ducked into the dim coolness of a nearby tavern for a quick midday meal.

It was a poor choice of establishment, for as our eyes adjusted to the dark after the brilliantly sunlit street, we found it already patronized by a handful of red-doubleted Guards of Cardinal Richelieu, with whom all King's Musketeers at all times had a smoldering rivalry that at the slightest excuse might, and often did, flame into sword fighting and bloodshed.

It was no real surprise, then, when one of the Guardsmen rose from his seat and bowed toward us in the exaggerated manner of a stage performer. I instantly recognized Jacquar from previous unpleasant encounters. Beside me, I could feel Montego tense as Jacquar raised his wine tankard to us and declaimed loudly, "Well, if it isn't Ponzo and Montego, the King's favorite whoresons and the greatest fools in all of France!"

Montego yanked his sword out of its scabbard and crossed the tavern floor in one great leap. I reached to stop him, but he brushed me aside. Jacquar drew his sword, and so too did each of his companions.

Fortunately, the innkeeper was a jovial giant well accustomed to stopping fights in his place before they had a chance to begin.

He quickly stepped between the would-be antagonists, saying, "Come now, Jacquar, surely such an ill-mannered tripe as yourself can find something kind to say to these gentlemen. Perhaps you could start with an apology and an offer to buy them drink?"

Jacquar winced as the innkeeper's huge hand clapped down upon his shoulder. He murmured something that might have been an apology, tossed Montego a silver coin, and sat down. Mollified, Montego found us a table, and we ate our meal in angry silence, as did Jacquar and his band.

When the Guardsmen left, Montego growled, so low that only I could hear: "Ponzo, what possible reason can you have for attempting to stop me from slitting their deserving throats?"

"I have two reasons, my dear Montego. One, I knew our fine host Girard would break your handsome face to pieces for fighting in his place. And how would you fare with the ladies if he did so? Two"—I lowered my voice further—"before we were so basely insulted, I heard one of the Guardsmen mention something about 'Buckingham' and 'rue de Plumet.' I thought it best not to kill them just yet."

"Capital, my dear fellow," roared Montego, his good humor instantly restored. "I say we follow these red jaybirds, for they may indeed lead us to the nest we all seek!"

For a child, summer is a farm's most fascinating season. The fields are filled with thousands of grasshoppers ripe for catching, the trees are cool and leafy and begging to be climbed, and the running streams are full of amphibious creatures. Katie and I explored them all, slashing our bamboo swords before us from time to time to wave away swarms of attacking insects.

"I love this time of year," Katie said absently, apparently oblivious to the pungent smell just wafting over from the pig shed.

"You do?" I'd always thought of summer as hot and boring.

"Of course," she replied, swiping masterfully at a fat bumblebee that was hovering too close. "No school."

"Lunchtime!" Katie's mother hollered from the door. "Y'all hurry now!"

The house seemed dark after the bright, sun-drenched fields, but once our eyes adjusted, we groaned at the sight of two smaller boys already sitting at the table. We were going to have to eat lunch with Katie's monstrous little brothers, Jeffrey and Richard, with whom we at all times had a smoldering rivalry that might, and often did, flame into smacks and punches at the slightest excuse.

As we slid into our seats, Jeffrey rose, bowed, and said ever so solicitously, "And how are the two Mouseketeers this morning? Have you seen Mickey today?" Richard, always eager to torment us, started singing as loudly as he possibly could: "M-I-C, see you real soon! K-E-Y..."

This was too much insult to be borne. Katie lunged for Jeffrey. I tried to quash Richard by stuffing a paper napkin down his throat. Mrs. Hanson came in with a plate of sandwiches and a pitcher of lemonade and calmly assessed the situation.

"Don't sing at the table, Richard. Katie, sit down. Jeffrey, don't antagonize your sister. Becky, your napkin belongs in your lap. Now y'all eat nice and quiet."

We did, limiting our attacks to glares and ugly faces when Mrs. Hanson wasn't looking. Katie and I ran outside as soon as we were excused.

"Maybe we shouldn't have tried to kill them," I said as soon as we were out of earshot.

"Why's that?"

"It's too nice a day for you to get in trouble for punching your dumb brother. Besides, I'd probably have to go home if you got grounded."

"Oh. Yeah."

"I say, Ponzo, does that not look like our red-breasted friends up yonder?"

"In faith, Montego, that it does! And right here on the rue de Plumet, too! What a wonderful coincidence!"

"Methinks those vain popinjays are about to enter that house. Mayhap their presence is not entirely welcome within. Shall we put the entire nest to flight?" There were six of them and only two of us. But after all, we were two of the King's finest Musketeers and they were merely ... cows. The odds were most certainly in our favor.

"But of course, my dear Montego. Let us make their fur — I mean, feathers — fly!"

We drew our swords and attacked Jacquar and company with a vigor and style that would have done any of our Musketeer brethren proud. After our first rush, they were only four in number, two having been cut down where they stood with a satisfying thwack to their hairy butts from our flimsy bamboo swords. Soon, two more hobbled off the scene, clutching a deeply wounded arm apiece, the result of perfectly matched sword swipes from Montego and myself. After a short engagement, during which one could hardly see swords attack and parry, they moved so very quickly, Montego dispatched Bossy — I mean Jacquar — with a nasty sword thrust to the chest. The poor remaining Guard (whom I had been merely toying with, waiting for Montego to finish) fled into the afternoon shadows, running as if the Devil himself were in pursuit, mooing indignantly as she went.

The odds were most certainly in our favor.

"Well," said Montego brightly, barely panting from his exertions, "now that the pigeons have flown the coop, shall we go in?"

The door of the barn, which had hitherto been barred by the presence of the Guardsmen, was now open to us, and we crept inside, careful not to let anyone in the street see us...

"I hear voices in the back of the barn," whispered Montego. "I wager you a bottle of the best, my dear Ponzo, that we have found one wayward Duke of Buckingham, and may now offer our services to safely escort him out of unfriendly Paris."

"Unfriendly for the Duke, I vow," I whispered back. "But I bet it's your stinky brothers."

Our swords were still drawn from the short battle in the barnyard, and as we came to a closed stall door (through which we plainly heard voices), we gripped them harder. I nodded to Montego, and with a sudden sharp pull I opened the door and found myself face-to-face with George Villiers, Duke of Buckingham, the second most powerful man in England. Behind him, a lovely dark-haired, dark-eyed lady withdrew into the shadows. She twisted a small lace handkerchief between her fingers, but said nothing.

As one, Montego and I swept off our chicken-feather-plumed hats and went down on one knee, saying, "My lord, Duke of Buckingham!"

Katie's father did not look amused; in fact, his face was turning purple and the veins in his forehead were beginning to swell. Dr. Aaron, the local veterinarian, stood next to him, looking perplexed. I guess he wasn't used to having eleven-year-old Musketeers pop out from nowhere and salute his eminence in the middle of a dirty old barn.

Katie and I did the only thing we could. We jumped up and ran like crazy until we reached the middle of an open field, then fell onto the soft, sun-soaked grass and laughed and laughed until our sides ached.

We escorted the Duke and the mysterious dark-haired lady to an abandoned hut at the edge of town, where, to our surprise, a small band of English soldiers and their horses waited silently in the growing shadows.

"I will be safe from here to London, my good fellows. Thank you for your aid, and tell Monsieur de Treville I am once again in his debt." He turned to the lady. "Beloved, I pray for the day we need never part. Until then, know that you hold my heart and soul in your care." He kissed her hand, then clasped it to his forehead as if it were the most precious of gems.

Turning to mount his horse, he beckoned Montego and me closer. "The lady," he said sadly. "I have no right to ask, since our countries are preparing for war against each other, but would you..."

A lump in my throat kept me from speaking. Montego spoke as softly as I had ever heard him speak when he answered for both of us, "Your lady will come to no harm, my lord. We swear it."

"It is well, then," said the Duke. He lifted his hand in a gesture of farewell and rode away.

"Incredible," I said to Montego later in our favorite tavern. We had somehow convinced Katie's mother to let us take our sleeping bags and pillows to the hay-filled barn loft to spend the night.

"Wha'?" Montego was pondering the depths of the tankard in his hand, perhaps wondering who had refilled it when he wasn't looking. He was more than slightly drunk. So was I — on Dr. Pepper, which we believed was the exact color and consistency of burgundy wine. Montego had a leg of fowl in his other hand and a comely wench on his lap. So did I.

"The Duke. To risk his life for love's sake. Would you be as brave, or as foolish, my friend?"

"To risk my life for love? No. Absolutely not. Never." He drained his tankard in one long swallow and slammed it decisively down on the table. "Well, mayhap were she as fond of me as I of her, and she as lovely as the Duke's lady. Mayhap I would, Ponzo!" He rose from his seat and gestured expansively to the gathered company, accidentally dumping the wench to the sawdust-covered floor as he did so. "But come! The night is young and so are we! Drink up, all! A song, let us have a song to celebrate true love and another to tell of our glorious deeds! Sing with me, Ponzo! Sing!"

And sing we did, happy for a time in each other's company. When the Dr. Pepper was gone, Katie and I lay back on our sleeping bags, itching some from the soft hay that had already worked its way into them, and gazed through the open hayloft

"Sing with me, Ponzo! Sing!"

door at the summer stars and waning moon. The caffeine from the burgundy wine kept us awake and singing for hours, songs we made up — to the tunes of John Denver ballads, Christmas carols, anything but the Mickey Mouse Club theme song — about Musketeers in general, Dumas's four Musketeers in particular, and, of course, ourselves especially.

We were finally drifting off to sleep when Katie rolled over and said quietly,

"Good night, Ponzo. Sweet dreams."

Good night, Montego, wherever you may be. Sweet dreams to you, too.

Air Displacement

Franci McMahon

Pirates was the only game I liked playing with my sister when I was young. Merry played the captive lady and did all the right things: swooned in my arms, wore piles of whooshing petticoats, and screamed often.

I wore an eye patch, a loose white blouse, and black tights. And, best of all, a pair of rolled-up socks tucked into the front of my underwear.

It's clear to me now that the socks gave me the authority to boss my older sister around — the only time I managed it. I considered wearing the socks in my jeans at other times to see how that changed the power. My mother quickly let me know that wasn't done.

"You're a girl." I came to dread hearing those words. That refrain was meant to put a stop to the racy, exploring side of life. Hearing it filled me with anger, resentment — and the sense that somehow, something was wrong. At the time I thought it was my body.

This confused me, because my body seemed to work well for me. When I ran through the apple orchards, pretending to be one of a herd of racing horses, I could jump wide ditches, weave between the tree rows, and slide to a hoof-planted stop or turn on a dime. Everything worked just fine.

And when I rode horses, it was through my body that they understood what I wanted. We had an unspoken language made up of subtle shifts of weight or a leg closed against the horse's side. My hands were light as I held the reins. After the ride, I would curry and smooth the big animal's coat to a high gloss.

Horses were a girl's best friend. The attraction wasn't just their intangible power or their unfettered freedom. A girl could also take on their spirit: wide nostrils sifting a sage-scented wind, hide flicking to shake off the pestering fly, a flint-hard hoof pawing the ground.

Even before I had a horse to ride, I would gallop through the sagebrush, my arms, the front legs of the wild horse; my strong legs, the hind. I would toss my sweat-flecked mane, flare my nostrils, and neigh my challenge to the sky. I looked for mares to herd, other stallions to fight.

Recently, I found a black-and-white photograph of me. *Franci, 1947, 6 years old,* read my grandmother's frail script across the print's white border.

My face glowed. My hair, cut in a short bob, lifted lightly on a breeze. I sat tall, but my feet didn't reach the stirrups of the western saddle, so they rested in the loops of the fender straps. The black horse was a riding stable nag: head like a suitcase; short, jackhammer legs.

This horse was my favorite. We could go anywhere. Exploration took us along irrigation ditches, across creeks, on a gallop through sagebrush and tumbleweed into the low hills. We moved with authority, parting the air, taking our space in the universe.

I think at first Merry rode with us, but I soon left her in the dust. Her preference had always been paper dolls and thumbing through our mother's *Vogue* magazines.

By the age of ten I had decided that the life for me would be on a horse, accompanied by my faithful dog (who would look like Rin Tin Tin), living in the wilderness. This job description fit precisely that of the red-coated Canadian Mountie.

I told Merry, who being a year older, quickly called on her worldly big-sister knowledge to tell me the way things were.

6 years old
1947

"You have to buy your own horse and gun," she said smugly. To this day I don't know how she knew this.

"I can get a job. I'll save my money."

"You also must have two hundred dollars."

As I started to respond to this, she added, "And be born in Canada."

My face fell, I know. Then I thought of our mother. "Mother was born in Alberta. Maybe that will be enough."

"And you have to be a man, silly."

That was it. No way around it. At that moment I felt the rope drop around me, lasso pulled tight.

There are times now when I feel that pure tomboy persona in myself. It takes an equine shape as I walk down the street, my body displacing air, moved by powerful legs. An echo of flint-hard hoofbeats follows me. I break the trail.

I spent most of my childhood learning about laws — physical laws — gravity, momentum, and the one about two objects not being able to occupy the same space at the same time. It seemed to take eons of misadventures for me to realize that I had a body and needed to preserve it while I tried all the things that my mind knew I could do.

I knew that I could run like the wind. I knew that if I wore a sail, the wild Santa Ana winds of southern California would race my bicycled being down the road. I knew that I could build a city of roads in the hardpan soil. I knew that I could be the cowboy hero of any story I created. I knew that I could build a camouflaged underground fort. Or attach a pair of rollerskates to a low platform and make a turnable scooter. I knew that I could pedal my bike as fast as I could and stand on the seat to sail free, a circus acrobat revealed.

Some of what I knew worked and some didn't.

–Kisa, from "On Account of Being a Tomboy"

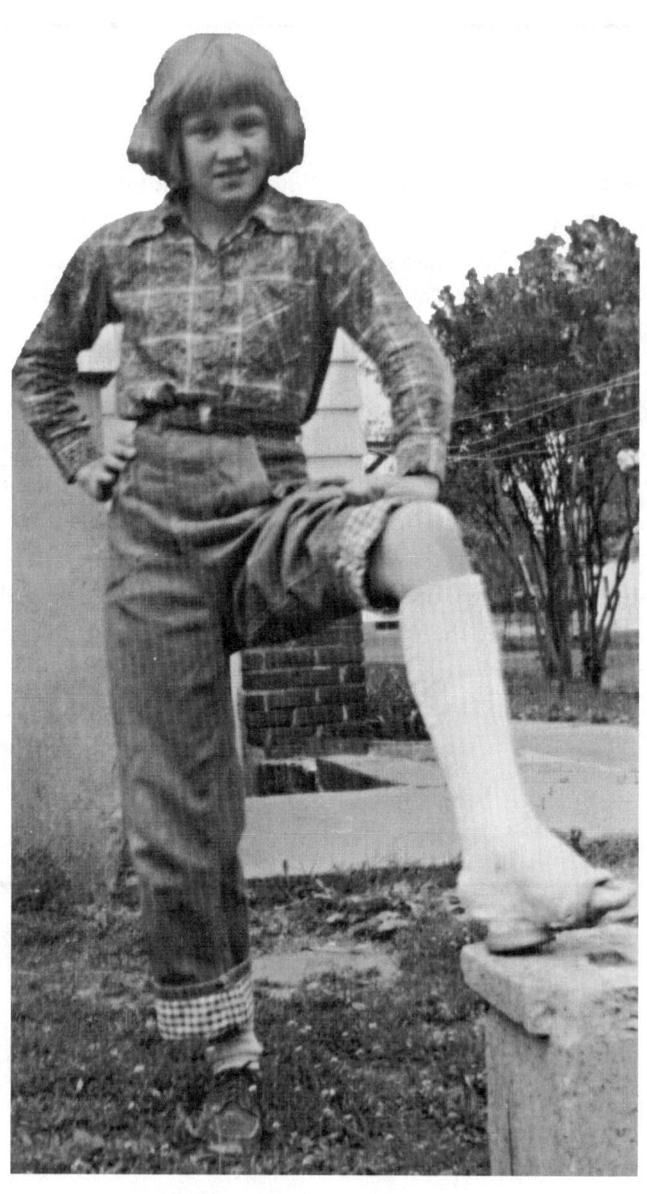

I got this broken leg as the result of a dare. The neighborhood boys were taking turns jumping off of a creek tunnel onto a sandbank. They dared me to jump, and though I was scared to, I was more afraid of what they would call me if I didn't. So I jumped. My foot came down with a snap on a rock and I felt a sharp pain. I rolled over, groaning and cussing, but did not cry, because, well, only sissies cried. The boys thought I was faking. I crawled out of the creek onto the bank, where I sat for the better part of an hour with my leg throbbing, thinking it was a sprain. When everyone left, I looked and found my ankle more swollen than with any sprain I'd ever had. I hopped, then crawled, across a cornfield home. When I saw my mother — out of the boys' sight — I cried. I wore the cast for a month and was the school hero: Karol had broken her leg on a dare — something that girls didn't do — and had only cussed.

–Karol D. Lightner, 1954

Stingrays

Giovanna (Janet) Capone

At age twelve, as "Summer in the City" tops the charts, I spend my summer Saturdays taking a crash course in bike mechanics. First, I carefully observe my father fixing our bikes in the driveway. Then, I teach myself. I sit for hours on the gravelly blacktop in the heat of the New York summer with Dad's toolbox beside me and the back wheel of my old red bike clamped between my knees. Dad got this clunker for me at the Salvation Army and I gotta fix it up. I'm proud of myself: learning bike mechanics, sitting there cursing and yelling, just like Dad always does.

I grip the wrench hard on one side of the wheel, while holding the other side tight with a pair of pliers that keep slipping off the nut when I squeeze. If the pliers slip, you can end up stripping the nut, so I hold them as tight as I can and turn the other side with the wrench. The bike keeps wobbling back and forth between my knees. Finally it crashes to the ground for the third time.

"Goddamn sonofabitch! I'm sick of this piece of shit! All morning I've been trying to fix this stupid thing!" I kick it with my sneaker. I swear, one more try and that's it. Off to the junkyard!

Wrench biting hard, pliers biting harder. Turn. The damn pliers slip again. That's it. I fling my tools clear across the driveway. I hate this shitty bicycle!

Next thing I know, my friend Max is walking up the street, wheeling her sister Christina's heap of junk in my direction. She's looking at me, shaking her hand like it's on fire.

"Hey, Mooch," she says. That's short for Martimucci. "You're gonna bust your father's tool set."

Her real name is Catarina, but she changed it to Max, which she got from a Superman comic book. The boys in the neighborhood still call her Catarina, though, just to rub it in. I don't blame her for changing it. Who'd want to walk around with a name like Catarina, unless you're ninety-five years old? Her parents named her after her grandmother, who still calls her that. She's from Italy. Most days she sits on their front porch in a black dress, rocking and praying. Sometimes she bakes a huge tray of cookies for the neighborhood kids: chocolate chip, and butter cookies sprinkled with powdered sugar, and cookies made with sesame seeds or pignoli. She always gives me some. She says, "Francesca, take a dis. Take a dis," kind of rough. She can be nice like that, but if you ever make her mad, watch out. She starts yelling and flipping out in Italian and I don't know what the hell she's jabbering about, so I just leave.

When Max hears her real name being called, she rolls her eyes. This happens every day, because she lives right around the corner from us and her grandma is always hanging her head out the kitchen window, yelling. First she whistles real loud. Then she yells for Max, and Max's brother and sister, all in a stream of old-lady Italian that sounds like one long name:

"AntoneeyaCatareenaChristeena, venite qui!" Every day at 5:30 on the dot we hear her whistle, then:

"AntoneeyaCatareenaChristeena, venite qui, subito!" Max, her brother, and her sister come from all parts of the neighborhood, tearing ass to make it home on time for dinner. If they're late, they're in big trouble.

Sometimes they invite me over to eat. I love it. Their food is just like ours: macaroni and meatballs, steak bizziola, stuffed artichokes, pasta fasule, and crisp, warm Italian bread right from the oven.

Seeing Max in the driveway reminds me that today's the day I'm supposed to fix her sister's brakes and patch her front tire. The bike's been in the cellar all winter. It's been collecting dust for months, and nobody should be without a bike that long, even your little sister. Plus, I owe Max a favor, because she did such a good job putting a decent pocket in my new mitt, oiling the leather and tying it up real tight with a hardball inside. Don't get to use it much, though, thanks to those creepy neighborhood boys who won't let us play ball with them in the lot across the street.

When I stand up, the backs of my legs look like the face of the moon, craters and all, from sitting on the gravel in my shorts all this time. I push the toolbox aside and walk over to where Max has leaned the bike against the wall.

She covers her eyes with one hand. "I know. It's a piece of shit."

"Needs some work all right."

It's a Stingray, a twenty-incher. Same size as mine, only newer and a girl's. I run my fingers along the chain. Too much droop — gotta put more space between the back wheel and the sprocket up front. I comb my fingers through my brown hair, like Dad always does. It's just now growing back since I cut it. I had to even it out after Dad's cousin Freddy botched my haircut. My father is so cheap. To save ten bucks, he takes me to his cousin Freddy's so-called beauty parlor. "Let's go see Freddy," he says. "He'll cut your hair and style it like a professional." A professional axe murderer. He gave me this cutesy cut with wings on both sides. I came home and got out the big, black scissors. It's short, but it'll grow back soon enough.

It's short, but it'll grow back soon enough.

I'm looking at Chris's bike and realizing I've got a job ahead of me.

"Pass me that wrench over there. Pliers, too."

By noon, we have the back wheel and brakes fixed. It's a miracle. Why was my own bike such a hassle? I'm patching Chris's flat when pesty Franky MacIntyre comes by with his skinny head and four eyes, and starts throwing pebbles at us from behind a parked car. It's Mr. Ionatti's son's car, a gold Impala with the back jacked way up. Franky throws larger and larger pebbles until pretty soon he's chucking rocks and aiming above the waist. We put up with it a minute longer before we lay down our tools and walk over. He's had it coming to him ever since he and his punky friends began hanging out in that dirt lot across the street, playing baseball and leaving bottles and trash. There're two baseball diamonds in the neighborhood, but they gotta play where we ride bikes.

Max covers one side of the car; I cover the other. Franky's ducking behind the trunk. We blast him with a "Get lost, punk!" and the crybaby's gone, tearing home to Mommy. His red head looks like a cantaloupe bobbing down the street. He lives only a couple of houses away.

A few minutes later, we hear him singing from his front porch — "Figaro, Figaro, Figaro" and "Let Me Call You Sweetheart." Then the yelling starts: "Wear a bra, tomboy. You need one. Wear a bra."

He yells that at me a lot, especially lately. I'm getting nubs. I wear loose sweatshirts, but it doesn't help. Last month, Ma yanks me to K-Mart to buy a bra. No way am I standing near her while she picks one out. We take it home and it's this stretchy, hookless job called a training bra. The elastic snaps like a slingshot. One size fits all, from the mighty to the small. What are you in training for anyway? Whatever it is, I don't wanna join.

I end up wearing the bra for one day. I'm in the old gray tree behind the church, carving my initials. I've just finished a perfect carving, higher than anyone else has ever climbed. On my way down, I swing from the bottom branch. Next thing I know, the damn bra is around my neck. I almost strangle to death! The minute my sneakers hit the ground, I reach inside my t-shirt and fling that stupid thing off me. I'm no poodle and I don't need training.

"Wear a bra, tomboy!" Franky hollers again. He can yell till he's blue in the face. We go back to fixing that tire.

We have the wheel off now. Max peels out the inner tube and pumps it full of air. She pumps and pumps. Her arms are as thin as spaghetti, but her muscles are rock hard. Her hair is pulled back in one long brown braid down her back.

We go into the basement and fill a tub of water, then submerge the tire tube and listen for the sizz. Millions of tiny bubbles ripple to the surface.

"She musta run over some glass," Max says, looking at me. I can tell by her look that we're both thinking the same thing.

"Coke bottle glass."

"We been cleaning up glass and cans ever since they started playing ball in that lot!"

"Shit."

It's like that for most of the summer. We keep patching flats. I finally get around to fixing my bike — and I mean fixing it up like new. Work on it a good two weeks before I finish. I fix the hole in the tube and buy two new tires with treads as thick as my boot soles, white walls and all. (I saved up my allowance. A lousy quarter a week for drying the dishes, whoop-de-doo. It took me forever.) Next I sand the old, red paint off the frame and keep on sanding till I hit steel. I spray-paint it jet black. Then I cover all the chrome with silver sparkle racing tape and plant a brand-new silver-and-white banana seat on it, add a wheelie bar, reflectors — the works. I name it the Black Python. Max says it looks wicked.

We fix up her bike, too. Sometimes the floor of our garage is a mess. I get yelled at one night when it's pouring down rain and Dad can't pull the Buick in when he gets home. It's got alternator problems and if the wires get wet, he has to go out early in the morning with Rosemarie's blow dryer to get it to start.

Max and Chris bring their bikes over and we fix flats all morning. We spend every last penny we have on patch kits and paint. When we finish, we take the bikes for a spin around the driveway. If they ride okay, we go through the neighborhood collecting stuff — milk crates from the A&P, a couple of bricks off Mr. Ionatti's crumbling porch steps, a bag of gravel scooped from the used-car lot around the corner, a shovel. Whatever we turn up that day we haul across the street to the lot. We spend weeks building a dare-or-die bike course, making ramps and gravel pits — right through the half-assed baseball diamond the boys have set up. We start out in left field and zigzag in. We even have a tunnel at one end of the course. That was my inspiration. One day, we were rolling around inside Mrs. Nardone's Maytag refrigerator box when all of a sudden, the bottom split open. There we were, sitting in this long box with no windows and two open ends.

"Hey, we got a tunnel!"

"All right!" Max said. "Slap me five!"

I'm in the driveway one morning, putting the finishing touches on my bike. I'm painting a yellow lightning bolt across my back fender when Max and her sister come dragging this splintered old door down the sidewalk. I swear, they find the best things in the neighborhood. They drop the door smack in the middle of the driveway.

"Hey, Mooch!" Max says. "Know that trench we dug yesterday?"

"The alligator pit?"

"Here's our bridge. Pop threw it out with the trash."

"Great!"

The course is getting bigger and better, weaving its way across left and center fields like a boa slithering toward third base. We give it a test run every so often. Franky and his gang are always there playing ball, batting away, laughing whenever one of us falls, but catching our good runs out of the corners of their eyes. No denying it, we're getting better. We coach each other. Two of us spread out in either direction. The rider pedals from one end of the course to the other, up the ramps and over the bridge. The other two watch for rough spots — patches of glass or weeds. The glass is always there.

One day, we're out there doing some last-minute work on ramp number three, a big old stone slab from the graveyard behind St. Ursula's that was hell to dig up. (We had to get a shopping cart from the A&P to haul it.) I'm standing at the end of the course, with Chris in the middle and Max at the starting line calculating how much speed she's gonna have to build up. I can hear my stomach grumbling. We've been at this all day long. I give the hand signal. Off Max goes, bombing down the course, her tires spitting gravel all the way. Her braid is flying straight out behind her like a raccoon tail when she disappears through the tunnel. The first ramp is no problem — she's up it and down, clipping along for the bridge. When she hits the second ramp, I think she just might take off into the wild blue yonder and wing it the rest of the way.

"Go, Max! All right!" Even the punks are watching now. Max comes zigzagging past Chris, down along the boys' left foul line, when suddenly I get a bad feeling in the pit of my stomach. That third ramp is way too steep for the tight landing space after it. Their damn baseball diamond is cramping us. I signal Max to slow down. She makes the curve, comes flying off the ramp, and hits her brakes. The bike skids, slipping out from under her and sliding across the dirt, past third base. Max lands on her butt. A second later, we hear her grandmother's long whistle in the wind.

"AntoneeyaCatareenaChristeena, venite qui!"

"Catareena, venite qui!" Franky mimics her. He makes some Italian hand gestures and the boys bust out laughing. I give 'em the up-your-ass, first one arm, then the other. Who do they think they are?

Who do they

Max gets up and looks at me. It's dinnertime and we're both hungry — on top of being pissed off and embarrassed — but no way are we leaving now. We've got some changes to make.

Between runs, we pick things up, rearrange that last ramp, and make the curve leading up to it a little smoother. The boys are at the top of the ninth and the pitcher is hurling fastballs.

"Okay, strike 'em out, strike 'em out!" we hear them yell.

My turn is up. Chris and Max get into position. I'm at the starting line. As soon as I see Max's signal, I start pedaling. I gotta pick up enough speed to get me through the tunnel, up the first ramp, and over the alligator pit. I fly over the ramp and come down pretty hard. My back tire barely clears the ditch and those alligators are snapping at my heels. I'm heading up the second ramp now. Max and Chris are rooting like mad.

"Mario Andretti! Indi five!" Max screams.

Next thing I hear is the crack of wood on hard leather, followed by yelling. Sounds like a home run. Franky MacIntyre is running for first, screaming a blue streak.

"Off the field, tomboy. Your tits are jiggling."

His ball nicks my back tire, throwing the bike off balance for a second. I regain control without losing too much speed. By this time, Franky is halfway to second, then going for third. His team is screaming like mad. I'm zipping down the left foul line. I could flatten him like a roach in a hot second, but I'd have to swerve off course and I'd never make that third ramp. I see Max rooting for me at the end of the course, and I go for it. I whip around the curve leading up to ramp three and aim full speed ahead for my buddy Max.

"All right!" she hollers, leaping in the air.

I'm flying over the last ramp when they get him. Tagged out at home plate. "Watch out, you suckers!" I yell as my wheels touch down. "I claim this lot for the girls! It's a bike course, not a baseball field." They shout in protest while I skid full circle, wrapping a giant fishtail right around home plate.

Who
do
they
think
they
are?

Confessions of an Unrepentant Tomboy

Marianne Dresser

As a small girl, before I lucked into the pixie haircut that I would later insist on, I used to stuff my long, sun-blonde hair up into a baseball cap and beg my mother not to reveal my true gender on outings to the Safeway. When I grew up, left home, and turned out to be gay, Mom, with uncanny hindsight, traced the roots of my queerness to the persistent desire I had for my teenage brother's long-since-outgrown Cub Scout shirt.

It was dark blue, emblazoned with colorful patches. I bargained for it by serving as my brother's grease monkey when he worked on his constantly-in-need-of-repair Jeep. I would pass him wrenches or sort through oily metal parts as a steady stream of obscenities emanated from under the hood. Once my servitude was over and I had earned that shirt, I wore it constantly and even slept with it at night. From such humble beginnings was born the cross-dressing career of a dyed-in-the-wool tomboy.

Quick and compact, all of three and a half feet tall, I went by the unlikely name Big Moose. I could run fast and knew the escape routes — the loose planks and torn chain-link in backyard fences, the easily corruptible guard dogs and sympathetic housewives. The gang of boys I ran around with came to rely on my ability to get us safely away from our ambushes and strikes into enemy territory. We lived on the white-trash fringe of a flat, dry Central Valley town, part of the last frontier, where generic American house-and-yard plots gave way to untended orchards and fields gone fallow or choked under crisp, tough weeds. These remnants of valley farmland were fast being compressed by the encroaching suburban grid, but to us they were unexplored continents, our Wild West, war trenches, tropical jungles.

Our turf was the four-block territory bounded on the north and south by Platt and Laurel Streets, on the west by an abandoned turkey farm, and on the east by the much less interesting elementary and junior high schools. From time to time the gang staged pitched battles with other groups of kids across the border, two blocks away. Small framed, towheaded, perpetually scruffy in jeans and t-shirt, I was undeniably the leader of this ragtag collection of neighborhood boys — not because I was the strongest, or even the biggest physically, but because I was the toughest mentally. I didn't so much seize power as receive it. I was a tough little tomboy, not a *real* boy, so I stood outside their constantly shuffling male pecking order and gathered up the reins when they were done. I had authority because I was not afraid to take control, willful as any dictator and as needless of external sanction.

We were all used to a lot of turmoil and a nearly universal lack of adult supervision — to being on our own in a terrifying yet endlessly fascinating world, cast adrift with only our wits and an abundance of dirt clods for survival. Fed a steady diet of domestic violence and TV, our imaginations turned to games of danger and survival. We played war and cowboys and Indians; we reenacted *The Fugitive* and *The Man from U.N.C.L.E.* In my genuine coonskin cap with its tail flopping rakishly off the back, I *was* Davy Crockett leading the frontiersmen through the Kentucky backwoods.

One Christmas, my parents finally got me something I actually wanted: a miniature army camouflage uniform complete with tiny plastic grenades on a carabineer belt, and a toy machine gun. Later, I pedaled to the store countless times balancing loads of deposit-return soda bottles on my handlebars, to earn enough money for an official *Man from U.N.C.L.E.* collapsible toy rifle. This I brandished while skulking around the yard wearing a black Ilya Kuryakin–style turtleneck. At twelve, I certainly didn't want to be the show's other character, wearing suits and kissing girls. I was to discover those pleasures much later.

Down the street from my house was a run-down clapboard cottage rumored to be inhabited by a mysterious, crazy old lady who reportedly took potshots with a rifle at anyone who trespassed into her overgrown yard. Of course, we saw in this a perfect opportunity for a display of idiot bravery. Just like Jim in *To Kill a Mockingbird*, I took a dare and ran all the way up to the porch, earning a fast flight to safety and the gang's queasy admiration. Poking around an abandoned tower next door to the turkey farm, we discovered a hobo's recent half-eaten meals, vaguely disturbing girlie mags, and other musty, discarded junk. No backyard volleyball set could compete with that. When I visited my pal Tommy at his middle-class family's ranch-style house, only the pool held my attention on 100-degree-plus summer days. In *my* neighborhood, there was adventure around every corner, across every muddy ditch and scrubgrass field.

By the sixth grade, though, boys and girls were inexorably migrating into separate societies. I regrouped in a girl gang, the power behind the throne occupied by Kristin, our ostensible leader, a cute blue-eyed blonde from the "good" part of town. Once, in her parents' white-on-white living room, we devoured the sexy parts of their John Updike novels. It was my idea for the gang to wear pants — forbidden attire for girls — en masse to school one day, to the shock of our staring, whispering classmates. The principal drove us home, and one by one we were made to change into skirts or dresses. Despite the public humiliation and parental wrath we suffered, our juvenile act of protest started a minor revolution. Within a year, the school dress code was changed and girls were allowed to wear pants.

forbidden attire

In my early teens, playing sports meant that I could always dress in comfortable, loose clothes and avoid the increasing social pressure to wear skirts and blouses. My best friend, my companion in negotiating the dangerous waters of adolescent tomboyhood, was a freckled, redheaded girljock of considerable talent. Elaine and I played on the junior high girls' volleyball, softball, and basketball teams, and fed quarters into the humming overhead lights for night games of tennis at the public courts. We rode our bikes to the mall to look at sports equipment we could never afford to buy. Once, we encountered an oily man sitting in his parked car who slyly showed us the ugly little sausage lying limply in his unzipped trousers. We rode home fast, taking the shortcut through the fields, and didn't talk about it.

One moist spring night, Elaine and I ventured far out into the flooded field behind her family's rambling old farmhouse, testing our fence-walking skills. The waterlogged pasture writhed from edge to edge with masses of fucking frogs. We perched on the narrow ledge of the fence, savoring the horror of tumbling into the amphibian muck below, and contemplated nature's rank fecundity. It was weird, we decided. I had never told her about the strange bellyache I sometimes felt during sleepovers. Elaine's father was a teacher from New York, so she was a great deal more worldly than I. She was as painfully aware of the threat of being called a "lezzie" as I was oblivious to the notion. But that night, amid the sea of frantic, slippery bodies and the cacophony of grunting frog-lust, I caught a glimpse of nature's reproductive imperative and began to wonder at my place in it.

I hit high school. My athletic career was soon eclipsed by one smoking pot in the parking lot with an ad hoc association of stoners. I was the sole female member, one of the cool rebel boys. I had long since outgrown my childhood tomboy name, but I now had a new moniker: Mao, after the Chinese Communist leader (someone else was the obligatory Ché). The shift from tomboy sports clothes to the androgynous hippie look was easily accomplished, so for most of my adolescence I avoided having to wear dresses or any kind of girlish clothes. (One horrendous exception:

an unspeakably humiliating floor-length, sleeveless *pink* monstrosity I was coerced into wearing at my brother's wedding.) But the summer before my senior year, the shock waves of adolescent lust rocked the gang. Once I started to have sex with a fellow doper, I was demoted overnight to the status of his "girlfriend" and exiled to the cold fringes of the guys' clubby society. I liked fucking, but being a "girl" came at too high a price.

And social pressure and high school rules were becoming harder to get around. Despite my straight-A status, the powers above threatened to refuse to let me graduate with my class because I insisted on wearing my own clothes instead of the degrading blue jumpsuits required during phys. ed. A well-meaning but overdramatic school counselor took my intense teenage boredom and bullshit-weary attitude as an indication that I might soon turn to "bombing banks." (He obviously had me confused with a certain rich-white-girl-gone-bad.) To graduate and escape to the greener, and presumably cooler, pastures of college, I toed the line, enduring the last few weeks with the secret pride of having successfully skirted the system for nearly the entire year. A few months later, I migrated to a beach-town university I chose specifically for its beautiful, forestlike campus and reputation for good pot.

After two years, I dropped out of college, moved to the big city, came out, and cut my hair. It was the late seventies, and in the urban punk underclass I joined, androgyny was the norm: *everyone* had cropped hair and wore the same black clothes. But in the wider world, the range of social acceptability was still alarmingly narrow, and I rarely fit within it. So I learned to brave alarmed stares from older ladies on entering public rest rooms, learned to never look at anyone directly or even at myself in the mirror to avoid inadvertently meeting a gaze. I honed my pat responses to the inevitable question, not always from children — "Are you a boy or a girl?" — and was ready when the answer was met with a kind of primal hostility. Somehow, having been a tomboy had taught me that the other side of "not fitting in" is a subtle subversive energy — the power of *difference*.

In the expansive realm of young tomboyhood, I had my first and sweetest taste of this power and its rewards. Boys didn't have to wait to be given a place in the big world. It was their birthright to strut, talk tough, and play rough; to play outside, get dirty, get physical, get into trouble. I knew that I wanted what the boys had, and on a deep level I understood that to gain the keys to their kingdom, I had to collapse all outward signs of "girlishness" into some private interior space, for retrieval later, as needed. Being a tomboy meant being teased, made me subject to a constant stream of none-too-subtle attempts to fit me into a "proper" female role. But it also revealed the power of self-image and self-definition and trained me well in creative resistance to the status quo.

Now, pushing forty, still a classic androgyne, I am grateful for my youthful gender transgressions, proud of my inner tomboy. She is with me still, a strong, playful little being at home in her body and in the world. In today's parlance, this is called being "empowered." I call it just being alive.

Sally Sotomayor, c. 1944

Band members got to wear *pants*.

A Tale of Two Brothers

Jeanne Córdova

It was showdown in West Covina, California, where the pavement plains baked under the same orb that had blistered the plains of Little Big Horn. Like General George Custer, I had readied my troops for my last stand. And so had Billy, my Chief Sitting Bull of a little brother. The men were restless, my soldiers lined up at Chetney Drive's west end, his warriors camping on three adjoining front lawns to the east.

It had taken all morning to gather the infant-ry from the neighborhood and to get Billy to agree that I would get to be General Custer and he would be Sitting Bull. He'd finally given in, pouting, "What's the difference — I'm gonna kill you anyway."

"Maybe Custer didn't really die," I yelled, waving my cork rifle in his face. "Maybe I'll kill you first!"

Billy drew his freckles together below his flattop and narrowed his eight-year-old blue eyes. "You gotta play it like it really was. This time your guys die."

"I don't *gotta* do anything!" I turned and strutted toward my soldiers. "Let the best man win."

Thirty child troops of the Seventh Calvary of Chetney Drive plowed into the Little Big Horn tepees that day. But Billy's warriors took cover in the trees and bushes, using collapsed grocery boxes to ward off the pellets from my men's berry shooters.

My calvary, ages four to eleven, all went down under arcs of rubber-tipped arrows.

I escaped.

Cheating history that day was easy. Trying to cheat time wasn't.

I was First Son

Bill and I began life together easily, born just twenty months apart. Both of our birth certificates read, "Child born abroad of American parents, Bremen, Germany," and it would be many years before I understood the critical difference: his read "male"; mine, "female." Until then, in the golden childhood years before gender labels came to distort the truth of who I was, my knighthood was in flower.

I was born the second child (technically, daughter), of "the mother with twelve kids." First in line was France, a space cadet sister eleven months my senior. Billy was third in line, First Son, according to the rules. But between us, I was First Son, Billy's big brother. Fortunately, physiology was neither Billy's forte nor mine. France was the girl; Bill and I were *pals*.

As Billy's older brother, naturally I had to teach him everything he needed to know. Like how to pick cactus thorns out of his butt when we finally landed in the uncivilized grasslands of presuburban California. And where to find Bamboo Land — far from home, down around the block, the hideaway of forts and cowboys and hidden treasures — wild, reed fields where Mom could never find us.

In Bamboo Land, sometimes even Billy and I couldn't find stuff — even our own — and he knew that. He broke my heart for the first time when he buried one of my new chrome-studded cowboy boots in the land of reeds. It had taken me eight years of wish-fairies and Christmas pleadings to get those boots. Now one — he would bury just one — was gone.

Of course I beat him up for that. He needed reminding that I was Arthur — he was Lancelot.

By the time Mom read us *The Knights of the Round Table*, there was, in addition to "the Big Three" (France, me, and Bill), also a "Middle Kingdom": three little sisters for Bill and me to torture.

Marianne, the oldest of the Middle Kingdom, often volunteered to be Guinevere. My kingdom now included enough neighborhood knights to surround the dilapidated Formica table that had become our glorious Round Table after Mom tossed it into the garbage, and if on any given day there were too many knights, Guinevere would offer to give up her seat at the table and sit on the floor with her ladies-in-waiting, Leslie and Louise. The Middle Kingdom was always deferential.

All that mattered in those Camelot years was that the sun came up every day, school got out while there was still daylight left to play in, and Billy and I ruled the neighborhood.

The orange groves were gradually replaced by stucco gray, tan, and pink tract homes. Bamboo Land was leveled for the classrooms of Monte Vista Elementary School. I had to move my knights out of the disappearing fields and onto the streets. I lost the land but still kept my dominance in the neighborhood. With Billy's help, of course.

I was still older, bigger, faster, better than Billy at the important things: catching, running, batting, even tackling — though, once, he broke my ankle downing me. Billy was still my second lieutenant in life.

He taught me the meaning of the word *friendship:* the honor and duty of being there for a friend, no matter how tough life got. Friendship was why he and I built our last hideout high up in the garage rafters, and why we had agreed that our cave up there amidst Mom's trunks and boxes would have no ladder so that no one would know where we shared our secrets and kept our childhood loot. We climbed up by a series of ready-made toeholds on Dad's tool wall. It was four years before anyone discovered us. Billy never gave me away, even when Mom grounded him for a whole weekend for refusing to tell her where I was one night when

I "ran away from home." That was friendship — not just words and promises but the flesh-and-blood hanging together in the trenches, even when the whole world said you were wrong. Grounded for a whole weekend — that was love.

And it was family when Billy helped me subdue the rebel masses the year our neighbor, Joey Bush, led a revolt trying to replace the Córdova clan as lords of the Chetney fief. Billy taught me that tough guys hang tight. Even when the tight got tough.

In those golden years I never heard the word *tomboy*. When I did, sometime in late grammar school, my clear child mind was offended. I didn't like the word. *Tomboy* seemed to describe a hybrid, a sub-boy, an alternative girl.

Not the real thing.

I also saw the faint sneer that came with the fake smile and the "Oh, isn't she cute." As I grew older, even Bill's love and devotion, his constancy at my side as my comrade in age and gender, couldn't protect my place in a world from which I would soon be expelled.

There came a day, shortly after my last stand at Little Big Horn, when Bill, now a "man" of nine on the Little League team, found it impossible to explain to his buddies why his sister was his best friend.

I found my situation increasingly confusing. I was the same, but my world wasn't. I was suddenly stumbling through life, while all the boys seemed to be hitting their stride. Even the rebel dimwit Joey Bush was getting better grades than I. And though he couldn't kick a football through a plate glass window, now he was "training for the Olympics," swimming for hours in the pool every day.

By this time, I had another set of baby brothers and a duet of baby sisters. In a house cramped by noise and chaos, I had no space to contemplate the meaning of *tomboy* or to wonder if my parents had noticed that I was one. I was simply number two in their grand scheme of now twelve offspring.

Luckily, I had enough skills to win some measure of identity in my newly changing world. Bill or no Bill, I was a damn good

Grounded for a whole weekend— that was love.

softball player. I became the youngest girl at St. Christopher's grammar school to make the girls' varsity softball team.

But playing softball couldn't keep the world out.

Trouble was brewing. My girlfriends had boyfriends with whom they "flirted." I hadn't a clue as to what the big deal was.

My teachers started calling me a "ruffian" and telling Mom I ought to learn "grooming."

"I feel stupid wearing fingernail polish!" I wailed as Mom blocked the doorway between me and the school bus. "Grooming is for dogs." I would have been happier being reincarnated as one.

High school is hell for tomboys. Tomboys under thirteen are derisively "cute." Those who are still tomboys beyond thirteen are just weird.

In high school, the vacancy Billy had left at my side was filled by a series of prom-queens-in-training. To these young girls, I represented safety, someone who would always listen and worship, and never compete. I passed quickly into the role of Prom Queen's Best Friend. This role provided good cover from the exigencies of dating. Sharon, Margaret, Cathy — they all simply arranged dates for me with the buddies of their boyfriends. It never mattered to me who the guy was: that I got to double-date with my prom queen on Saturday nights was enough.

I suppose I went underground in high school, as I would again later, in my lefty days when we warred against the military-industrial establishment. In high school, I was fighting the religious establishment of nuns and peers screaming, "Girl! Girl! Girl!" at me.

I learned to fake it long before I learned to enjoy it with women years later. I faked writing notes to boys, because Margaret did. I faked losing Ping-Pong to Mike, because Sharon said, "That's what girls do." I buried my grief and myself everywhere but on the baseball field.

Fresh into college, living at last away from the soul-ravaging eyes of nuns, priests, and parents in that den of iniquity the state university, I celebrated my freedom by buying a motorcycle. Shortly thereafter, Bill bought his first bike. Now a senior in high school, Bill had just come back into my life. He was in trouble: his girlfriend was pregnant. And I, his newly out dyke sister, was the one he came to for my expertise on sex and girls.

A few years later, Bill, now a young man flunking college, sat with me in the hippie tie-dye living room of my tiny, newly purchased house with a pre-boycott Coors in one hand and cigarettes in the other, and asked about bondage. Fortunately, I had just learned about the "B" word from my butch mentor.

"Well, first thing is to find out what she wants and what she doesn't want." I huddled toward him, whispering as though Sister Mary Vincent were lurking outside my open front door. "Every woman is different. Some like that kind of thing. Some don't. Here's how you find out..."

Bill and I were close again. In my early twenties, before feminism, I could be a boy with him again; we could understand each other. Never mind that I understood so much more about him than he did about me and my world. By that time, I was also woman enough to know that understanding men more than they could ever understand women was one of the many things that gave women their edge.

One thing I understood about Bill soon after that day of Coors and bondage talk was that he was destined to love strong women. My first clue (tap me with a sledgehammer) came shortly after I'd broken up with Janie — one of those we-were-best-friends-and-should-have-left-it-at-that relationships. Only she didn't feel that way about me: as her first, I was her "true love."

That's why I almost went into shock a few months later when I went over to Janie's house to console her and found her in bed with ... yes, brother Bill.

I was furious with her. (At twenty-two you get mad at that sort of thing, even if you don't want to be lovers.) And I was so riled at Bill that a full year passed before I confronted him.

"She wasn't your girlfriend anymore. Why don't you ask her why she wanted to screw me?"

"Well, if it makes any dent at all in your ridiculous male ego, I did ask her." I was spoiling for a fight.

"Yeah?"

"Yeah!" I shouted. "She said that if she couldn't have me, she'd settle for another Córdova."

"Fuck you!" Bill was more shocked than angry. Lesbian games and female emotional intricacies went way over his head.

"Well, I guess we both got had." I fell to the floor laughing, and Bill finally joined me. I was still his big brother, and now also his big sister.

brother sister brother sister
brother sister brother sister
sister brother sister

My fraternal relationship with Bill went into the closet with my silk tie collection and other politically incorrect things when the lesbian-feminist movement arrived in Los Angeles in 1972. I became a "sister" instead, and a "dyke" instead of a "tomboy" — or, goddess forbid, a "butch."

But blood is thicker than politics. I snuck out of the movement and back to West Covina to offer Bill my shoulder to cry on when his first wife left him. A decade later, disguised as thirty-something adults, we huddled on a rain-soaked porch as he told me his second wife was finally pregnant. "It's because we did it with her on top!" he proudly explained. And, finally, in the summer of '95, my first knight rode back into my life to deliver the "best man" speech at my own lesbian wedding. He stood beside my "best dyke," Robin Tyler, who had taken his place as Lancelot in my lesbian world, and said, "It couldn't have happened to a nicer guy — er, girl!"

"Boo and the Boys, 1968"
Becky Thompson (right), a.k.a. Boo, Bruce, Sasquash, Male Hormone...
London, Ontario, Canada

Alan and Me

Sharon Lim-Hing

"Shh, we've got to be on the lookout," Alan hissed in the Scottish accent of his forebears. "Them heifers been on the loose." We sat down and were engulfed by the thick grasses and weeds of Alan's backyard. Sunlight was pouring down on us. When the wind moved, the grasses swayed like forests of seaweed. Alan looked over at me and smiled. I pushed back my Stetson, wiped the sweat running down my cheek, and smiled back at him. We were lost on the prairie.

Curly light brown hair framed Alan's face, with its chubby mottled pink cheeks like bowls of raspberries in cream. His smell was that of his parents' house: clean cotton sheets, shortbread just out of the oven, bacon sandwiches, new plastic toys, baby powder. He had long brown-to-blond eyelashes that curved out and up and ended in a point like a scimitar. Skinny, taller, and older, I always won when we wrestled. This seemed to annoy him, to be beaten by a girl. Sometimes I felt a twinge of pity for him as I got up and brushed bits of grass off my clothes.

"Aaah," Alan suddenly yelled, jumping up. I stared at him as his hands seemed to frantically search his body. "Help!" he yelped. "Ants!" Trails of tiny black dots snaked up his pink legs. My feet began burning. I leapt up, and began desperately throwing off my cowboy regalia and brushing dozens of ants off my skin.

Crying, scratching, and brushing ourselves off, we ran to Alan's back porch. The maid came running out and helped us undress and wipe the angry insects off. Soon we were naked and crestfallen, both of us covered with tiny red *o*'s.

"You lucky is not red ants," the maid said, kindly. She helped us out of our gun belts, bullets bulging from every side. Sniffling, we shook our clothes to get rid of any remaining ants, snapping the fabric at the crest of the motion. We got dressed again. Alan said good-bye mournfully and followed his maid into the house to get some first aid. I walked home, dragging my guns behind me. Some prickles — what Alan called "burrs" — caught the skin of my toes, and I had to stop to pick them off.

By the time I got home, it was dusk.

Every day after school, Alan and I would call to each other from our adjacent houses and meet at the hibiscus hedge that marked the boundary between his father's and my father's property. Silently we would stalk thieves, snakes, Indians. Sometimes we were on the same side: the cows were stampeding, or the renegades were attacking. Sometimes one was the sheriff and the other the outlaw, and we dodged each other until the sun went down behind the mountains on the other side of his house. Then we would go to Alan's house, and the maid would serve us tea and biscuits that his mother had baked.

"Sharon!" Alan's voice preceded him. We met in the curve of the driveway, in the dip where rotten guavas rested after their comet ride, their hard rain down on concrete. After thundershowers, a lake would form there, around which we drove our Matchbox and Corgi cars. I had a Batmobile, a James Bond Aston Martin and a Lincoln Continental with a TV. Alan had a Rover V-8 sedan, a Jaguar, and a fire engine — and an appendage called Lois. Whenever he came round the bend, his shorts pockets bulging with cars, sure enough, his little sister would be trailing after him.

an appendage called Lois

Lois was three and afraid of our dogs Rex and Rebel, two mongrel German shepherd brothers. They towered above the little blonde child, panting into her eyes while she, not daring to move, trembled. Lois was a baby tag-along. I didn't like how small she was and I hated her frilly pink dresses and her blue eyes wide with fright. Sometimes I waited two or three seconds before shooing Rex and Rebel.

"Alan!" I called.

"Sharon!" I heard Alan reply.

We gathered our forces on the carpet in Alan's living room. American astronauts were about to walk on the moon for their first time, but Major Matt Mason had been there and back a hundred times. He had strolled around its equator nipping whiskey out of a tin canteen, while simultaneously singing Elvis Presley songs, strumming on his guitar, and drawing on a Lucky Strike stuck to his lower lip. With light brown wavy plastic hair framing his pink plastic face, Major Matt Mason was six inches tall but loomed large in our imaginations. The Major possessed a space station, a futuristic missile launcher equipped with a sharp spring that enabled it to shoot gunboat gray plastic projectiles, and a moonmobile that lumbered forward on Maltese cross legs powered by four C batteries. Alan had the space station. I had the missile launcher and the moonmobile. We each had our own Major Matt Mason figure (not "doll"). I had another figure in the series, too, an alien, also six inches tall, with a bulbous, green, translucent head and a name full of strange letters. The alien wore a spacesuit over a skinny, humanoid body. To make the alien gun work, you squeezed the barrel. Propelled by air, a bright green string whooshed out and back in again, looking like a laser beam.

Out of breath, Zxxving ran across the rocky landscape and hid behind a hill. She was from a neighboring solar system, whose denizens spent most of their time debating intellectual topics. Their technology was highly advanced. She was her planet’s first intergalactic explorer.

On the deck of the space station, Major Matt Mason I saw the ugly green creature in his telescope. He fired a shot. It bounced off the alien’s back. He radioed Major Matt Mason II.

“Bring the missile launcher,” Alan deadpanned.

“Roger. Over and out,” I said.

Major I and II found the alien on radar. Since there was room for only one of them in the moonmobile, they donned their air helmets and pulled the missile launcher behind them. Gravity was low, so they bounded along quickly.

“It’s hiding behind the rocks,” Major I cried out. Major II silently loaded the missile launcher. The first missile landed in front of the hill. The second landed behind the hill. The third landed right on top of the hill. Even if Zxxving had not stepped out from behind the hill to raise her arms in peace, she would have been destroyed. The third missile carried poisonous gases and radiation. Her gun was no match: the soft thread dispensed only the peaceful and loving thoughts of Zxxving’s world.

“Let’s possess this planet,” the two majors said. They unzipped the flies of their spacesuits and peed in the clay. They bounced over to Zxxving’s highly advanced spacecraft (the only one of its kind) and shot it full of holes, laughing at its silly round shape. Then they went back to the space station and had tea and home-baked cookies.

Alan’s mother had baked some cookies and decorated them with icing. I picked up a cowboy. He had a white icing shirt, red icing pants, a blue icing cowboy hat, and a yellow icing vest. I smelled his cookie back. Lemon. I bit greedily into him. To my surprise, it was sour. I spat the Stetson out onto my plate and wrapped the cowboy in a paper napkin.

Then we decided to play cowboys. I ran home and came back with my guns and hat. This time, Alan was the sheriff; I, the outlaw. There was a big bounty on my head. But I swore I wasn't going down alone.

I hid behind Alan's father's pile of lumber. It exhaled the scent of pine into the heat, in slow shallow breaths like those of a dying man. I emerged with guns drawn, my trigger finger itchy, and a Tarzan knife in my waistband. I snuck up on the sheriff from behind. The brown locks tumbling down the back of his neck looked as soft as a vine's new tendrils feeling the head of a stone cherub. Alan was crouched in a tense ball, craning his neck around the corner of his house, a jackrabbit ready to spring. I drew a bead on his heart.

"Turn around real slow," I drawled.

He twirled and tried to go for his six-shooter, so I shot him several times in the chest and legs.

Alan cheated and claimed I'd missed him. At pointblank range that was impossible, and we both knew it. We spent the rest of the afternoon arguing about whether I had killed him or not.

When the sun lowered itself orange and heavy into the hills, a tiredness came over me, as sweet and thick as Lyle's pancake syrup. We said good-bye. I walked home through lengthened shadows and dappled golden light. Tomorrow, I would beat Alan at wrestling and show him who was boss.

I researched *tomboy* in my *Funk and Wagnall Standard College Dictionary* (Canadian edition), the very same volume I was awarded in high school some twenty years ago for being studious and athletic (read: tomboy). I won't pretend I wasn't a little disappointed at first: "Tomboy: a girl who prefers boyish activities or dress." True enough, but hardly subversive. I read on and was referred to a surprising synonym: *hoyden*. Hoyden? How could I have come this far in my manly life and not known a synonym for *tomboy* was *hoyden?*

I wasted no time in flipping to *H:* "Hoyden: a tomboy; a boisterous and ill-mannered girl." Aha! Now we were getting somewhere!

Hoyden though I have been since I was small, I have never been rude or ill-mannered, this fact confounding those initially determined to despise me for my deviant gender behavior. To my credit, I can report I have always, unless provoked otherwise, been polite and courteous to others, especially my elders. And my courtesy has not gone unnoticed: "Why, thank you, young man" is a phrase quite familiar to me.

What could Mr. Funk and Mr. Wagnall know of the pleasure of trucks over tea parties, sprinting over skipping, shouting over giggling? What could they know of the joy of outperforming one's playmates in sports? And of the similar delight of taking Mark Prime by his shirtfront and propelling him across two rows of desks in eighth-grade geography? (I'd warned him often enough against calling me unflattering names.) These and other memories are the rewards of impolite girls who prefer boys' duds.

—Andrea Lowe, from "A Girl's Boyhood"

Being called tomboy took away the sting of being "encouraged" to not play with the girls in kindergarten through elementary school. It buoyed me through the times I was not allowed to wear pants to school. It created a sense of self-worth when I was forced to get my hair curled and put on a stiff, red organdy dress. Or when the boys showed me their wienies and how far they could pee. And when they razzed me because I didn't have one or anything they could see.

–Kisa, from "On Account of Being a Tomboy"

Marta's Magic

Sally Sotomayor

Marta shifted her weight on the hard bench, noting wearily that the green floor tiles still outnumbered the white ones. She probably knew the ratio better than any other student at San Andrés's, given the number of times she had sat here waiting for Sor Francisca to usher her into her office. Let's see. At least ten times. One for every year of her life. Like when she had wanted to play kickball with the boys. And when she split her uniform up the middle on the jungle gym and had to go home early. And then there was her disagreement with Padre Gabriel about eating fish. And the elevator affair. And Sor Beatrix's wimple. And that didn't count the times she'd been sent here for asking too many questions — what the sisters called impudence. "And I thought I was getting better," she sighed, scooting to the edge of the bench so that her toes could tap the floor.

Marta had discovered when she was very young that she was different from other children. In the first place, she couldn't stand to see people or animals or even things mistreated. She was forever rescuing frogs and chickens and puppies from boys who tortured them. When at Carnaval the *vejigantes* beat upon the inflated cow bladders, Marta felt every striking of the *vejiga* as a blow to her own body. Once, as other children — and some adults — laughed at her, Marta had tried to piece back together the torn wrapping paper that her cousin had thoughtlessly ripped from his birthday gifts.

In the second place, Marta never understood that girls had limitations. She always wanted to do the things her brothers did. She had made a careful study of her body and theirs and had determined that, with one small exception, she had the same apparatus they did. And that one exception seemed to have nothing to do with being able to run and yell and climb and wrestle. Even as a crawler, she had gravitated to her brothers' toy truck instead of to her sister's doll.

So she had balked at wearing frilly Sunday dresses and at being imprisoned indoors to play house while Juan and Miguel were set free to play ball. To their credit, Mami and Papi and Abuela (who took care of the children while Mami and Papi worked) had all given in a lot, allowing Marta to do more things than other girls her age. After all, Mami and Papi had lived for a while in New York and had absorbed some North American ideas, and Abuela often let Marta play wherever she wanted to, just as long as she was within calling distance. Still, even her parents and Abuela had their limits, particularly when it came to being criticized by the neighbors or other parents. So Marta negotiated very carefully for every one of her special freedoms.

Very shortly after she discovered that she was different, Marta began deliberately to hide her feelings and to wait until no one was around before doing something the grown-ups wouldn't approve of. She never wanted to be disobedient, and certainly she loved Mami and Papi and respected her teachers, but sometimes there were things she just had to do. And when that happened, she ended up in big trouble.

Like now. Mami and Papi were right this minute talking with Sor Francisca and Padre Tomás about her playing baseball. And this was the most important decision ever, because, like so many

Marta believed that baseball was the most important thing in the world

Puerto Ricans, Marta believed that baseball was the most important thing in the world.

Way back in the first grade, when she had walked with Mami and her brothers and sister by the big field where the Babe Ruth and Little League teams played, Marta would hold up the whole family by stopping to press her face against the wire fence so that she could watch the practice. The smack of the ball when it landed in the glove, the stretch of legs in a hard run, the freedom of an arm sailing the ball in from the field — she was entranced by it all. She wanted to do it for herself.

Even the crack of the bat hitting the ball gave Marta a special thrill — though she also felt sad for the ball. It seemed to love being pitched or caught — that was like being massaged — but she could feel it hurt sometimes when the bat hit it. Then Marta would talk to the ball, trying to make it feel better. She would tell herself that this was her imagination, that the balls probably felt fine about being hit ... didn't they?

Marta was eight years old when she realized that if she wanted to be a baseball player, she would have to practice in secret at first. She began formulating a bold plan: on her own she would learn to run, throw, catch, and hit; then, when she became really good, she would present herself to the school team and they wouldn't be able to turn her down!

And so she began running, running everywhere she could: to and from school, around the playground, even in the halls. And whenever she could get her homework and house chores done early, she would hang around Juan and Miguel and their friends as they played catch, chasing their missed balls and watching very carefully the way the boys pitched and caught. Sometimes, when there was no one else to play with and there was an extra glove or an old fence board she could use for a bat, her brothers even let her join in their game. Since Marta threw left-handed, she was forever trying to adapt to her right hand a glove made for left-handed catching.

Marta's girlfriends refused to join her, saying that baseball was silly or that they were tired or that they didn't want to dirty their uniforms. So it was her neighbor, Mario, who became Marta's conspirator and teacher. At first his help was simply an act of kindness, but a day or two of her perseverance convinced him that she might really be good. So he began spending whatever time he could with her in the vacant lots behind her house. He taught her how to swing a bat, how to throw overhand and sidearm, and how to field fly balls, grounders, line drives, high-hoppers. He even lent her his battered catcher's mitt so that she could hold on to fastballs and sliders. One day he handed Marta a small grungy aluminum bat that he had won in a contest. "Here," he said. "I'm too big for this now. You can practice with it." Then he was off.

That same day, Marta made one of the most important discoveries of her life. Since Mario had taken his ball, she picked up a small rock and tossed it in the air. When she tried to hit it with the bat, she missed completely. She tossed up the same stone again, and swung at it in her best imitation of the coaches who, in fielding practice, could place a ball anywhere they wanted: right, left, or center; outfield or infield. She missed again. Frustrated, she scooped up the stone, threw it up a third time, swung the bat even harder — and missed.

She was angry. "Crazy rock!" she growled, searching the ground for the culprit. She scowled as she tossed it up once more. This time the bat connected with a satisfying click and sent the stone sailing yards away. Marta was ecstatic. Then, suddenly, a sharp pain shot through her whole body, as if she had been hit head-on by a truck.

Letting out a cry and doubling over, she dropped the bat and fell to the ground. She lay there a moment wondering why she hurt so, all over. "I broke my back!" she moaned.

"Naw, you didn't. You'll live." The voice seemed to come from all around her.

She sat up. "What? What did you say?"

"I said you'll live." Now the voice was coming from behind her.

She spun around on all fours. There was no one anywhere near. "Who said that?"

There was a silence, and then a long sigh. "I'm over here. Where you sent me."

Marta couldn't believe her ears. "It's devils!" she thought, crossing herself.

"Naw, not devils. Just me." Now the voice was clearly coming from the stone — at least, since she couldn't see it, from where she thought the stone had landed.

Her body was still ached, but she pushed herself up to her feet and began cautiously following the sound of the voice.

"I'd like a kiss," the stone said.

"A kiss!"

"Yeah, a kiss and a little love, doncha know, just to say you're sorry."

Then Marta saw it. She would have recognized it even without the dull silver glow that surrounded it. She crept toward it.

"You can pick me up. I'm okay now."

Slowly she squatted and stretched her hand toward the rock. "Gee," she said, "I'm really sorry." And as if to testify to her remorse, big tears started rolling down her cheeks. "I used to know that swatting you like that would hurt. I guess I just forgot."

The stone shimmered a little. "Thanks. It's okay. I'm tough. Been through a lot."

Marta carefully picked up the rock and held it to her cheek and kissed it. Then horror began rising in her. "Oh, no!" she cried, collapsing into a sprawl on the ground.

"What's up?"

"Stone, I'll never be able to play baseball! I can't ever hit a ball like that! And think—"

"Don't be crazy. Sure you can play. And sure you can hit the ball. You can hit me again, too, if you do it right. But you've got to be my friend. I've got to know you don't want to hurt me."

"Ohhh." Marta was puzzled.

The stone sighed. "Figure it this way. You're the hitter, doncha know. So what are you feeling? Are you mad? Or worried?

Are you excited? Are you maybe respectful? Wrap up a baseball in love and respect, then give it a good clean stroke, and it will sail up and away for you every time, sometimes even out of the park. And it'll love doing it, too, doncha know. Try to kill it and you'll probably miss. Or if you accidentally hit it in that mood, you can really hurt it."

Wrap up a baseball in love and respect, then give it a good clean stroke, and it will sail up and away for you every time

"Stones too?" Marta grinned.

"Stones too. It's got to be an agreement, doncha know. A dance. Tennis balls, golf balls, punching bags, drums, *vejigas,* maracas, castanets. You've got to talk to them, listen to them. You've got to be a friend to them if you're gonna hit them or shake them."

Marta kissed the stone. "You're right, Stone! Mario does it that way! I'm sure of it!"

"Any good hitter. Watch 'em. Most do it without thinking, but they do it. With their attitudes."

"Oh, Stone!" Marta closed her eyes and clasped the stone to her heart. "Will you stay with me forever?"

"Forever? That's a long time."

"Well, yes. Just so I can remember today. Today I think I learned something magic!"

The stone's dull silver glow brightened into a soft, radiant sparkle. "Yes," it said. "Yes, I can stay with you awhile."

Marta knew that the news was good the moment the door to Sor Francisca's office opened. Mami and Papi were smiling, and even Padre Tomás's thin face looked softer than usual.

"Well, Marta" — Sor Francisca sighed — "this has been very difficult." Then she almost let herself smile. "But we have decided that just for this year you may take your exercises with the baseball team. And, of course, so may any other little girl if she wishes."

Marta beamed and ran to Mami's side. Mami clasped her close.

"But you must understand that this is only for this spring, Marta. Probably by next year you will have lost interest in baseball." When Marta said nothing, Sor Francisca went on. "And there is one condition." She paused for emphasis. "There must be no trouble, I repeat, no trouble whatsoever, between you and the boys on the team. Do you understand that?"

"Oh, yes, Sor Francisca," Marta answered. "The boys like me fine. I can hit." She looked at Papi for confirmation.

Papi nodded. "They came to see us, Sor, and asked that we let Marta play."

Padre Tomás cleared his throat and addressed Sor Francisca. "Señor Covina is right," he said. "The boys are looking forward to winning every game with rival schools this year. Perhaps because they now will have Marta." He actually smiled.

Mami put a proud arm around her daughter and looked at her husband as if to say, I don't understand our little one. But I am happy.

And so it was that San Andrés's Elementary began its rise to fame. For not only did Marta not lose interest in playing ball the next year or in the years following, but three other girl students also joined the team. By the time Marta was in high school and challenging the city's Babe Ruth and Little League Associations to include girls, San Andrés's had seven girl students on its baseball squad and a glowing reputation as the home of San Juan's best school baseball team.

After heated controversy, and publicity that reached even newspapers and magazines in the United States, Marta was finally granted permission by San Juan's Babe Ruth League Association to play with the Guerreros, one of the league's best teams. With that, Puerto Rico's hundred-year tradition of all-male baseball was officially shattered.

And Marta did not let the association down. Because she was a fine first baser and a speedy runner, and because her batting record was unexcelled, the Guerreros chose Marta as their Most Valuable Player for three consecutive years. In the third year, the whole league voted her that title. Fans not just in San Juan but in all Puerto Rico cheered her on.

Those were glorious times for Marta: she got to do the thing she loved best, and the whole world seemed to love her for doing it. Best of all, her teammates ceased to be in awe of her and accepted her as one of them. There was the matter of Arturo Tacones, of course, a boy in her class who played third base. He was a good player, but even the other boys knew he was a bully. He seemed to hate Marta's exceptional skills. Often he would crack jokes when she was at bat just to rattle her, and sometimes on a double play he would hesitate a moment before throwing to second base so that the throw to her at first would be late. Or he would purposely throw badly to her so that in catching she would look awkward or unbalanced. One day during base-stealing practice he actually tripped her. That was when Coach Anza had to intervene and force an uneasy truce between the two teammates. After that Arturo was still arrogant, but he stopped giving Marta a hard time. Marta simply avoided him when she could.

Much as she loved playing ball and the fame that came with it, Marta was most enchanted with two other miracles. The first was the amazing development of her body into that of an accomplished athlete, capable of extraordinary feats of endurance and skill, not only in baseball but in other sports as well: basketball, soccer, swimming, rock climbing, gymnastics. Her whole body seemed daily to thank her, to sing its good health with every step of her happy life. The second was the discovery that loving herself so enthusiastically brought her into a harmonious relationship with the world, with other people, with animals, with things — including, of course, baseballs.

In all the years since her conversation with the stone, Marta had told none of her Guerrero teammates the secret of her extraordinary hitting power: the proper attitude toward a pitched ball. She helped her teammates (particularly any other girl) in many ways, like teaching them to watch the red seam on the ball when the pitcher released it to discover what it was going to do when it reached the plate, and showing them how, without peeking up the catcher, they could sense when he (or she!) was setting up outside. But somehow she always feared that if the whole world knew what she knew about how to talk to a baseball, then she, Marta, would no longer be special. And she had to stay special, she thought, to keep on playing and to keep baseball open to girls. Several times she had been tempted to tell, but then she would consult the stone that she always carried in her pocket and always the stone would just glow dully and tell her, "No."

Then arrived the biggest game of her life: Puerto Rico's top Babe Ruth League team — the Guerreros, of course — versus Mexico's, the visiting Charros. The stands were packed. The game was being televised. Parents were wild with pride and anticipation. And, naturally, the score became tied in the bottom of the ninth, with two Guerreros out, nobody on base, and Marta's friend Mario Méndez coming up to bat.

Marta and her teammates paced and shouted and repeatedly hiked up their britches. The crowd echoed and amplified their anguish. Marta sent Mario two thumbs-up as he stepped out of the on-deck circle and up to the plate. "If he can just get a hit," Marta muttered. Then another thought struck her: "Who's up next?" Frantically she reviewed the batting order in her head. She knew she was number six. Not much chance she would be up this inning.

"Who's up next?"

Then she saw him, swinging his bats and approaching the on-deck circle: Arturo! Arturo Tacones! Her heart sank. Arturo liked to kill the ball, and for that reason, she was convinced, he was only a sometimes hitter. A sometimes hitter wasn't good enough right now. If the game went another inning, then the top of the Charros' batting order would be up and all hope would be lost. If the Guerreros were going to win this game, they had to win it now. Marta shot a glance down the third base line at Coach Anza. He was worried, but not about to make any changes.

"Stee-rike!" shouted the umpire. Mario bounced his bat on the plate, unperturbed. In a flash of intuition, Marta knew that Mario would hit. Mario would single, maybe even double. And at that same moment she knew what she had to do. She fumbled in her uniform's pocket and finally brought out the stone. It was sparkling, radiantly silver. She held it tightly and closed her eyes, blocking out the fiery sun and the voices of the crowd. The stone's answer was unequivocal. "Yes," it said. "Now."

Marta opened her eyes. The pitcher was winding up again. Above her she could pick out her family in the crowd. Anita, her special friend, was sitting with them and even now waving to her in support. Marta waved back. She kissed the stone and slipped it into her pocket.

Then, for the first time in all her years of playing baseball, Marta Covina boldly disobeyed one of Coach Anza's most sacred rules. Like a streak of lightning, she broke from the makeshift dugout and her teammates and made for the on-deck circle. "Arturo!" she shouted.

Arturo's astonishment tempered his usual arrogance. "You're out of line, *nena*. I'm busy." He dropped one of his bats and took a loose swing with the remaining one.

"Arturo, I have to talk to you." Marta glanced at the coach. He hadn't noticed her yet.

"Ball one!" intoned the umpire.

"Miss Ballplayer, I am about to win this game for us. Now leave me alone."

"Arturo, you'll never win this game for us if you don't listen to me."

"And if I listen to you, we'll win? You guarantee it?" Arturo sneered.

Marta took a deep breath. The stone in her pocket almost burned her leg in its bright affirmation. Marta looked straight at Arturo. "Yes," she said. "I guarantee it."

Something shifted inside Arturo Tacones. Marta saw it happen. Without a word he stepped outside the on-deck circle and stooped, as though picking up the bat he had dropped. Marta squatted beside him, both of them now farther out of Coach Anza's range of vision.

"Arturo, you've joked a lot about my hitting, saying I'm too lucky, saying — well, once you even said I was a witch. You remember?" Arturo nodded. "And once you asked me how I did it, how I always seemed to connect." Arturo nodded again.

"Ball two!" The crowd was roaring.

"Well, Arturo, there is a secret, and I'm gonna tell it to you right now if you'll listen."

"You better hurry, 'cause here comes Coach."

"Ball three!" The spectators were on their feet, shouting.

"Good eye, Mario!" Coach Anza's words barely reached his batter over the roar of the crowd. Looking for his next player up, Coach Anza started down the third base line toward home plate and the on-deck circle beyond. What he finally saw as he neared the plate was a very strange conversation between two of his young players who were supposed to be enemies. He slowed his step. Those two were squatting together just outside the circle. Marta Covina had her arm around Arturo Tacones, speaking close to his ear. Arturo's eyes were growing very wide. Arturo asked Marta some question, gesturing with both hands. Marta nodded furiously. Arturo shook his head, equally furiously. Marta shook Arturo, said something more in his ear. Then Arturo nodded, very slowly. And Marta laughed and hugged him.

The crack of the bat hitting the ball galvanized the coach. Mario was on his way down the first base line, legs invisible in their motion. Three outfielders were running in, three infielders were running out, and the ball was bouncing in the middle of them all. Mexico's second baser recovered the ball and fired it to first, but long after Mario had touched in. The winning run was on base. And the tension rose to a new level.

Coach Anza outshouted the crowd, gesturing for Mario to stay put. Mario could score on a double, the coach knew, even from first base, as fast as he was. It was all in Arturo's hands now.

Arturo was a different player as he moved toward the plate. Gone was his usual arrogant stride. In its place was an almost casual sweet assurance. Coach Anza watched with amazement as the boy known as a bully smiled and spoke to the catcher. Just before he entered the batter's box, Arturo looked toward Marta. She was taking something out of her pocket and holding it up for

Arturo to see. Arturo nodded and grinned, and then stepped up to face the pitcher.

The rest is history: how the rattled Charro pitcher narrowly missed hitting the batter on his first pitch, how on the second pitch Arturo Tacones eased his loving bat into a happy baseball and sent it deep into center field for a triple, how two Charros rushed back in vain to capture the ball before it touched earth, how Mario Méndez sped round the bases to score well before the ball came back from center field, how the stands exploded in a victory celebration even before Mario's toes tapped home plate.

Cheering loudest of all for Arturo and Mario was Marta Covina, who at that moment decided that from then on she would share her batting secret with the whole world. She looked down at the stone in her hand, a stone that was pulsing with a bright silver splendor.

"Yes!" said the stone. "Yes!"

Girls and boys were separated at recess by a big ol' white line right down the middle of the schoolyard. I used to stand on that white line. Not behind it or in front of it but on it. Dared not stand in front of it, because I'd have to stay after school for being on the boys' side. Didn't want to stand behind it either, because that meant I was one of the girls and, by golly, I wasn't. Standing on it gave me a sense of having my own identity, not defined as boy or girl. How many of us still feel like that today?

—Denise K. Earley

No Fear

Lucy Jane Bledsoe

From my earliest memories I've been both a tomboy and a femme, with the two coexisting almost symbiotically, working together to make me whole. And yet, in my relationships with other women, I've always kept them separate: I'm either the femme lover or the tomboy pal.

That started to change, however, just last weekend when I met Monica.

I pulled Seashell, my new Saturn, into the turnout near Castle Peak in the Sierras, and looked around for the trailhead. A couple of guys were getting their gear together in back of a truck, so I pulled up and braked. Seashell embarrassed me by laying down a little rubber. The guys looked up and I realized they were women. I smiled. They stiffened, probably thinking that *I* was a guy. "Which way to the trailhead?" I asked. The bigger girl, who had a long, dark brown ponytail and broad, squarish features, pointed in front of her truck. Not too friendly.

"Thanks." I turned Seashell around and parked in back of them. Then I pulled on my hot-pink "Choice" cap and smiled again at the girls. This time, the big one shifted in her body. The other, a thin woman with blonde hair and a stern face, turned away.

The big woman kept looking. Finally, she asked, obviously impressed, "You're skiing *alone?*"

The tomboy in me was pleased to have impressed another woman. The femme in me picked up flirtatious energy. Together they did a few perfectly synchronized inner cartwheels. "Yeah," I said. "I'm skiing alone."

Two strides and she was at my car door. "I'm Monica." She pumped my hand. "That's Bridget." She cocked her thumb in the direction of her companion.

"Lucy," I said, weakly. Nothing like the firm grip of an authentic butch to turn my legs into amoebas. And Monica was the real thing: about five feet ten inches tall, burly, and muscular. There's a way that long hair can seem more butch than short hair. Maybe it's the contrast of all that butchness next to the ponytail. Or maybe I'm just endeared to butches who think they're not.

"1994 Saturn," she announced. "Can I have a look?"

I scooted out of the driver's seat and let her in. She asked questions about how the car ran, then commented on how I had only one cup holder.

"All I need," I answered.

Monica strode back to silent Bridget, who hadn't once spoken to me or even smiled, though I'd tried twice to include her. Monica locked up her truck at the exact same time I locked my Saturn, and the three of us walked to the trailhead. I felt awkward about the coincidence. I didn't want them to think I was trying to join them.

Then Monica asked, "What do you have for lunch?"

"None of that peanut butter and dried fruit stuff for me," I boasted. I saw Bridget's face tighten and figured she must have packed exactly that. I went on: "I have barbecued chicken. I have fresh grapes. I have half an avocado. I have homemade oatmeal cookies. And I have fresh walnut bread from the Acme Bakery in Berkeley. The best."

Monica's face went slack. With desire, I bet.

"And you?" I asked. No answer.

By now Bridget, struggling with her skis and poles, had fallen several paces behind, though she was well within earshot.

"Where're you staying?" Monica asked.

"I usually snow camp," I bragged. "But I'm staying in a cabin up the road this time."

"I usually snow camp, too," Monica said in her tough, no-nonsense voice.

I stopped walking and turned to face her. "You *do?* I mean, snow-camping women are nearly nonexistent! Look, I'm always looking for women to snow camp with. What's your last name? Are you in the phone book?"

I loved how bold I was being.

Monica glanced over her shoulder at Bridget, then answered, "Rutgers. I'm not in the phone book. You can get me at work, though. I work for PGE. Call the main Oakland office and leave a message for me." She hesitated, then said, "Leave your number, too."

We stopped and waited for Bridget to catch up.

"Just go on," she snarled. "I'm coming."

We reached the trailhead, and knowing I'd overstayed my welcome — with Bridget anyway — I said, "See you out there. Maybe."

I snapped my boots into the bindings and skied away, pleased with myself. I'd indulged my femme by flirting shamelessly, and at the same time, I'd indulged my tomboy's mean streak by doing it flagrantly, in the girlfriend's face. Having my femme and tomboy selves working in concert like that made me nervous, though; I was glad I had gotten away without giving Monica my phone number or last name.

As I skied up the mountain, watching the clouds break and then close in again, I thought about how I would never call Monica at her PGE job, because my tomboy doesn't date. My tomboy is the most authentic me, the only me who inhabits my body fully. It's me as tomboy who goes to the mountains, who works in the garden, who loves reading science, who wants to know and feel the exact material

My tomboy is the most authentic me

makeup of trees, soil, the moon. Ironically, though my tomboy is the me most closely tied to my body, no one touches her physically.

Or, I should say, no one has touched her physically in twenty-five years, since my first love, Nicole.

I was a lesbian prodigy. I came out when I was six years old. Nicole was a new girl in the neighborhood. Within the first five minutes after we met, she bragged that her mother was French. I suggested she prove it by demonstrating real French kissing. I knew about French kissing because I had a lot of older brothers and sisters. Nicole told me, hostilely, that the French kiss just like Americans.

"Not at all," I argued. "They kiss like this." I rested my six-year-old hands on her chubby waist and leaned forward to press my mouth against hers. Before she could grunt and push me away, I slid my tongue between her lips.

Nicole smelled like grass and sweat. As I French-kissed her, a sweet syrupy feeling rose from my feet right up to my head. I remember thinking, "*This* I've gotta do again." The next thing I knew, pain exploded in my belly. Nicole had slugged me. She ran home crying.

She had to get over my forwardness that day, though, because I was the only girl her age in the neighborhood. When she came back a week later, I suggested we play Barbie and Ken. I detested that game, but I had ulterior motives. After a few minutes of foreplay — like Ken coming in the pretend front door saying, "Honey, I'm home," and Barbie sashaying about a pretend kitchen putting the last touches on dinner — I had Ken give Barbie a quick chaste kiss.

"Was that a French kiss?" Nicole asked.

"Oh, no," I said, as if I'd never think of anything so dirty.

"Time for bed," Ken said.

"What about dinner?" Barbie countered. "I've made fried chicken and potato salad."

I sympathized with Ken, who sighed and resigned himself to dinner before sex. Nicole led Barbie and, therefore, my Ken, through a prolonged dinner conversation. Finally, Ken firmly set down his knife and fork and walked to the other side of the table. Ken's hands couldn't actually do anything, so after making them fuss about Barbie for a second, I used my own hands to pull the hot-pink rayon blouse off her shoulders, revealing two nippleless plastic points. I expected Nicole to get mad, but she didn't, so I pushed Ken down on Barbie right there at the dinner table. I pressed his slight bulge against her V and felt the heat swell in my own V.

Nicole astonished me by saying, "Let's do what they're doing."

I dropped Ken, ready.

But Nicole had a condition. "Let's pretend I'm the most beautiful girl in the world," she said.

I was six years old. What did I know about my lesbian identity, let alone the *nuances* of that identity? Twelve years would pass before I claimed my sexuality as a femme, but even back then, something inside my gut rebelled. "No," I countered. "Let's pretend *I'm* the most beautiful girl in the world."

Nicole and I stood face-to-face, Barbie and Ken on the floor at our feet.

"No," she said. "I won't play unless I'm the most beautiful girl in the world. You're the boy."

The tiny latent femme dwelling somewhere in the pit of my stomach screamed, "Help! Help!" But Nicole had discovered her power over me: I wanted to play this game. I accepted her conditions. I became, for the next six years, Michael.

Nicole and I played what we called "it" or "boy and girl" as often as we could, all the way through the sixth grade. The game was most fun when we had a context: I was a basketball star and she was a cheerleader; I was a rock musician and she was a fan; I was a ranger and she was a park visitor; I was a photographer and she was my nude model; I was a woodsman and she was a young girl lost on her way. I was always Michael, but she adopted various exotic names, usually after movie stars, like Zsa Zsa or Annette or Joanne.

I learned to relish being Michael, but as Michael I worshipped and nourished not the femme Nicole played, but the femme in myself, my sexual self. In Michael, I created my own adoring tomboy to love me. At night I would lie in bed, hugging my pillow, plotting elaborate fantasies in which Michael passionately loved a carbon copy of me. I named her something other than Lucy, because I couldn't imagine anyone directing that kind of passion toward me.

The years passed. Though Nicole and I were inseparable, we were an unlikely pair. Nicole made mostly D's in school and I made mostly A's. She was passive, except with me, and I was aggressive with everyone except her. We had frequent and fierce fights, and Nicole could, and on several occasions did, beat me up. I never gave up trying to share the role of "most beautiful girl in the world," but Nicole wouldn't relinquish it for a moment. Not even once.

The sex was hot and always included elaborate scenarios. She would sit on the swings and watch me shoot baskets for a long time. Through dialogue, we'd create teammates for me, as well as an opposing team. I'd star in play after play until I won the game. Then Candy (or whoever she was that day) and I would go out on a victory date. I'd take her in back of my house, where we would sit among tall pines and pretend we were watching a drive-in movie. I'd put my arm around her, then slowly slide a hand up under her shirt. I'd start kissing her neck, breathing in her musky (French, I thought) smell, then kiss her on the mouth. She had come to like French kissing, though I took care, in deference to her mother, never to call it that again. Sometimes, if it was summer, we'd remove our shirts and I'd lie on top of her and rub my flat pink nipples across her flat dark brown ones. Then, because we couldn't yet imagine what was supposed to happen next, we'd change games.

"Want to play doctor?" I'd say, and we'd switch gears smoothly and quickly. I'd pull down her pants and put my fingers up her vagina. "I think everything's okay," I'd say after a long examination, "but I'd better get a closer look."

I loved Nicole. She had beautiful long, dark eyelashes and a lovely mouth, with wide, curved lips. In the summer, brown freckles covered her face. I loved her thick brown curls and her firm, chubby body. I hated that she won every physical fight we ever had, but her strength made me respect her body and added voltage to our touching.

"I'd better get a closer look."

One day, the summer we were eleven, we decided to build a fort in Pete's Woods, a small nearby forest. We spent whole days walking around Portland looking for construction sites we could steal from. Once we found one, we had to wait until no one was around, and even then we could carry away only small boards. We would hide the lumber near the construction site, then go back at night to drag the boards to Pete's Woods, where we hid them again in some brush near a creek.

Nicole had an astounding belief in what was possible in this life. She truly believed that we would build the elaborately planned fort and eventually live in it. I now know that I scorned her belief because I was deeply envious. I knew that I could never really be loved by a girl. I knew that I could never really live in the woods with Nicole. When I finally lost faith in the fort altogether and told her so, she threatened to find another friend to help her build it. So the next day I was back in Pete's Woods with the family hammer and a sack of nails, building. We put in shelves for boxes of cookies and other things we'd need. Sometimes, after a whole day of hammering, I'd almost believe.

Then skepticism would creep in again. "How're we gonna keep the animals from eating our cookies?" I'd ask.

"We'll keep the door shut," she'd say.

"They can get in through the cracks, Nicole." Her ignorance infuriated me.

She just kept hammering.

I remember the last day we worked on the fort. It was late August of 1968. School would start the next day. The fort had no roof and only three walls. I was amazed no one had discovered it and torn it down.

We spent the day gathering handfuls of mud from the creek and carrying them to the fort to caulk the cracks between the boards. It was a hot day. Mud and sweat covered us both.

At around four in the afternoon, Nicole suddenly took off all her clothes and sat in the stream. I joined her. She scooped up big handfuls of mud from the streambed and smeared them on my chest. We worked on each other's bodies until we were both plastered chocolate brown. Then we lay on our bellies and squirmed like salamanders moving upstream. I slipped behind Nicole and squirmed up onto her behind. She rolled over, and covered with mud, we humped each other right there in the stream. We weren't a construction worker and the lady of the house. We weren't a biologist and his assistant. We were Lucy and Nicole. Sex had never seemed dirtier.

We washed off the mud in the stream and took our clothes to the half-built fort to dress. Before dressing, though, I sat down on the fir boughs we'd put on the floor. The scratchy branches felt good on my bare behind.

Nicole said, "Let's pretend I'm the most beautiful girl in the world."

We never did return to the fort in Pete's Woods. School opened and we abandoned it. The next summer we began digging a hole in the vacant lot next to Nicole's house. Once the hole got deep enough, we planned to dig parallel to the ground and make a tunnel that would lead to a big chamber. We would furnish the chamber with an easy chair for me and an ottoman for her. We would carve shelves in the walls of the dirt cave for our boxes of cookies.

I began changing that summer. My mother told me that twelve was too old to be digging holes in vacant lots. My grandfather, the only person in the world who loved me unconditionally, died. And my oldest brother dropped out of college, making himself vulnerable to the draft. Death and war became immediate realities in my life. At the same time, my resentment toward Nicole's faith in life's possibilities grew. I tried to destroy her lyrical reality by telling her we would not only never live in the cave, we would never finish digging it, just as we never finished building the fort. I told her we couldn't play boy and girl anymore. It wasn't natural.

Dense Nicole didn't seem to hear a word I said. She still pressed to play boy and girl and I usually succumbed. She begged to continue with the cave and the next day I found myself with a shovel in the vacant lot, digging. And responding to the name Michael. And melting into Nicole as we made out in the dirt at the bottom of our hole.

Then, on July 20, 1969, the same day that Neil Armstrong walked on the moon, Nicole learned a new word. That night, I stood alone in the middle of my street and stared up at the fat crescent moon. I wore Converse high-tops, Levi's, and a boy's t-shirt, and I'd just cut my own hair to one-inch long all around. A man was walking on the moon, though most of the moon wasn't visible. I wondered if he was on the dark or the light part.

I ran the two blocks under the two-pronged moon to Nicole's house. Out of breath, I banged on her back door. Nicole answered and said, "Shhh, we're watching the news."

"Let's pretend," I whispered, feeling strangely desperate, "that you're the most beautiful girl in the world and I'm Neil Armstrong. I've just come back from the moon. You see me on the street. Then we..."

Nicole pushed me out of the doorway and into the dark. She came out after me and I took her hand. I tried to pull her into the night, but she pulled back.

"No," she said. "I'm not a lesbian." Then she disappeared back into her house. I didn't even hear the door shut.

I stood in the middle of her yard, looking up at the moon and thinking about Armstrong's footprints: how, with a couple of steps, he'd changed the moon from poetry to science. My body felt the same way. Building, digging, loving Nicole — all this had been poetry. But Nicole's new word had turned it into science, like Armstrong's footprints.

I had depended on Nicole to convince me that our imaginings were real. I wanted the poetry back in my body. I needed something real in my hands.

I pushed through the bushes separating Nicole's house from the vacant lot and jumped into our hole, which by now was about ten feet deep. I reached over to the little shelf we'd carved in the dirt and found an opened package of Oreos and a box of Diamond matches. I tried one of the cookies and spit it out. Then I pocketed the matches and climbed out of the hole, using roots as handholds and carved steps as footholds. I ran to Pete's Woods.

The slice of moon cast little light through the trees, but it didn't matter. I could have made my way to the fort in total darkness. It was still there, all three sides standing, though the mud caulking had washed away in rainstorms. I crawled inside the fort and sat on the fir boughs, now brown and dry. Something inside me screamed. Nicole was the most beautiful girl in the world and I was the one who loved her. But who loved me?

Who loved me?

I didn't know this then, but sitting there in the fort, my tomboy, the most authentic part of me, the part of me who lived in every cell of my body, had to face my femme, the sexual me, the me who felt the meaning of the word *lesbian* to my core. We, me the tomboy and me the femme, were finally alone. And I was terrified by the gap between them. At the same time, I was thrilled by the rawness of their meeting.

When I stood to go, I lit one of the Diamond matches. I held the very end of the match and watched it burn all the way down to my fingers. Then I threw it on the dry fir boughs.

The fire started gently. I could hear the soft crackling. I could smell the sweet scent of burning evergreens. Soon the fire hissed as it sucked away at the sap in the bigger branches. I stepped back and continued to watch. I waited until the flames filled the fort, then backed off slowly. The fire was hot, bright, and hungry.

I left the woods by the opposite end I'd entered them and walked home the long way. I sat on the fence in front of my house and waited. Five minutes later, I heard the sirens. I saw the reflected flashing red light of the fire truck even before it rounded the bend. It stopped at the mouth of the dirt road that led into Pete's Woods, too big to go any farther. I ran to join my neighbors gathering near the truck. The firemen unrolled the fat canvas hoses and heaved them up the road. We all wondered whether they would be long enough to reach the fire. I wanted to follow them. I wanted to see how big my fire had become. I would go tomorrow to inspect the ashes.

My tomboy didn't go away. Over time, she developed into a kind of bodyguard for my femme, working behind the scenes to negotiate power and vulnerability for her. To my tomboy, I'm the most beautiful girl in the world — even when I'm running fast, wielding a hammer, or covered with streambed mud.

Every once in a while, when I'm alone, usually in the mountains, my tomboy and femme selves meld, and I become simply me. That was me watching the moon the night Nicole disappeared. That was me burning down the fort in Pete's Woods. And that was me, tomboy and femme united, flirting with Monica near Castle Peak.

When I returned to the trailhead late that afternoon, I popped off my skis and carried them to my Saturn. Monica's truck was still there. The thought of Monica, and how I'd carried on that morning, filled me with terror and desire. Both my tomboy and my femme wanted her. That fire in Pete's Woods blazed for a moment in my head. Talk about having all your eggs in one basket. I was so glad I hadn't given her my name or phone number.

Then, as I was unlocking my car door, I saw her walking toward me, skis laid across her shoulders and crossed behind her head. Bridget stumbled along twenty yards behind.

"Hiya!" Monica whooped. My legs felt again like amoebas.

I smiled and looked away quickly. I started chanting silently to myself, *She's got a girlfriend and the girlfriend's right here. She's got a girlfriend and the girlfriend's right here.*

Monica kept her distance, unlocking her truck and stripping off her ski gear, but I saw her looking every chance she got. Bridget threw her skis in the back of the truck and ripped off her gaiters. She jumped in the passenger seat and slammed the truck door after her. Monica lingered behind the truck, cleaning the snow off her skis.

Then I noticed, for the first time, her bumper sticker: No Fear. The message stunned me. I felt as if I'd just had a vision. Those two words seemed so simple, clear, and somehow necessary. I took them literally, like a command, and grinned at Monica. "Wanna try driving the Saturn?" I offered.

Monica's eyes blazed. "Yeah," she said, without so much as a glance over her shoulder at Bridget, who sat rod straight in the truck's passenger seat, waiting.

I cleared the dirty socks and gaiters off the front seat and opened the driver's side door for her. Then I walked around and climbed in the passenger seat. Monica put Seashell in reverse and backed her up. She pulled out onto the highway, spewing gravel from the parking area.

Only then did Monica glance at Bridget in the rearview mirror.

"She'll be okay," I said.

Monica looked at me and smiled her big old tomboy smile.

I rolled down the window, though the breeze was cold this late in the day. A slice of moon hovered over the mountains to the west. I liked the look of Monica's hands on the steering wheel, the weight of her foot on the accelerator. I wondered just how far she would go.

Alison Bechdel, 1969

I probably spent half my childhood mowing our huge backyard. I didn't mind, though, because I felt like such a stud on that Cub Cadet.

Playing House

Karol D. Lightner

Playing house was a source of holy terror to me, growing up, but sometimes it was unavoidable. Inevitably would come the dreary day or other dismal occasion when the little girls in our neighborhood would drag out their miniature tea sets, doll carriages, and furniture, and commence to set up a mock-adult household. After attempting to drag in by the ears as many little boys as they could locate, they'd finally come looking for me, the neighborhood's token tomboy.

I was the last to give in to playing house, considering it the lowest of the low, an oppressive invasion of my childhood fortress. I much preferred the exotic and faraway — cowboys and Indians, pirates, cops and robbers, soldiers, jungle adventures, sports of any kind — and often chose to play by myself rather than endure all that nuclear-family nonsense. Alas, sometimes my need for human companionship overrode my revulsion to playing house, and I would consent to it.

But they had "casting" problems with me, those future domestics who set it all up: I adamantly refused to be "Mother," that beaten-down, tired, overworked figure I saw around me every day in everyone's mother. And god knows, I didn't like the part of "Father" — he was bossy, fussy, hairy chested, and creepy. What's more, each and every day he had to take his lunch bucket and disappear to some heinous place called "work." With the exception of two boys whose parents ran a local pizza parlor, no one seemed to know much about this place and didn't know what to do when they went there, so that was boring. True, Father didn't have to pretend he was cooking or cleaning house, or pick up dolls, but still, he was out of my scope of interest. Playing "Little Girl" was as bad as playing Mother — she had to help out, for one thing, and, worse, if you played house for any length of time, she was apt to grow up, stage a wedding, and become a bride. Gross! "Little Boy" might seem a better choice, but little boys just grew up to be fathers.

Now, our families were such that one could not opt for being a maiden aunt, or Uncle Albert, or Grandma — we played it straight midcentury Americana: little nuclear families honed to essentials, no extensions. Grandmas didn't live with you — grandmas were people you stuck in nursing homes.

And so I would create my own role — usually consenting to be the family dog or, if I was in a particularly churlish mood, the family horse. To this day, as a result of all the hours I put in as a family pet, I can bark, growl, and snap well enough to provoke dogs, and whinny and kick better than any humans I know outside of some cast members of *Equus*.

Being a pet was the perfect "out." I could inject into what was normally a boring routine any kind of adventure I wanted: I could attack burglars; warn the family of fires, earthquakes, or tornadoes (we did live in Iowa); rescue the children from backyard quicksand or from giant anacondas that invaded the household at night (my poor mother could never understand why she had to buy a new vacuum cleaner hose every two years, unaware of my snarling fights with that giant snake). Best of all, if things got too boring, I could "get lost" or run away from home. Ensconced in the body and psyche of an animal, I could always "become wild."

Being a pet was the perfect "out"

One day a crisis occurred. It was raining and we had elected to play in someone's attic. We were indoors, so my being a horse was a no-no: in the adult world we were imitating, horses did not come into people's homes. Saloons, yes; houses, no. There was already a real live dog present and no one felt there should be two dogs. Plus, I tended to intimidate dogs with my growling and groveling on the floor with them.

And so I had a problem: I could not be a dog or a horse and wasn't interested in being a person or a cat. What, then? I looked around the attic. It was littered with old furniture, boxes, trunks — and an old abandoned radio, the tall floor-model type popular in the thirties that now sells for hundreds of dollars. It had a wooden frontispiece backed with soft cloth and brandished fancy knobs and a little red dial on the radio band. It had been gutted, its back beaverboard torn off, its tubes and wires strewn about on the floor. I found that if I knelt down, my eight-year-old body fit perfectly in its hollow inside. I promptly slipped into the back and announced to my surprised playmates that I was going to be the family radio.

Yes, the radio. From inside, I could vaguely see the children who came to turn the knobs. I could hear the click when they turned it on or off, and could see the red dial move as they changed stations, so I knew when the radio was being played and what station it was on. Being a fair sound-effects maker and a decent storyteller, I had found my niche. When someone turned the knob and moved the dial, I made a static noise, a sort of *Chhhhhh,* and as soon as they set the dial, I became a station broadcasting any number of programs:

> "On, ya huskies! ... Well, King: this case is closed!"
>
> "Who knows what evil lurks in the hearts of men: the Shadow knows ... Heh-heh-heh!"
>
> "Gramps, he left a silver bullet. Who was that masked man?"
>
> "Shucks, Suzie Mae, don't you know who he is? That's the Lone Ranger!"
>
> "Hi-yo, Silver, away!"

Or even (to the tune of "Blue Danube"):

"Use Rival dog food — Arf, arf, arf-arf;
Use Rival dog food — Arf-arf, arf-arf!
Your dog's eyes will shine, he'll be fine,
When you use Rival dog food."

It worked! Not only had I managed to sidestep the monotony I was facing, but my performance as a radio so fascinated the neighborhood kids that they stopped playing house and began to play the radio. I was home free...

home free...

Diana Le Blanc, 1965

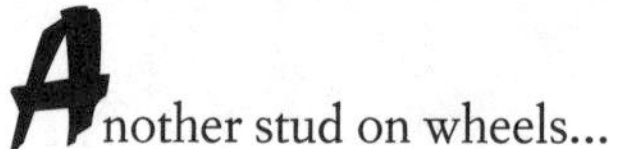

Another stud on wheels...

Like many New England girls of the fifties, I had a proper collection of dolls, a long line of them sitting neatly in order of size against the wall. My dolls were fresh and clean-looking—from lack of use rather than from any endearing attention on my part. Though I had a tender heart for animals, sad people, and underdogs, my mothering instinct was faint from the beginning. What I liked to do was bring my fine dolls over to the Lawrence girls across the street, who would exchange playing time with the dolls for my use of their big blue tricycle. I'd say to them, "Let's play house. You be the mommies. I'll be the daddy, and now I have to go to work." I'd pump myself down the street and they wouldn't see me again until suppertime.

—Diane F. Germain, from "Tomboy of New England"

Occasionally, I would play with dolls, but that wasn't much fun. I preferred to spend time with my imaginary friends of unspecific gender: Fruit Cocktail, Crewcut, and Butch. We were all the best of friends. Cowboy was our favorite game, but army was a close second. At first, my parents refused to buy me any boy toys, so I was forced to improvise. There is a picture of me looking fiercely at the camera. I am brandishing a rifle made from a crib rail. An ancient leather football helmet is scrunched on my head and my eyes are hidden behind a pair of welding goggles. Later evidence of my love of make-believe — and that my parents finally relented and bought me some of the toys I wanted — was my Roy Roger cowboy outfit and my Zorro cape and mask.

—Barbara Ann Wray, from "Swamp Fox and Me"

There's No Girl in Tomboy

Denise Carmen Paquin

At four years old, I stood at the foot of my bed and declared that I wanted no more dolls for Christmas. "I'm a boy and I want boy things!" (By this, I meant Lincoln Logs, Tonka trucks, and a western town kit with cowboys and Indians.) "If you give me a doll, I'll rip it up!" The next Christmas was the best. In fact, over the years, my parents often gave me what I wanted, despite many struggles, especially over clothing. Mom secretly bought me boys' underwear, but at Easter she'd try to get me into girlie outfits for large family gatherings.

It seemed that to get the things I wanted and to do the things I felt inclined to do, I had to choose one gender or the other. I think my dad was glad I chose to be a boy. All the butch photos of me, including a recent one of me wearing a double-breasted linen suit at my sister's wedding, he took. My femme photographs were all taken by women: my mother, my grandmother, friends. Sometimes I feel lucky to have had parents who respected my boy choices. At other times, I wish they could have found a way to foster my female side more.

Tomboy was never a term I chose for myself. It was a word people used to fit me into society's strictly defined gender classifications. It allowed me to exist. People think a tomboy is cute — within limits. But why is there no correspondingly cute janegirl concept for queenie boys who want to play dress-up and dance? In the short run, *tomboy* serves the nontraditional girl's desire for typically boy things. In the long run, however, the label perpetuates misogyny within the very girl it appears to liberate.

I tried to convince Mom that it was "gym day" at kindergarten. She did not believe me, probably because I'd lied before just so I could wear pants and sneakers. This time I was telling the truth, but she forced me into black patent leather shoes and a frilly dress. The gym teacher wouldn't let me play, because I hadn't come prepared. I cried. Later, I vowed never to wear a dress again. "I am a boy, and boys wear pants and sneakers!" I fought hard and won. Mom even cut my hair short, much to my grandmother's chagrin. I think Mom was just as relieved as I was to do away with grouchy hair-combing sessions spent untangling snarls.

In second grade, I was transferred from the tyrannical public school to an experimental, "open" classroom, ironically, in a Catholic school. There, I was free to explore the art materials, the science room, and the games in the math room. (I generally avoided the reading room.) I entered the new school with a fully established boy identity. I played kickball and smear the queer at recess and made friends with boys and one girl — Kerry Kelly, another devout tomboy.

In third grade, I sang in chorus and loved it, especially at Christmas, a joyous time for an eight-year-old whose family respected her toy wishes. We spent weeks preparing for a holiday concert at the local church. I was really excited about it until they announced the dress code for performers: boys were to wear black pants, a white shirt, and a green tie; girls were to wear a green skirt, a white blouse, and tights. I wanted a green tie, but the teacher said I had to wear a skirt and blouse if I wanted to sing in the concert.

In the long run, the tomboy label perpetuates misogyny within the very girl it appears to liberate

I cried and cried. "Well, I'm just not going to sing in the stupid concert!" But I really wanted to sing in it. I still remember my tear-flooded phone conversation with Miss Muriel: "But why can't I wear pants? ... It's not fair! ... Dresses are soooo uncomfortable! ... I *hate* them!" I felt as embarrassed and traumatized as a boy forced to wear a dress would have.

I wore the ugly skirt and sang my heart out. I especially remember the airy, spirited echoes of "Do You Hear What I Hear?" As soon as the last note was sung, I left it to hang in the air while I slipped into the safety of my blue jeans in the backseat of our big Chevrolet. Kids and teachers teased me about the dress the next day, and from then on I rejected chorus, my love of singing squelched by the limits society set on the tomboy's cuteness. My "boy" clothing was tolerated on the playground, but for important events I had to conform to society's dress code for girls.

The next summer, a boy in my neighborhood told me they were letting girls try out for Little League. Dad brought me to tryouts and I made Wayne's Exxon. I remember the first cold day of practice and Wayne's speech about teamwork, welcoming the only girl who would play on his team for four years. With my very short haircut, I tried to fit in, and the experience further reinforced my boy identity.

In fourth grade, the school's tolerance for my tomboy behavior on the playground waned. They regulated recess by drawing a line through the playground, separating girls from boys. I was not confused about where I belonged: I played on the boys' side. Not for long, though, as I was straightaway sent to the principal's office for breaking the rules. I was outraged. "That's not fair!" My friends were boys, and the kickball field was on the boys' side, which was almost twice as big as the girls' space and more level. I spent many days in the office crying hard and arguing against the nuns' illogic. I vividly remember Miss Savageau shaking me hard out in right field on the kickball diamond and shouting at me: "Girls' bones get more fragile as they grow older! You should learn to play with other girls!" Through my tears I could see my

best friend, Tom Hurley, staring at us, scared. *Do something, will ya, Tom!?* I thought. He didn't. I think he was too afraid of her.

At first, only Kerry and I were allowed on the boys' side, but by the fifth grade the other girls had caught on, and slowly the line disappeared. Playing with the boys never felt the same after that.

I entered junior high school a boy inside and out. "Hey, Denise! They let girls play on the soccer team," Paul Gagnon told me in homeroom. My Little League experience had made trying out for a "boy" sport feel natural to me, but no other girls joined the team. It was a new sport for me and I wasn't the best player. The coach never helped me in practice and would play me only in the last few minutes of a game — if we were winning by a lot. Kerry convinced me to try out for basketball. I was hesitant to play on a girls' team, but after getting a lot of attention in practice and actual playing time at games, I left the soccer team for basketball. I think a part of me was afraid of girls. I knew subconsciously that I was different in a big way and that fitting in would be a struggle.

For the first time in my life, I began to identify with girls. Under pressure from my teammates, I asked my mother for a bra. (I was so nervous, I went along with her on some benign errand so that I could ask her in the privacy of the Dodge Colt. Still, my palms were sweating and I could barely breathe.) I even started to shave my legs. In the spring of seventh grade, I chose to play softball instead of baseball as I began to enjoy girls' company over that of boys. And I was thrilled when Ellen O'Neil, the star of the basketball team, invited me to her house for a sleepover. It was the first time in my twelve years that I'd been invited to a girl's house to spend the night. My fear and anxiety soared when I discovered we were to sleep in the same bed.

Fear of being labeled a lesbian exacerbated my situation, and I felt a strong pressure to date boys. My first date took me roller skating. I had never gone before. I was wearing blue jeans and a green-and-white checkered shirt, typical attire for me. We walked up to the window together to get our skates — black for both of us — then flew around the rink. Though sore from repeatedly falling, I was having fun. Then the music changed and they called for couples out on the floor. As at any junior high dance, there were a few awkward moments as the slow song kicked in. We left the floor and leaned on the railing to watch. I could smell his sweaty body as he moved closer to ask me to skate with him. Since we were officially "on a date," I said yes, and we skated out. My black skates caught the eyes of the rink monitors, though, who wagged their fingers at us and told us that two boys couldn't be a couple. "Whaaat? I'm a girl!" I replied. They were incredulous as they checked my hands — for daintiness, I guess. "What do you want me to do? Take off my shirt to prove it!? I'm a girl!" They kicked us off the floor anyway. Humiliated, I said to my date, "Why didn't you tell me girls were supposed to wear white skates?!" and whacked him in the stomach. "I dunno," he replied earnestly. "It doesn't matter to me!"

"I'm a girl!"

My parents divorced the next summer and the basketball team became my surrogate family, with the coach, "Mr. G.," as surrogate dad. We played fifty-two games and five tournaments in eighth grade and won them all. I was awarded nine trophies that year, including one for Best Sportsmanship for all of St. Joe's. I became the coach's favorite. In the meantime, my home life was falling apart as Mom lost her job, then landed in the hospital for weeks with hepatitis.

"Mr. G.," I asked late one night as he drove me home from a game, "if boys are so much more important, why do you coach girls?" "Because girls are prettier," he replied with a funny smile that confused me and made me uncomfortable. Mr. G. sexually abused me over a period of about five months. It scarred my sexuality in the obvious ways, but it also further isolated me from the only other girls I was beginning to relate to — my teammates.

The change to high school helped a little. Mr. G. had inspired me to work toward a basketball scholarship as a way of going to college. I had never thought about college before meeting him, but throughout high school, the prospect drove me to achieve in academics and in sports and other college-track extracurricular activities. I played four sports a year, all on girls' teams, and made some new friends. It was relatively easy to make friends among my teammates with all the time we spent sitting on buses and chowing at McDonald's. A few of them were even as butch as me. I went to some jock parties and even to the prom with the soccer-softball gang.

I always wanted to be closer, somehow, to my girl friends. One reason I wasn't closer was that my sexuality had gone dormant as a result of Mr. G.'s abuse. Part of the distance also came from my fear of being identified as lesbian and from my skewed gender identity. I still believed deep inside that I was supposed to be a boy.

Eight of us girljocks lined up for a group photo at the prom (four of us are now lesbians). I did wear a gown and never more proudly, because my dad and I designed and made it together. (He had sewn dresses for my mom when they were married. How ironic that he could engage in such a "female" activity and yet give me so little approval for my femaleness: his approval was all for my boy self.)

I went to the prom with David Pezzini, my closest friend in high school and the only boy I ever liked in a romantic way. He loved to dance as much as I did and dared to do the fox trot and the waltz during slow songs. Though we were "boyfriend and girlfriend" for a short while, our relationship was fairly platonic. Our first day in homeroom I'd asked him to share a locker with me, and he'd agreed. We were lockermates for three years. Normally, girls shared lockers only with other girls, and boys, with other boys. As a result, we bore a lot of pressure to be a couple. The best times I had with him were going out for ice cream sundaes, jogging for miles to get in shape for soccer (he played too), passing notes to each other in class, and singing "Chestnuts Roasting on an Open Fire" while cross-country skiing around the lake. He was a gender-bender like me and we found a special place together somewhere in between male and female.

I began to like my lost female self

When I went to college, I began to like my lost female self, with the help of feminist friends who encouraged my developing lesbian sexuality. I grew my hair long and became active in both the gay and the feminist movements. Something was missing, though — a love life, for one. I felt pretty isolated as an "out" lesbian-feminist at conservative Boston College. I was lonely for romance, yet unable to be intimate with other lesbians. I had a long, convenient crush on a straight woman, my best friend. During a year in Paris, I had an affair with a woman sixteen years my senior. In the eight years following, I had a few short relationships with basically unavailable women. I was "out of the closet" politically but imprisoned emotionally. Some of the blame rested with my parents' divorce and Mr. G.'s abuse, but it was not until I dealt with the internal hatred I felt for myself as a girl that I could truly develop an intimate relationship with another woman. At Boston College, I had skipped a step between growing up a boy and becoming a feminist "womyn."

In 1989, I started therapy, shortly after beginning a career as an elementary school teacher. I was working in an after-school program, where we focused on play and building social relationships, when I was confronted by a group of eight-year-old girls: "You only do boy things ... You never want to play with us ... You hate us..." The first part was true: I did spend most of my time playing with the boys, essentially repeating my tomboy habits from elementary school. I also disliked dealing with the girls' conflicts and could hear boys' arguments with more tolerance. But, though I appeared to the girls to hate them, what I really hated was what they brought up for me about my past.

Since then I have been doing things to show my girl self that I love her while still attending to my boy self's needs. I made a soft doll, for example, who wears sneakers and blue jeans. I have learned to play guitar and sing even the high notes. With the help of a professional massage therapist, I have learned to listen to my body in ways beyond a jock mentality.

My work with girls greatly improved while interning at the Cambridge Friends School, a Quaker establishment that works diligently against racism, sexism, and homophobia. The teachers were delighted to have an out lesbian working with their team. I came out to students during their gay pride celebrations and developed close relationships with all of the students in the class. During my internship, I learned new ways to teach girls and boys sports and foster equality through literature, math, science, and the arts. Currently, I work in a new after-school program with an equal following of girls and boys in such activities as hockey and woodworking with power tools. My professional work provides me many opportunities to liberate my inner child from the constraints of the tomboy label.

Growing up a tomboy allowed me to pursue sports, build a clubhouse, wear comfortable clothes, ride a motorcycle, and go without a shirt in the summertime for much longer than most girls in the 1970s — but at a cost. I don't want to be a lesbian who hates girls. We must raise our boys and girls to like their whole selves, with loosely fitting gender labels applied purely in an anatomical sense. I am a kinesthetically inclined lesbian woman with both male and female traits. It is with this new definition of myself that I have been able to create gratifying relationships with the children I work with, with my family of origin, and with a lover. There was no room for a girl in my definition of a tomboy. So now I would rather not use the term at all.

the POWER of PRAYER

UNTIL THE SPRING OF SECOND GRADE, I WAS A CAREFREE, GODLESS CHILD. THE WORLD WAS MY OYSTER.

THEN ONE DAY AT SCHOOL, THE TEACHER DIVIDED OUR CLASS BY SEX.

NOT EVEN MY WORST SUSPICIONS PREPARED ME FOR WHAT WAS TO FOLLOW.

I WENT THROUGH THE MOTIONS IN ORDER TO AVOID BEING SINGLED OUT FOR SOME EVEN **WORSE** FATE.

BACK IN THE CLASSROOM, I THOUGHT MY HUMILI-ATION WAS OVER... BUT I WAS WRONG.

ALL THAT WEEK, I ENDURED THIS ASSAULT ON MY DIGNITY AND SELF-DETERMINATION.

BUT FINALLY THEY WENT TOO FAR. ONE DAY WE WERE WERE GIVEN NOTES TO TAKE HOME.

FRIGHTENED, I CONCOCTED A SHORT-RANGE SOLUTION TO MY PLIGHT.

I WENT STRAIGHT TO MY ROOM AFTER SCHOOL AND CHANGED FROM MY GIRL COSTUME INTO MY REGULAR CLOTHES.

AFTER POCKETING THE TEACHER'S NOTE, I PICKED UP A TROWEL FROM THE GARAGE AND SET OFF FOR THE WOODS.

AT THE ABANDONED RAILROAD TRACKS, I STOPPED AND DUG A DEEP HOLE...

TORE THE NOTE INTO AS MANY PIECES AS I POSSIBLY COULD...

... AND BURIED THEM.

THE NEXT DAY, HOWEVER, I HAD A BAD SCARE.

I PLAYED IT COOL, AND SHE DIDN'T SUSPECT A THING.

BUT THE DAY OF THE GYM SHOW WAS FAST ENCROACHING. DESPERATE NOW, I HOPED FOR A MIRACLE.

ON SATURDAY, I ATTENDED MY REGULAR WEEKLY CHURCH SCHOOL CLASS. I HAD NEVER PAID MUCH ATTENTION BEFORE. IT ALL SEEMED SO ABSTRACT.

BUT THAT MORNING, CATHOLIC DOCTRINE FELL INTO PLACE FOR ME.

THE NIGHT BEFORE THE GYM SHOW, I SAT UP IN BED SAYING A HUNDRED "OUR FATHERS."

AND I AWOKE THE NEXT DAY WITH DIVINE INSPIRATION.

MIRACULOUSLY, IT WORKED.

AND EVEN MORE MIRACULOUSLY, WHEN MY MOTHER RETURNED FROM TAKING MY BROTHERS TO THE GYM SHOW THAT NIGHT, SHE DIDN'T MENTION MY CLASSMATES' LITTLE PERFORMANCE.

YES, I HAD BEEN DELIVERED FROM THE SCARF DANCE. BUT SOMEHOW I COULDN'T RECAPTURE MY FORMER CAREFREE ABANDON.

AFTER ALL, GOD ONLY KNEW WHAT FURTHER EVILS THIS LIFE HELD IN STORE.

Cowboy Heaven

Marlene H. Lipinski

Three brown-haired girls sat on the couch in their best Sunday dresses, patiently waiting for the clock to read seven. Francine, the oldest at fourteen, sat nearest the Christmas tree in a pink-and-black taffeta confirmation dress with matching black flats. Kathleen, nine, sat in the middle wearing a crisply pressed, red floral-print dress with a white Peter Pan collar. Amy, who had just turned seven, was in the only dress she could tolerate from her limited wardrobe: a navy blue sailor dress with front pockets where she could keep her small plastic horses, reaching in occasionally to pet them. It was her favorite because it was neither frilly nor a hand-me-down from her sisters.

Fifteen more minutes before their grandparents would arrive and the opening of the presents could begin. The three girls stared at the gifts as Bing Crosby crooned "White Christmas" in the background. Francine, who had just started high school and was in love with *American Bandstand,* had asked for clothes and records. Kathleen was hoping for a kitchen set, complete with a stove, refrigerator, dishes, and baking tins. Amy had asked for only two things — Tinkertoys and cowboy boots — and now she studied the packages that, earlier that afternoon, she had scouted out as being for her. There were three for each girl — her mother prided herself on treating her children equally — but Amy's three were exceptionally large.

Amy knew her mother had gotten the gifts, just as she knew there was no Santa Claus. She had made that discovery at the age of three when, on Christmas eve, she had unexpectedly walked in on Stanley, her father's maintenance man, sitting in the kitchen in a Santa suit with his beard off, unshaven and drinking a Schlitz with her father. She had loved to follow Stanley around, watching him fix the plumbing and paint the walls.

Amy loved to build things, take them apart, and, if possible, put them back together differently. After coloring the white dots on her dominoes with her favorite bright crayons, she would use the dominoes to build forts and skyscrapers. Her wooden blocks had been one of her most precious treasures until her father used them to prop up a broken leg on her sister's bed.

"Mom, if I could have Tinkertoys, I could build an airplane," Amy had told her mother. At the time, Amy was kneeling on a kitchen chair, fishing for the Cheerios in her breakfast bowl.

"Why would you want to do that, honey?" Her mother didn't look up from the sink, where, wearing pedal-pushers and a blouse with rolled-up sleeves, she was doing the dishes.

"So I could fly like Superman or Sky King and Penny." Amy could see only one side of her mother's face, but her mother's voice had sounded indifferent.

"Why can't I have little-boy toys?" Amy asked, grumbling more into the cereal bowl than at her mother.

Her mother stiffened slightly. "Because you're a little girl." Her mother cocked her head to one side and looked over at Amy, her eyebrows wrinkled above her clear blue eyes.

Amy felt her true thoughts breaking out of their corral and stampeding from her mouth. "I don't want to be a girl, I want to be a boy. They get to do all the fun things and they get all the fun toys." Amy's voice had risen to a shout.

Her mother put down the dish she was washing and turned toward Amy, putting one wet hand on her hip. "You're not a little boy; you're a little girl. Now, finish your cereal."

Amy got up and crossed the living room, peering out the front window for signs of her grandfather's car. She thought of last year's Christmas presents: an iron, an ironing board, and a sewing machine. She hadn't asked for these gifts: they'd just appeared. The sewing machine was okay; after all, it was a machine, and later, she discovered she could load colored thread on it and sew colored lines onto paper. Her mother demonstrated ironing handkerchiefs, which Amy immediately denounced as boring.

Amy decided her ironing board made a nice bar in the frontier saloon that she imagined her bedroom to be. Cowpokes could come up to the bar and order shots of red-eye. And the iron made a good art tool for melting crayons, which got her in more trouble with her mother and with her sister Kathy, for melting all the crayons. She used to freely drip the melted crayons onto pieces of scrap paper to make beautiful abstract designs. Once, she tried blending the colors in her Cisco Kid coloring book, but the iron was so big, it was hard to stay within the lines.

"Real cowboys don't wear skirts"

As the clock ticked closer to seven, Amy's gaze wandered to the top of the TV set, where white plastic reindeer encircled a December calendar candle slowly burning its way to December 25. The reindeer reminded her of wild white stallions, the kind cowboys were always trying to catch in Saturday-afternoon movies. She thought of the cowboy boots she wanted. The largest package — did it hold the boots? She remembered the gun and white cowboy hat she had gotten two Christmases before, along with a cowgirl skirt with fake leather fringe.

"Real cowboys don't wear skirts," she had argued as she sat watching her mother brush her curled brown hair.

"But it's an authentic Dale Evans skirt." Her mother picked up her hand mirror to look closer at her tweezed eyebrows.

"Real cowboys leap onto runaway horses, they jump from balconies onto their horses, they chase bad guys at a gallop. How can I do those things in a skirt?" Amy moaned.

"Dale doesn't do those things," her mother said. "A little girl should be a lady, like Dale Evans. Why, she can even ride a horse in a skirt."

"But, Mom, I don't *want* to be Dale Evans; I want to be Roy Rogers. Besides, I play with Bobby and Joey, and if I wear a skirt, they'll see my underpants, and no lady should ever let someone see her underpants," Amy had insisted.

Her thoughts were interrupted by a shout from Kathy: "They're here! Grandma and Grandpa are here!"

Amy's grandparents adored all three of their grandchildren, continually showing it in tender glances, caresses, and encouraging praise. But Amy knew there was no chance of her getting Tinkertoys and cowboy boots from them: Grandma was very old-fashioned, known for her embroidered pillowcases and the floral-print skirts she sewed for the girls each year. Amy was happy to see them anyway. Besides, their arrival meant that opening the presents was close at hand.

After the usual greetings and hugs, Dad and Grandpa got their beers, and the girls, their orange pop. The homemade Christmas cutout cookies that Kathy and Amy had helped frost and decorate were passed around. When everyone was settled in place, the opening of the presents could at last begin.

Orderliness was a priority. Amy's father hated chaos under the tree. Only one present was opened at a time, with Amy's mother distributing the gifts.

Amy, being the youngest, was always the first to open a gift, another reason Amy and Kathy didn't get along.

"I'll play house with you, but only if I can be the father or the older brother," Amy would tell Kathy — if it was raining and Amy couldn't play outside. Kathy loved dolls. Amy thought them useless except as a makeshift football.

"Amy, what are you doing?" her mother had yelled, catching Amy drop-kicking her doll Susie across the bedroom. "I'm ashamed of you, treating your doll that way." Her mother had given her a look that would make a small animal freeze. Amy often got these looks from her mother and her sisters. Sometimes she felt like some sort of a Martian.

Oh well, at least they stopped giving me dolls, she thought.

"Well, now." Her mother rose and moved over to the Christmas tree. "I guess it's time to start opening some of these presents. Let's see if I can find anything under here for the youngest."

Amy took her cue and moved to the middle of the living room to wait for her mother to hand her the first gift. She stood watching her mother move slowly around the tree, pretty in her brown plaid skirt, brown wedgies, and a see-through pink blouse that revealed a white lacy slip underneath. Neatly parted dark brown curls framed her well-powdered face, and the touch of rouge on each cheek matched her red lipstick. Amy loved to sit by her mother's vanity and watch her put on her makeup. Amy also got a lot of spankings at that vanity, for coloring on surfaces she wasn't supposed to color on.

"Let's see. This one says, 'To Amy from Santa.'" Her mother picked up the flattest of the large boxes Amy had been studying all evening. As if by reflex, Amy's hopes soared. *Tinkertoys?*

She searched her mother's face for a clue as to what the box held, but her mother's face was neutral. Amy immediately curbed her hopes, recalling that awful day last summer when her grandparents had rewarded her with some money for earning several A's in first grade. She was allowed to go to the dime store by herself to pick out the toy of her choice.

She had come back shouting, "Mom, look what I got!" running into the basement, where her mother was doing the weekly wash. "A shaving kit!"

Her mother stopped loading the clothes into the washer and turned. The look on her face was both puzzled and shocked.

"You got what? What did you say you got?"

"A shaving kit, so I can shave like Dad and Grandpa."

Her mother stepped forward and took the box from Amy's enthusiastic hands. "This is a little boy's gift. You can't have this." She was shouting suddenly, horror in her voice. "You have to take this back and exchange it. Little girls don't shave. You take this back to the dime store right now." Disgust filled her face.

Amy walked dejectedly back to the store, stepping on every crack in the sidewalk, reciting, "Step on a crack..." She didn't understand her mother at all. She didn't understand why there were right toys and wrong ones. She did understand that she kept picking the wrong ones.

She looked at her mother placing the Christmas present in front of her. What did her expression mean now? Was she peeved at her for even asking for cowboy boots? Was she trying to tell her, No little boys' toys in this box, young lady?

Amy gazed at the box at her feet. The white-bearded, cheery-faced Santa on the red paper seemed to wink at her, raising her spirits again. She began to dig into the box like a dog digging for its bone. She shoved the lid off and pushed aside the white tissue paper, catching her breath as her gaze fell upon the most beautiful pair of six-shooters she had ever imagined.

She smelled the real leather as her fingers gently touched the holsters. Two large silver ornaments with rubies the size of quarters shone at her from the center of each holster. Spaced around the belt were small plastic hoops for bullets. The buckle was very fancy and bore the same kind of ornate drawing as the metalwork around the jewels. The handles looked like ivory, with Roy Rogers's face carved in one and Trigger, his horse, in the other. Amy carefully withdrew one gun from the holster, brushing her hand over the surface as if she were cupping her hands around a newly hatched baby chick. The guns glistened under the Christmas tree lights like her mother's finely polished silver candlesticks. Amy rolled the gun over in her hand, examining every detail. Next to the trigger she found a small latch that opened the cylinder, revealing a small space for a roll of caps. *They even shoot,* she thought.

She slowly removed the guns and holsters from the box and strapped the belt to her waist. Her mother adjusted it to its smallest slot. *How could there be anything else?* Amy wondered. The gods had already visited her once that Christmas eve; there could be no need to open any other boxes. But after Kathy had opened her Betty Crocker baking set; Francine, her poodle skirt; Dad, his green trout necktie; Mom, her embroidered pillow cases; Grandma, her dusting powder; and Grandpa, his bottle of Christian Brothers brandy, it was Amy's turn again.

She returned to the center of the living room, hesitantly taking her hands off her pistols to unwrap the second package. Another wave of ecstasy washed over her. There in the second box was a black felt cowboy hat, and under it were the boots, genuine black leather with red and white stitching to match the holsters. She kicked off her brown oxfords and plunged her feet into the boots, transported by the softness of the leather. She felt transformed. No acts of courage were beyond her now. She could perform with the best of cowboys. Rusty, of *Rin Tin Tin* fame, had nothing on her anymore. Jeff and Timmy of *Lassie* would envy these duds. What heights she had attained!

She no longer noticed what other gifts were being opened. In her mind, Amy was already out on the range roping steers and shooting rattlesnakes quick-draw style.

The last box was the pot at the end of the rainbow: the entire authentic Roy Rogers cowboy outfit, complete with black jeans, a red-and-black plaid flannel shirt, a canteen, and a pair of rawhide-fringed leather gloves. The only disappointment was a red-and-yellow silk scarf with Roy's picture and signature on it. She would have preferred plain cotton.

Before going to bed, Amy cleared off the bar of the saloon and put the ironing board next to her bed, arranging her treasures on it so that she would see them all as soon as she opened her eyes in the morning. Something was puzzling her, a question darting like little fish through the stream of her wonder as she set each beautiful thing out. Her mother came and tucked Amy in. After she had kissed her good night and was turning to leave, Amy's question slipped out. "Mom? I thought you didn't want me to have little-boy stuff."

Her mother sat back down on the bed and patted Amy's leg through the covers. "Well, one of Santa's elves reminded me that when I was a little girl, I used to play with my brother's toys."

Amy hesitated before answering. If there was no Santa Claus, how could there be elves? "Boy, I'd sure like to thank that elf."

Her mother smiled. "Maybe you can give your grandma a big hug when you see her tomorrow."

The family album over the next two years testified to Amy's devotedness to being a tough hombre of the Old West. Summer pictures showed her in shorts, sleeveless blouse, cowboy boots, hat, and guns. Winter pictures showed her guns bulging out from under her gray car coat and her angora knit cap peeking out from under her cowboy hat. Even on Easter Sunday she posed in black jeans and boots between Kathy and her cousin Mary, both in their Easter dresses.

She spent countless hours riding her bike, which she imagined to be her horse, Lightning. She ran and reran her fantasies like movies, seeing herself returning the Wells Fargo cash box to the townspeople, saving women from runaway stagecoaches, catching the bad guys, and, of course, sneaking up on her mother in the kitchen and challenging her to a showdown, which her mother tolerated with surprising good humor.

As the years passed, Amy traded her guns for artists' brushes, the boots for athletic shoes, the cowboy clothes for warm-up suits, and faithful Lightning for a red pickup truck. Those two glorious years of cowboy bliss, when her mother had let her play out all those wonderful fantasies, seemed to have satisfied her need to be part of the rugged West. Still, seeing other lesbians at coffeehouses, bookstores, and bars, she felt an immediate bond with those wearing western boots, flannel shirts, and silver belt buckles. The only item that remained from her two years in cowboy heaven was her canteen, that trusted companion that, filled with lemonade in the summer and hot chocolate in the winter, had sustained her and Lightning through many a hard trek through the mountains and desert. Now, thirty years later, it hung from the corner of her dresser mirror, along with her Nikon camera.

That Christmas, Amy's parents came to visit her and Beth in their new home.

"Mom, come upstairs and see our new bedroom set," Amy said.

The two women were walking around the room discussing the beauty of oak when Amy's mother suddenly stopped, her gaze resting on the canteen that hung next to the bureau mirror. Amy watched from the other side of the room as her mother reached for the canteen and gently pulled it toward her heart.

"Your canteen," she whispered, barely loud enough for Amy to hear. Her face grew softly somber. She gazed at the canteen as if it were a crystal ball casting up images from her past.

Amy felt as if she were witnessing her mother in prayer. Then, her mother, with tears in her eyes, turned to her grown daughter, slowly pointed her index finger at her, cocked her thumb, and said, "Stick 'em up."

TOMBOY
by Dianne Reum
©'94
I GOT DIANNE A "CINDERELLA" COSTUME.
YOUR DIANNE?
YOU MARK MY WORDS: I'M GOING TO TURN HER INTO A LITTLE "LADY" YET.
I RECKON I'D BEST BE SLIPPIN' OUT THE BACK DOOR.
BOO
Happy Halloween, Pardner.

There was crick walkin', fort buildin', books and knees meetin' mud, occasional detentions, cubby-hole hideouts, bat capes at Halloween, invincibly Mercurochromed forearms, a legacy read in scars...

Tom was nowhere near as unsettling a moniker as *boy*. *Tom* was just another name, an expedient truncation, but *boy* was the kind of insult to bring blood to the face. I mean, I knew who I was, and who the hell were they to voice scorn and invoke censure? It may have been different for those who wouldn't charge nets or contest calls once they reached the high school prom, but for the rest of us, the appellation wasn't benign — it was meant as a warning.

—Marie Elizabeth Dolcini, from "Their Word – Not Mine"

What Good Is a Doll If Her Clothes Don't Come Off?

Elena Sherman

Growing up a tomboy in post–World War II Chicago wasn't easy. Growing up a short, Jewish tomboy in post–World War II Chicago was even harder. The fifties were not a good time to be different. All "good" little girls played with their dolls while dreaming about Prince Charming, who was waiting to take them away to a life of baking apple pies and raising children.

I just wasn't built that way.

To me, dolls were things you removed clothes from, whether they were removable or not. When I was four, my parents tried to convince me that some dolls were meant to be played with as is. I replied, frustrated, "What good is a doll if her clothes don't come off?" But I dropped dolls for radios. Taking apart radios was a lot more fun. They had tubes that glowed and a lot of mysterious wires.

The summer I was four, in 1946, I was sent to an eight-week residential camp. I won the Best Junior Camper award: a leather headband with my name burned on it and a feather sticking up in front. Perhaps I won it because I was fully four years younger than the next youngest camper — my memories don't lead me to believe that I, in any way, deserved the award. I recall spending an entire day, from breakfast to bedtime, sitting in the dining hall being watched over by a succession of counselors, engaged in a battle of wills over whether or not I would eat the disgusting oatmeal. I won.

I remember sticking my finger in the mouth of a fish with a lot of teeth. The blood dripping down my arm was annoying, but not as annoying as the silly girls who were screaming and the dumb adults who wanted to drag me off to the nurse. I was busy peering at the fish trying to figure out how a dead fish had bitten me, and I wasn't interested in being interrupted.

Most of the time I hung around with the nine- and ten-year old boys. I carried the various toads, lizards, and other creepy crawlies they wanted to collect but were afraid to touch. Even now, my neighbors call me when they see a snake in their yard.

I never made the "good little girl" category. Going to a total of nine elementary schools and five high schools made me too independent to conform. My father was a magician and artist, and as our fortunes rose and fell, we moved. At each new school I had to defend myself and my father, frequently by fighting.

Socially, life was easier for me when I was the only Jewish kid. The other kids viewed me as an oddity and didn't expect me to behave like them. I expect I was odd to them, a short, round, dark child in a sea of skinny, tall blonds and redheads.

Our favorite game in 1948 was, reasonably enough, war. The boys would choose sides to fight and expect all the girls to be nurses. Since none of the boys was ever willing to be wounded, the girls didn't get to play. Well, I wanted to play. So I told the boys that they needed a front-line medic and that it was going to be me. After I wounded a few of them personally, just to give them the idea, they stopped resisting and went along.

Being a fair-minded child, I did show the boys how, by scraping the powder out of caps and adding a fuse, they could blow a tin can into the air, creating a satisfying bang. After that, I was in great demand as a medic and frequently worked both sides.

The combination of always being the shortest and youngest in my class and not being especially meek led to a certain amount of assertive behavior on my part.

In third grade, I watched two fifth-grade boys regularly take one of my classmates behind the building during recess and beat him up. He told me they threatened to beat his little sister if he told on them, so he wouldn't and begged me not to.

I didn't. Instead, the next time, I waded in, having no brothers or sisters to worry about. I broke the arm of one and gave the other some bad scrapes and a bloody nose. Fortunately, their fathers dropped the issue when they found out both boys had been beaten up by one tiny, younger female. That's my earliest memory of a long list of things my parents never knew.

When I was nine, I decided three things:

I would never marry.

I was going to travel around the world with a female companion.

And, later, I was going to be an eccentric old lady with wild clothes and an outrageous attitude.

I was assured by my parents and their friends I'd never do any of these things. They laughed at how "cute" I was.

That same year I haunted the neighborhood park, studying the boys playing baseball. Then I would go home and practice throwing the way they did — only, I had to practice in my bedroom when my parents weren't home. I used a rolled-up pair of socks and threw at a spot where two cracks intersected on the wall. There was no hope that I, a girl, could expect to get a real ball. Hearing boys taunt other boys on the playground with "You throw like a girl!" kept me practicing. No one was ever going to say that to me.

When I was ten, the world caved in for my parents, great-aunt, and grandmother. I needed glasses. My parents were already upset because I was two years ahead in school. But this was too much. After many adult-level conferences, including long-distance calls to far-flung relatives, I was given the verdict — I had better plan to be a teacher or a librarian. Glasses and intelligence were too much of a handicap to overcome. I was destined to be an Old Maid! For months, my mother would cry every time she looked at me wearing glasses.

I was destined to be an Old Maid

Privately, I was elated. I took glasses as a sign that I could forget about boys (ugh!) and live my own life. If I couldn't get married, I reasoned, I had to be able to support myself, which meant I had to go college. There was no longer a choice, even though, at that time, most colleges didn't accept Jews, and those that did had a quota. For the first time, life looked promising.

Conformity was everything in the aftermath of World War II and with the advent of McCarthy's House Un-American Activities Committee hearings. Night after night my parents and their friends discussed how, as Jews, they could best protect themselves. Where to live, what jobs to apply for, where to shop were all evaluated on the basis of what was safe for a Jew to try.

I became a major topic of discussion. My parents and their friends were afraid for me — I was too different, too outspoken. McCarthy was a real threat — everyone knew someone who had been blacklisted. And so, in an effort to scare me into behaving "properly," they all continually drummed into me McCarthy's message: TOMBOY = BOHEMIAN = HOMOSEXUAL = COMMUNIST. I didn't know what the homosexual part was (and no one seemed interested in explaining it), but the rest sounded interesting.

My parents didn't have to tell me. All around me was the evidence of what being different meant. Many of my neighbors had haunted eyes and ugly numbers tattooed on their arms. There was the old lady who lived in a makeshift room in the basement of my apartment building, who fell apart if anyone in a uniform tried to get near her. The mailman didn't want to scare her, so I took her monthly check to her. Then there was the old man who had been blinded by the Nazis. I walked him to and from the synagogue for services every morning before I went to school.

The message was ASSIMILATION = INVISIBILITY = SAFETY. Even then I knew it was a lie. I could never assimilate enough to become a tall, blond, Protestant, white man.

I was deeply angry and upset. The adults in my life were trying to make themselves believe a lie. I had been taught in school that people like my father, who had been stationed in England and was a B-17 pilot, had fought this war to save the world for democracy and freedom. And now I was being told that this freedom didn't apply to me. I decided to hide who I was, not from the world, but from my parents. I was determined that someday I would be accepted as I was and that was that.

My desire for physical activity was what had led to the charge of tomboy. Other than walking a lot, physical outlets were a no-no for young ladies in the fifties. When I decided I wanted a bicycle, my parents told me that first I had to learn to ride one, then I had to earn the money to buy it. A big challenge for an eleven-year-old.

I talked a neighbor into letting me take care of her five-year-old daughter four hours a day for the summer. That took care of the money. Next I had to learn to ride. None of the boys in the neighborhood would let me touch their bikes and none of the girls owned one. The college student on the next block let me sit on his bike, but I wasn't tall enough to straddle the bar and reach the pedals. I did some research in the phone book and found a place that rented bicycles. All it would take was one train, three buses, and the rental fee.

When I arrived, the shocked owner said no; he wasn't going to rent a bicycle to an unescorted little girl. Besides, he pointed out, I didn't know how to ride — I might damage his bicycle. Fuming inside, I patiently explained to him that, if I knew how to ride, I wouldn't be there, and pointed out that my money was as good as anyone else's no matter how young I was.

At this point, a beautiful older woman came out from in back. Laughing, probably at the look on my face, she introduced herself. She was the owner's daughter and went to high school. She offered to teach me. The next thing I knew, I was on a bicycle and she was running next to me, holding me up. Unfortunately, it took me only four lessons to learn, and the first of many beautiful women passed through my life.

Sherrie snottily told me she had made harassing me part of club rules

I spent most of my time on the streets, exploring and watching. I was a spy, a photojournalist, a famous novelist. I took my sketch book everywhere. I learned to make myself invisible so that I could observe and sketch people without being noticed.

Roaming an art fair on the Near North Side when I was twelve, I was fascinated by a photographer who would walk up to within a few feet of people and take their picture without their noticing. I began to follow him, trying to see how he did it. He caught me, but instead of being angry, he was delighted and showed me how he did it.

The next year I had access to a camera and tried his technique. I was so pleased with the results that I called him up (from a pay phone, like a good spy) and asked him to look at some of my photos. My life abruptly changed from pretend to real when he sold one of my photos. I was a professional photographer. I could be what I wanted.

By this time, we had moved into a predominantly Jewish neighborhood. It was too late. I was irredeemably different. To my non-Jewish classmates I was Jewish, and to the Jewish kids I obviously wasn't.

Usually, when we moved, the kids would stop hassling me when my father would come to school and perform some magic. But here, one clique of girls wouldn't let it go. Their leader, Sherrie, was considered the prettiest in the class, because she had already had plastic surgery on her nose. (Many of my classmates' parents made financial sacrifices to provide their daughters with plastic surgery and braces to ensure their marrying boys who would go to college and become professional men.) Sherrie snottily told me she had made harassing me part of club rules.

The harassment became so bad that I knew I had to stop it before my parents found out. If they did, I would be in trouble again, no matter what I might say. It was always my fault whenever my parents were forced to see that I was different.

After studying her for several weeks, I devised a plan. I went to the brat and told her if she didn't change her club's rules, I would tell the teacher how she cheated on tests. That part was true — she did cheat. She wrote the answers on a piece of paper that she rolled up and stuck in her sock. I had prepared for the showdown by making a paper cylinder the same size. I showed her the phony evidence, telling her she had dropped it in the girls' room. It worked. Sherrie got scared and called the other girls off.

I was seriously relieved. If I had had to make good on my threat, the teacher would never have believed me. She always held Sherrie up to the class as an example of a "perfect little lady," while I was "what can happen to you if you don't do what you're told."

This also was the year I made my worst slipup. It was eighth grade, and we were learning to write term papers in preparation for high school. Our subject was what we wanted to be when we grew up. Too excited to be wary, I blew it. By then, I wanted to be either an electrical engineer or an aeronautical engineer. I chose to write on aeronautical engineering, because I had a great collection of aircraft photos I had requested from aircraft companies.

I had been collecting them for two years, since I had learned to sign my letters Alan instead of Elena. My first request had been turned down with a letter telling me the company sent photos only to boys. Interestingly, the trucking companies I wrote to didn't have a problem sending photographs to girls.

Proudly, I turned in my paper, complete with photographs, convinced I had written the best paper ever. Was I wrong. The teacher shoved the paper in my face, screamed that I was taking jobs away from men, and called my parents in. Together, they agreed the best "cure" was to force me to sit in the library during math class. If I missed eighth-grade math, I couldn't pass the entrance exam for high school algebra. Not having algebra would stop me from pursuing what the teacher called my communist ideas.

That part worked. I wasn't allowed to take algebra that fall. But you can't not do what you have to do in life, so as an adult I became a systems engineer for IBM *without* an engineering degree. I also earned my pilot's license and have done maintenance on some of the planes that are now in the National Aerospace

Museum. I'm a reasonably good household and stage electrician. And, as a present to myself for my forty-fifth birthday, I went to a local two-year tech school and signed up for high school algebra (and geometry and trig). I loved it.

My first year of high school was crowned by my expulsion. The principal called it a social expulsion and even admitted to my father that, if I had been a boy, he wouldn't have done it.

Each fall we were issued locks for our lockers. We had to sign the paper with the combination and turn it back in. If you happened to forget your combination, you had to report to the office, never a pleasant experience. If you were a boy, one of the secretaries would write down the combination for you, chuckle how boys will be boys, and you were on your way. But, if you had the misfortune to be a girl, you were lectured by the assistant principal (a man who neither washed himself nor brushed his teeth) and were required to pay a dollar for a copy of the combination.

A friend of mine forgot hers. Paying a dollar was out of the question — her family was poor and money was budgeted to the penny, and I couldn't get a dollar without involving my parents. The solution was obvious — I would crack her combination. They caught me kneeling on the floor listening to the tumblers drop. I'm proud to say I was able to give her the combination before they dragged me off.

The advisor of the science club in my second high school brought home to me the impact of missing algebra. Though allowed to join the science club — I was their first female member — I wasn't eligible for any of the citywide science club events, because all participants had to be currently taking math and science. At that time, if you didn't take or pass a class the year it was scheduled, you were out of luck. And, without algebra, I couldn't take any science beyond general science. I was furious.

By this time I had figured out that, if I had been a boy, I would have been called a genius and given all sorts of privileges. As a girl, I was told constantly, from the time

By this time I had figured out that, if I had been a boy, I would have been called a genius

I was nine, to hide my intelligence because no decent boy (translation: doctor or lawyer) wanted to marry a smart girl.

With no role model for being a dyke, I had to invent it. The first time I heard snickers about people who wore green on Thursday, I went and got a green sweater to wear on Thursday. I didn't really know why — it just felt important.

In my early teens, I didn't fit in anywhere. My attitudes, proclivities, and by then eight schools left me outside of any mainstream I lived in.

While other girls giggled about boys, I was looking at girls. I didn't understand why they acted so silly about goony-looking boys when there were so many great women to look at. My instincts led me to believe this was not a subject to ask about, though. I had learned at an early age not to ask either of my parents for explanations when my view was different from the prevailing one.

I had been going downtown alone since I was seven, when I started art lessons at the Art Institute of Chicago. Now, besides attending classes there, I started hanging around looking at the female college students, especially one. She had dark, thick, curly hair that she wore in a braid down her back. And she wore pants or, sometimes, overalls. I followed her every Saturday for months, praying for an opportunity to rescue her from a dragon or two.

No dragon ever appeared, and the museum didn't catch fire so I could lead her out through the smoke, nor did bandits attack us. What did happen was that she lured me from behind the columns and cases where I skulked, out into the middle of the entrance hall. There she turned and grabbed me before I could run.

She marched me down to the cafeteria, bought us both dishes of ice cream, and made me sit at the same table with her. I saw her mouth moving, but all I could hear at first was the blood rushing in my ears.

As my panic subsided, I heard her saying I shouldn't follow her around. Clearly, she wasn't angry at me, so I happily listened to her lecture. With great cunning, I asked her about school and where she was from. She mentioned that she lived in Oldtown, and the next day I took the Clark Street streetcar from Rogers Park and went to investigate. It was great. There were coffee houses, artists, winos, and women, a lot of women. Not trusting myself to remain vertical, I put my arm around a lamppost and casually leaned. I watched and I learned. The really cute ones wore Levi's — the first women I had ever seen wearing Levi's.

I promptly dipped into my savings and headed off to buy a pair for myself. In 1955, young ladies did not buy Levi's. They were available only in the boys' department, a place young ladies didn't go. I wove a long story for an obviously disbelieving saleswoman about their being a gift for my cousin, who happened to be a boy exactly my size. I swore my parents had sent me to make the purchase.

After hanging out in Oldtown for several months, I figured out which were the women's places. But it was clear that to see any real action I had to be there at night. So, one Saturday night, after my parents went out, I put on my brand-new Levi's and a starched white shirt, wrapped a red silk scarf around my neck, and headed out.

I had guessed right. There were tons of them, all going down an alley and through a dark doorway. Unfortunately, it was a bar and I was thirteen. What could a hormone-struck baby dyke do?

I hung around listening, all my invisibility practice paying off. Eventually, I heard a group of women planning to continue their party in someone's apartment. That was my cue. I was right behind them when they walked off. Using my best spy techniques, I followed them down the street, into the courtyard, and up to the apartment.

I was there. Where, I still didn't know, but I did know that somehow I belonged with these women. I stretched out on the floor behind the couch and took it all in. I memorized how they talked, what they wore, their body language. It would be another five years before I found out that I had crashed a party of real, live lesbians, but that night I had my first sense that there might be a place I belonged.

I belonged.

Values Clarification

Mariah Burton Nelson

a true sports story

During a brief het phase in my teens, before I figured out that life would be infinitely more fun as a lesbian, I was seduced and molested by two married men. They offered the only sex anyone was offering this young Amazon, and for a brief time they provided me with a sense (albeit skewed) of heterosexual normalcy.

I was rescued from the first of these two confusing and devastating relationships when my parents happened to move the family across the country, to Phoenix, Arizona. It's the second relationship I want to tell you about, because in this case it was my fierce love of sports and my unshakable belief in equal rights for girl athletes that helped me escape the lusty clutches of the 42-year-old high school history teacher I'll call Joe Snodgrass.*

Joe Snodgrass was a balding hippie who had grown bored with the Civil War, the Revolutionary War, and other staples of American history. He taught us values clarification instead, ask-

* Author's note: I have changed this man's name for legal reasons. The rest of this story is true.

ing, "Which is more important: money, love, a good reputation, or integrity?" Oh, money is not important at all, I answered vehemently, chasing my written response with two carefully drawn exclamation marks. I liked that he asked.

It was the early seventies. I wore tight hip-hugger, bell-bottom jeans to school with tie-dyed t-shirts and, on my pinkie, a peace ring. The Vietnam War was not yet over. The Supreme Court was debating whether to legalize abortion. For a project in Mr. Snodgrass's history class, I made a mobile of the suffragists, pictures of Susan B. Anthony and seven other women dangling from a red coat hanger. He gave me an A.

Snodgrass — we called him by his last name — seemed to understand me. He seemed to understand my suffragist mobile, let it decorate the corner of his classroom, twirling slowly in the currents of students' comings and goings.

I was new to Phoenix, having just been transported there after spending my first sixteen years in rural Pennsylvania. To me, it was an exotic land of perpetual sunshine. Weekends, my new girlfriends and I would ride horses in the desert, climb the red rock of Camelback Mountain, and twirl down the Verde River in inner tubes. My face was always burned bright red, my hands punctured by the small wounds of cacti. After a lifetime in a too-small town, I was finally having an adventure.

In school I became known as the "women's libber," the one who, in English class, demanded to know why we were reading only novels by men. After school, I played pickup basketball with the boys.

In October, when tryouts for the boys' basketball team were announced over the P.A. system, I asked the boys' coach, my astronomy teacher, if I could try out for the team. There was no girls' team. The teacher and I stood outside his classroom door. He was tall, one of the few teachers taller than I. He looked at me carefully, quizzically. "Your breasts would get in the way," he said finally. He stood close to me; he riveted me to him with the magnetism of his large body and the shock of his words. "Your breasts could get hit with an elbow," he continued, and his elbow was close enough to my body to demonstrate the maneuver.

"I want to try out anyway," I insisted, taking a step back. "I played basketball at my old school. I'm good."

"Only if I can personally bind your breasts," he said, his eyes twinkling.

Girls didn't sue teachers in those days. The term *sexual harassment* had not been invented. I played intramural basketball instead, dribbling the ball downcourt against the leftover boys, the boys not good enough to make the varsity or junior varsity team. I was better than many of them, taller than most, and though occasionally one refused to jump against me or guard me, I tried to prove myself there, tried to demonstrate to this conservative southwestern city not only my own ability but the ability of girls in general to play sports.

I also found a women's team to play on, an Amateur Athletic Union team called the Phoenix Dusters that traveled around the Southwest competing against college and other AAU teams. As the youngest team member, I idolized these women, and was shocked and confused when one teammate told me that most of the other women were lesbians. "In fact, we're the only straight ones," she said. One woman in particular was dangerous, she warned me: this woman hung out in bars and picked up women and might "make the moves" on me. To my vague disappointment, neither that woman nor any other teammate made the moves on me, and two years would pass before I would realize that my teammate had been wrong to assume I was straight.

Meanwhile, back at high school, I infiltrated the Sportsman's Club, then tried to convince them to change the name to the nonsexist Varsity Club. Snodgrass commiserated with me when I failed. So that I wouldn't feel so alone, he told me about a girl who had graduated the previous year: she had also believed in women's liberation. He didn't call it "women's lib" like the other teachers: he even pointed out in class how derogatory that was, that we'd never refer to the civil rights movement as "black lib."

He asked me about basketball and played HORSE with me himself on his driveway court. His house was a gathering place for students, who on weekends would come to play games, talk, and drink screwdrivers. I lived just a few blocks away. By cutting through an orange orchard, I could be at his house in ten minutes. I'd arrive stoned on the pungent smell of orange blossoms. Sometimes we'd smoke dope, too, though Snodgrass had rules about that: it had to be outside, in the orchard, not in his house. We understood: wouldn't want to get this nice teacher busted for distributing marijuana to minors.

Snodgrass knew Bob Dylan. This was a source of great pride to him, and though "knowing famous people" was not high on my values clarification list, I couldn't help but be impressed. He and Bob Dylan went camping together each summer. Snodgrass showed us slides: Here's Bob clowning around on a sycamore tree. Here's Bob by the campfire with — sure enough — guitar in hand. I loved the photos of artistically fuzzy waterfalls and gnarled trees that looked like old people. I liked the pictures of Bob Dylan, big nose and all. While showing the slides, Snodgrass would play a scratchy version of "Lay, Lady, Lay" on his record player. I thought that was corny, but I couldn't help but be swept up by the romance of it all, and the immediacy. Here was Bob Dylan, practically in this house with us. It brought the revolution home, made the music and the culture of the sixties accessible to a group of kids who were born just a little too late to experience it directly.

Snodgrass had children, six of them. One was a year older than I, attending the same high school. One was a year younger. He had a wife, but they were separated, he told me. Still, I'd see her sometimes, a fleeting figure dashing across the upstairs hall while a group of teenagers sat in the dark living room watching bright images of Bob Dylan and waterfalls and trees.

I didn't love Snodgrass. I was intrigued, impressed. And turned on. Aren't all seventeen-year-olds perpetually turned on?

I loved my best friend, Charlotte, a small, powerful tennis player who drove a red Jeep with a sturdy roll bar that promised to save us when we'd careen, screaming, off-road among the desert saguaro. When Charlotte went away for summers, I'd sob uncontrollably. But I didn't realize I was in love with her. The closest we got to consummating our relationship was drinking vodka at high school football games, then, "too drunk to walk," leaning on each other while stumbling back to the car.

In Pennsylvania, where I'd done most of my growing up, I'd been in love with my swimming coach, the first man who seduced me. Yet even then, my strongest feelings had been for my girlfriends. So I arrived in Phoenix not only betrayed but confused, looking for love in all the wrong places.

One boy asked me out. His name was Rod, he was on my intramural basketball team, and he was the stepson of actress Amanda Blake. Though I didn't much care for Rod and had only a murky recollection of Amanda Blake's role as Kitty on *Gunsmoke,* I was fascinated because Blake kept African animals in her suburban Phoenix backyard. As I recall, a lion, a jaguar, and something smooth-skinned with hooves lived in sturdy cages just beyond Blake's back porch, in the place where most Phoenicians would have dug a swimming pool. Sometimes I could hear the lion roar from my own bedroom, a mile away. When Rod brought me to his house, the animals would eye us warily, pacing. He didn't have any particular rapport with them.

Rod didn't understand women's liberation. After basketball games, he'd take my elbow and escort me to his car. I didn't want him to take my elbow and steer me around like a cafeteria tray. When I tired of his wild animals, we stopped dating.

I was daring enough to ask other boys out, but most said no. Or, worse, they'd say something noncommittal, which I eagerly interpreted as a "yes," then they'd get "sick" the day of the dance. One of the few who did say yes died soon after my invitation, on the baseball field, of a brain aneurysm. I wasn't broken-hearted, but I was stunned and suspicious. Was God trying to tell me something? In my seventeen-year-old mind, God would do such a thing, kill off a teenaged boy just to make a point to a teenaged girl. But what was the point?

Snodgrass's seduction of me began in late October, when he started walking me home from his house. We'd walk along the neat rows

Was God trying to tell me something?

of orange trees and I'd touch the bark or the leaves just to be touching something. Occasionally I'd pluck a rotting orange from the ground and hurl it toward a faraway trunk, challenging him to do the same. We'd talk about school and drugs and, eventually, sex. I told him about the swim coach in Pennsylvania, hoping to find in Snodgrass an adult who could help me sort out what had happened there. Instead, he apparently heard the story as a sign that I was sexually available to him — which, for a while, I was.

One day we stopped talking and stopped walking. I backed up against a tree trunk, smacking my head on a low branch. I hoped he wouldn't notice. He walked toward me and stood close. I had a clear view of his shiny scalp. To make myself shorter, I spread my legs apart, a stance I had devised while doing dishes at low sinks. He came closer still, his pelvis touching mine now, the pants' bulge firm against me. We kissed. His mustache clogged my mouth. It tasted bad: of stale marijuana and vodka and maybe even that morning's bagel. Still, I liked the feel of that pressure against my crotch.

Snodgrass started asking me to meet him in other places, beyond the orange orchard. We'd each drive to the parking lot of the Mormon Temple, then I'd slide into his front seat and he'd drive me to the outskirts of Phoenix, where we would get high with friends of his, an unmarried couple in their twenties named something like Sunshine and Frank. On their bathroom wall was a poster that impressed me as risqué: "Save water, shower with a friend."

One time Sunshine and Frank left to "do errands" and Snodgrass led me into their spare bedroom. He stood on tiptoe and kissed me. This time no mustache hairs got in my mouth, and I liked the feel of his curious tongue. We sat down on the bed and he nuzzled his head between my breasts. I wondered about birth control. Snodgrass whispered, as if the word were sexy, "Vasectomy," adding, "Do you know what that is?" I was insulted. Yes, of course. Luckily, we'd just had that unit in anatomy class.

He unzipped my bell-bottoms and yanked them off. I knew that women's liberation had something to do with sexual freedom and even with sexual assertiveness, but I was at a loss as to how to respond. I watched, trying to smile. Next he pulled off his own pants, and I looked to see if his penis was up or down the way a meteorologist looks to see if a flag is waving or limp. It was waving. I took that to be a good sign. Now what? He lay on top of me and fumbled. Six kids, and he's fumbling? I was not impressed, and didn't know how or if to help him. He reached down and spread my legs apart. There was some urgency in the act, and some frustration. Oh, so the fumbling was my fault? How was I supposed to know you're supposed to spread your legs? He was panting now, and I felt my body fill with something blunter than a flag, and thicker. Soon the bedspread was damp and he was panting in a different way. He rolled off me, smoothing a few sweaty hairs over his bald spot. As we got dressed, I kept wondering about the stained bedspread. Would Sunshine and Frank notice? Did they already know?

The next week I followed him, zombielike, to the Mormon Temple again. This time we drove to an empty house that Snodgrass owned but had not sold. We parked a few blocks away "so no one will recognize the car," he explained. Apparently he had a system all figured out.

In November, everything changed. In November, the guys who hung out at Snodgrass's house, playing HORSE and drinking, began to talk about the Turkey Bowl, an annual Thanksgiving Day football game that included not only high school boys but also many of Snodgrass's friends and some other teachers. The astronomy teacher played. The boys on my intramural basketball team played. One year — it was unclear how long ago — Bob Dylan had even come to town for the occasion. As November wore on, not a volleyball game was played, not a screwdriver served, without some excited mention of the upcoming football game. Practices were held and teams were selected. Snodgrass began to grin and giggle with the pre-Christmas anticipation of a kid. Just the name itself — the Turkey Bowl — was enough to make all the men in my world smile.

It didn't take long before I asked Snodgrass the obvious question: "Can I play?"

It was just after seventh period, the last class of the day. We were in Snodgrass's classroom, housed in a trailer imported to Phoenix to handle the baby-boomer overflow. Through a thin partition I could hear the Arizona government teacher putting away his slide projector, packing up to go home.

"Can I play?"
"Can I play?"
"Can I play?"

"I've played football," I told Snodgrass. "I used to play all the time in Pennsylvania."

When he remained silent, I continued my plea, my voice gaining strength to breach the invisible wall I was detecting. "I can throw a football. Spiral. I'll show you. I can run. I can catch. You know I'm a good athlete."

He listened, not speaking, his eyes not meeting mine. "Aren't you going to let me play?" My stomach began to feel hot and agitated, as if water were boiling there. "You're not, are you? How can you not let me play? I *can* play football! Why can't I play?"

"I'm sorry," he said at last. "It's a male thing."

I stared at him. The suffragist mobile was shifting behind his head, the women twirling in swift swoops toward his bald spot.

"Well, then," I said, my voice rising. "I am never, ever having sex with you again."

Behind the partition, the Arizona government teacher dropped a tape reel. Snodgrass's face blanched the color of coconut milk. *"Shhhhhhh!"* he said, moving toward me as if to put his hand over my mouth. "Do you want to send me to jail?"

"Don't shush me," I said, backing away, my legs beginning to wobble. "I'm good enough to have sex with but not good enough to play in the Turkey Bowl?"

"Sit down!" he commanded, and in my mind I obeyed, folding my long legs under one of the small school desks. But I could see that if I sat, I'd soon be sobbing, and probably apologizing, and that Snodgrass would sit next to me and pat me on the head, transforming my anger into shame.

I didn't sit. "I am not going to sit down, and I'm not going to have sex with you, and I don't give a damn about your stupid,

stupid, stupid, stupid, *stupid* football game. I also don't care if you go to jail," I added, in a softer voice, because I did. Hearing myself say all those "stupid"s, I felt silly, but, wobbly legs and all, I managed to walk out of his classroom without looking back.

Still shaky but suddenly euphoric, I strode quickly — occasionally skipping — to the tennis courts, looking for Charlotte. Feeling free and energized and happy to the point of giddiness, I wanted nothing more than to go for a desert ride with my best friend in her bright red Jeep.

Tomboy Groupie

Allison Faust

The story of my Beatrice of Basketball begins with irreverence — my teasing my girlfriend about her liking one of the players on the local college basketball team — and ends with passion — but not for my girlfriend. And it is rooted in my long-standing appreciation of female athletics, or, rather, female athletes: those tomboys who still play hard when they're grown up.

What happened was that, despite my irreverence, I started hunting the sports pages for pictures of and stories about the team when I was by myself. Then, along with everybody I knew, I started focusing on one particular hot-shot freshman. But unlike everybody else, I made the fatal leap to fanaticism, rationalizing my devotion to this teenager by calling it religion.

My girlfriend and friends thought I ran out of bounds with this one. They wouldn't acknowledge my feelings for Beatrice, just because I didn't know what she looked like up close.

Now, I know you can't love someone you don't know. But you can idolize, idealize, fantasize, fanaticize, and pester. I'm sure John Hinkley felt similarly justified. So I have creep potential. I don't want to shoot the president for her. I can't be a psychopath, because I work for the state.

While flattery works on everyone to some degree, tomboys are tough. You can't slather them with compliments without making them wonder if you're a pantywaist weakling who can't throw a ball, who "learned the truth at seventeen," and so on, or some sagging former champ who wants to recount her own glory days on the court back before gals in jock haircuts ever dreamed of someday wearing hundred-dollar high-tops.

So the first card I sent my knee-brace-wearing goddess was restrained: store-bought and illustrated with a drawing of Artemis, its message formal and old-lady-like: "You're doing fine, dear; keep it up..." Subtle, not too gushy, not too lezzie. With the second card, I fleshed out the goddess theme by enclosing a "Mysteries of the Rosary" holy card (for credibility — she's Catholic); it depicted, with the help of Xerox, my heroine as the Blessed Virgin herself — flaming heart and all. Her angelic Fellowship of Christian Athletes smile made her perfect for the part; I just added a Sacred Flaming Basketball in the center of her sweet chest. I also threw in a few lines from Shakespeare to seem smart:

> Mine eye hath play'd the painter, and hath stell'd
> Thy beauty's form in table of my heart...
> Yet eyes this cunning want to grace their art,
> They draw but what they see, know not the heart.
> (Sonnet 24)

After an inspiring headline — "Beatrice lifts Texas" — appeared the following week, I made a collage depicting her as a saint levitating the Lone Star State with her sacred, if not stigmatic, hands. I included another poignant, friendly letter of encouragement that ended: "You may not be a saint, but you sure are a star."

Next came the poem "Driving to the Basket," my overextended sports metaphor, my letter of intent:

> in this sport that teams archery with combat
> I play the risk of drawing the foul
> or going down

wide as the paint I wait
key, rim, net
in case you look for an inside spot
and the chance to drive to the basket

anytime you put it up my stats
mount and fall:
air ball or rainbow arc
or your signature outside shot

my patience beats
any thirty-second clock

I'm open
whether you pass to me or not

But I couldn't send it. I kept it on my computer and peeked at it every day. I knew that I had it bad and that I'd better do something about this crush or get past it. I decided to risk just being myself in a letter asking to meet her. The rest would be up to her. As sensible as it sounds, I was terrified. I rewrote the letter thirteen times over several days but lacked the nerve to send it. So again I went with a gimmick: a whimsical "news" article that I wrote while listening to one of the conference tournament games on the radio.

BEATRICE TO GO ONE-ON-ONE WITH FAN

Freshman basketball sensation Beatrice shocked the sports world this week by agreeing to meet a fan despite her busy schedule. The 5′10″ three-point shooter from ———, who has gained national attention this season at the university, will grant audience to diminutive admirer Allison Faust "in the near future."

Faust, a university honors graduate in English currently employed at the Center for Environmental Exploitation, was hesitant at first to approach the celebrated athlete. Estimating that Beatrice must daily receive dozens of fan letters and pleas for personal appearances, the writer felt her chances of meeting her youthful heroine were slim.

> Then she conceived of an original tactic. In a bold and clever move, she presented her request for a meeting in the form of a news article — including in it the "news" that Beatrice was amenable.
>
> Beatrice admitted she was flattered by the effort. "Besides," she said, "Coach says it's okay to meet fans as long as they're short." Faust, 31, a long-retired competitive gymnast who now swims laps for fitness, is 5′1″ in combat boots.
>
> "I want Beatrice to know that while I may be nutty, I'm not crazy," Faust said from her office at the center. "I'm in good shape for our tête-à-tête. In addition to my usual workout, I've increased my caffeine intake by 43 percent in case she wants to meet at the university cafe," she confided.
>
> Beatrice has shattered school, conference, and national records in her first season with the Lady Bulls. Faust's brushes with basketball fame include attending high school in Lubbock with famous hoopster alum ——— and winning a game of HORSE in 1977.

The ball, so to speak, was in her court. Now all I could do was wait.

This latest devotion to an athletic diva has evolved from the awe, fear, and adoration I've cultivated for tomboys since girlhood. My first tomboy love was Liz, the formidable champion of a game called smear the queer. I revered her body (taller and denser than most of ours, arms and wrists stronger, eyes slyer and crueler, teeth bigger and whiter); her walk (toes slightly turned in, giving her a proto-butch gait); and, of course, her superior athletic abilities. Once, I beat her in a foot race, but she was sick.

Because I played with dolls, I feared that Liz would beat me up, but, to my surprise, she liked me. Not best, of course. Her best friends, after boys, were other tomboys. My insecurities about my dollhouse and canopy bed were curtailed when I saw her girlie room, complete with a frilly, floral dust ruffle and curtains. It

I beat her once in a cross-country race

made me feel less inferior, like she was only 98 percent cooler than I was.

I couldn't keep up with the tomboys, and I couldn't get into the girl groove, either, always somewhere in between what I tried to be and what my parents hoped for me. Then, in the middle of the sixth grade, it seemed as if one night someone put pods in some of the girls' basements and they came to school the next day wearing makeup instead of track shoes and opaque knee socks like me. The girlie types liked me less than the tomboys did, because I just didn't apply myself, so I became, and remain, a tomboy groupie.

One of my best early groupie memories is of Liz bestowing on me an outgrown pair of her straight-leg Levi's (an anomaly in 1971) with ripped knees and a patch on the butt that read, "LUV." Of course they were huge on me, so I wore them only on weekends, when my mother couldn't object. Then, after one last big all-girl party at the end of elementary school, Liz moved away.

Liz will reign as my Virgin Tomboy Queen forever, because I never saw her ford that treacherous river of puberty that swept away so many others of her kind. They developed boobs and forgot how to handle balls. Betraying themselves while depriving me of my rightful idols, these young women gave in to adolescence. Developing secondary sex characteristics seemed to signal the start of a secondary existence. Luckily, I escaped my own cruel judgments by belonging to a nearly puberty-proof group: gymnasts. We were athletic yet prissy, like Barbie's kid sister, Skipper, keeping ourselves free of body fat as long as possible while posing in darling outfits.

Next came Karla, confident, cute, popular, feared, and "foreign" (she went to another school): a tomboy dream. Over the years, we were Camp Fire girls together, teammates, friends, enemies, minors under the influence, and, eventually, lovers. She definitely went the other way with girl grooming in junior high, but nevertheless stayed my idol because of her athletic superiority. I beat her once in a cross-country race, but she was sick. Our

but she was sick.

favorite activities besides working out were arm wrestling, chugging beer, and necking at red lights. She managed that girljock-with-makeup-and-hairdo look much better than I did. My style leaned toward ponytails and jeans, and a little mascara if I was the one trying to buy the beer.

Since Karla, all my girlfriends have been tomboys. You could call them butch, but that's not exactly accurate. They tend to be ex-jocks with a preference for electric guitars and steel-toed boots. No makeup or girls' shoes on them — they've got that tomboy strut. As long as I'm the better-dressed one, I don't care what they wear. The thing they all have in common is the inner tomboy they won't give up, even if they give up on me.

As much as I feared silence from my Beatrice of Basketball, I dreaded running into her somewhere even more. My detours past her dorm were reverent yet anonymous — even if she was out front, I could gawk privately and move on. Eventually, of course, fate brought us face-to-face — over Tampax. I was in the drugstore muttering about the store's being out of o.b.'s when she strode up and grabbed a 32-count box of slender regulars. At first I didn't realize who she was: all I noticed was her height and bulky sweatpants. *For god's sake,* I thought, *it's 87 degrees out.* My mood was understandably foul. By the time I registered who she was, she had passed on to the painkiller aisle. Amazingly, I stayed conscious enough to watch her pay cash and head south out the door toward her dorm. I celebrated the miraculous sighting by buying a bag of Jolly Ranchers in assorted flavors.

If only I could have asked her if she liked my tributes. If horror had accompanied recognition on her face, I could have apologized, told her that I was there renewing my lapsed Prozac prescription, and promised not to bother her again. But all I ended up with was the receipt for tampons and ibuprofen that she'd left on the counter in what I assumed was her world of pain. I clutched the tiny slip to my swollen, tender chest like it was a sacred testament or a winning lottery ticket.

Summer hit this year like a damp woolen blanket. The students have gone, leaving yards littered with For Lease signs. I guess she's gone, too, because her dorm is closed down and she doesn't have to report back for practice until late August. Despite the angst I feel not knowing her whereabouts, my devotion goes on.

This current tomboy worship stands out in my personal herstory. Though I have not yet met her after practice with a clean towel and tiger balm — in fact, we've never met — this acute obsession makes me feel as special as if I were the one receiving the fan letters. Elevated by the reverence that surrounds the revered like a stadium, I delight in her skill and grace from my distance and plan next season's devotions.

Next year's season tickets teasingly showed up on this month's credit card bill. If I squint, I can picture her running onto the court through machine-generated fog to the beat of music from a basketball shoe commercial. I'm no star college athlete, but I know the drill called "running the lines" and how seasons and time have everything to do with everything, especially girls in sports. And my relationship to them. I'm waiting for the whistle to blow on this one. It's still a toss-up.

Cerisy's Sphinx

Brenda Brooks

I have a photograph of her from that time. She's wearing: her favorite pair of cutoff jeans, a striped shirt, a pair of gray tennis socks (many odysseys removed from their original white), and a pair of grimy sneakers I can still smell. She also wears a braid of fine sweetgrass looped around her wrist. You can't see this in the picture but it's there — I remember because I'd woven it for her earlier that day.

The picture is taken from above, from the branch of a tree just across from the one her swing is tied to. The rest of the kids are down below, all smiles, staring up from the very nifty clubhouse we'd built a few months earlier out of old bits of board and tar paper salvaged from the dump.

We had a chair too, found abandoned in the woods — a kitchen chair with rusty chrome legs and a ripped, turquoise plastic seat, the stuffing bursting forth like bulrush fluff. Despite its cuts and bruises, we'd found it sitting quietly under a chestnut tree looking oddly civilized, as if a well-spoken person in a torn coat had sat awhile reading from a book with missing pages, then continued on her way.

We kept the chair outside because it took up too much room in the clubhouse and, being the only one, caused a fair amount of division, or, more accurately, collision, among the members. Most often it was used by Shadow, my family's old black retriever, who would clamber up and observe our meetings through the window.

Shadow's in this picture too, just disappearing at bottom right, looking every bit the reason we named him as we did. But the photograph really belongs to Blue, looking the way I remember her. That's Evelyn "Blue" Winters. She's standing straight up on that swing, having pumped herself and her dusty cutoffs and her sister's secondhand sneakers as close as she could get to that most desirable place, that whispering, blue beguiling place, glittering between the oak leaves above her.

That's just the way her hair flew back in a tangle too, and how her hands gripped the swing's ropes and thrust them apart as she opened her mouth wide to howl into the camera, her swing reaching the top of its arc — that precise moment when it stopped briefly and then began to fall back again toward the upturned, landed faces below.

I recall her holler and how I thought she would catapult herself right out of that swing from sheer desire and glide off over the trees, over the playing field and the high bush blueberries, over the hollyhocks in her mother's garden, high over the rooftops, past the foothills, and disappear like a reckless kite over the forest and snowy mountains, never to be seen by any of us, most especially me, again.

That would have struck me in the heart and left a piece of cold, white neon in its place, I'd realized then. Not entirely because I wanted her to stay. No, mostly because I was dying to go with her, my heart already belonging to some distant, dreamy realm at once vivid and obscure. A place about which I knew nothing for certain. A nameless place that pulled and drew me to it from somewhere infinite and shivering and equally nameless within myself.

I never talked to anyone about this place; it seemed to defy dialogue and all usual manner of understanding. I contented myself with receiving fleeting essences of it from my books about wildflowers and fish and planets and trees, as well as in moments spent traipsing through marsh and woods.

Afterwards, in bed at night, I'd bring out my books and flashlight and proceed to give names to the individual essences of that compelling larger thing, whatever it might be: wood nettle, featherfoil, wild pine. Spring peeper, swallowtail, blue-winged teal. Wild hyacinth, owl and otter. Nebula, galaxy, Andromeda.

Or I'd lie and think about plunging to the pond bottom, then looking back up through the duckweed at the liquid green sky, as if through the long, calm eye of a mottled, silent fish.

I'd think about Shadow — his fur spiked and wet from the river, black and shining in the sun like the oiled feathers on the necks of nine crows bathing.

Perhaps I'd touch myself softly and dream about the day just past: climbing the oak's dark branches, Blue flying away on her swing, past the foothills, over the forests and snowy mountains, never to be seen...

But of course that didn't happen. The swing fell back in its predictable reversing arc and Blue finally came down, emptied of shouts for the time being and somewhat nauseated too. Shadow snorted and lapped her perennially roughed-up knees, his tail doing a wacky, circular sort of metronome. Then, by casting our spell across the doorless doorway, we closed up the clubhouse and all went home, secure and filled with faith in the strength of our own magic.

Unknowing.

Our mothers introduced "Evelyn" and me at her tenth birthday party. They were just getting acquainted themselves, since my family was new in town. One day they would be found murmuring over coffee that perhaps their daughters had a bit too liberating an effect on each other. But that was later.

At the party itself, Evelyn had no influence on me whatsoever. I'd been to a few parties by then — after all, I was ten also — and I saw immediately that this was the usual stuff: pin-the-tail, hot dogs, Kool-Aid, and a mix of ten boys and girls, including a kid with a brush cut and horn rims wearing a tiny blue suit I envied — coveted even — from within the itchy confines of my miserable poodle skirt. By this I mean a skirt which, on the off chance its overall effect wasn't silly enough, had a wretched poodle drawn on the front and a small rhinestone glued approximately where its eye might be.

I had resisted this skirt. I had resisted going to the party. My plan had been to explore my new environment by leaping onto the back of my best imaginary steed and doing a thorough scouting of the neighborhood, in full western regalia.

My mother assured me throughout my protests that my skirt would be "a hit, a regular conversation piece," and she was right: I spent most of my time at the party smacking other children as a result.

Evelyn's party was in June and the day was a hot one. We ate cake with pink icing and drank raspberry Kool-Aid under the linden trees while the lawn sprinklers whirled slowly, sending off lazy snake sounds in the heat.

My mother had brought Shadow to the party, and I watched as he panted along behind my little sister, who was steadily eating her way through the hollyhocks in Mrs. Winters's garden. My mother caught her before she started on the petunias, but these weren't her favorites anyway. It was hollyhocks my little sister made a beeline for, drooling all the way — her eyes widening as she tripped toward them, her arms spread, her tiny fingers flexing like famished sea anemones, as if the magic of these flowers was such that it wasn't enough to simply eat them; they needed to be absorbed through the eyes and skin, attended by the whole body, whose entire purpose was to open itself wide enough to consume them all — acres, hopefully.

And, once again, my mother found herself exclaiming that she didn't know what to do about this kid, and was there something vital missing from her diet, or what? All the while, she apologized to Evelyn's mom for the pathetic stalks with no flowers left standing in the garden — the same way she'd apologized to Mrs. Merwin, another neighbor, the week before.

Up until this point I hadn't thought much about Evelyn. She'd mostly been pestering her mother to let her get into her bathing suit so she could run through the sprinkler and "get the show on the road," as she put it. All in all, she was doing what I was usually doing just before somebody called me a pain in the butt.

But, as my sister was being chastised for munching the garden and my mother brushed the pollen from her child's chin and tried prying the remaining petals from her clutches (sea anemones turned to Venus flytraps), I noticed that Evelyn was taking careful note of these goings-on too.

Although we hadn't spoken to each other yet, she caught my eye and mouthed several words I couldn't make out, though I was to become practiced at interpreting these signals in the future.

I knew chances were good she was saying something rude to me, since that's how it sometimes goes when you're new in town and a stranger at the party. Especially if you're a stranger at the party and wearing a ridiculous outfit.

I squinted at her and frowned while weighing the possibility that she hadn't yet noticed the pooch on my skirt, then considered inching it around gradually to the back so it would be planted on my bum, where I felt it belonged, if it belonged anywhere.

She mouthed the words again and I resigned myself to having to smack her, birthday girl or not. Just then she got up, plunked herself down next to me, leaned over, cupping her mouth with her hand, and said:

"Hollyhockburgers and petunia pie."

"What?" I said, deciding to attack this head-on.

"Hollyhockburgers and petunia pie. That's what must be missing from your little sister's diet, don't you think? I'll ask my mom to make some for her next time she comes. And maybe a drink of milkweed too."

Pause. "Get it?" She smiled cheekily.

"Uh-huh. I get it," I answered, my own substantial cheekiness feeling vaguely stirred and encouraged.

Then, rewinding the Band-Aid on her finger, she asked if I liked horses (because she did) and remarked that I had on a real nice skirt, looking genuinely sorry I'd had to wear it on her behalf.

Three months later, we'd drawn a secret map showing each one of our favorite haunts. Green arrows indicated their exact location, and they were labeled MDPs, "most desirable places."

Six months after that, we'd changed our names to "Skeezix" and "Blue," both agreeing that our given names were the most boring and sickly ones that our parents could have dreamed up.

Promises we made: Never tell our horses' names. Don't tell any boys about the beaver dam we found. Don't tell anyone else what part of the body we mean when we say the word "nature." Keep a secret that we touch and show each other our "nature" when we sleep over. If one of us moves away, meet the other in twenty-five years at the Moonlite Motel. If one of us dies, the other buries her in the most desirable place, at dusk. Say the same two words, at the exact same time as each other before going to bed every night.

Know each other forever.

The two words were: Cerisy's Sphinx.

Cerisy's Sphinx is a moth whose wings can spread three inches or more. My book showed these wings opened wide and filled with swirls of gray, amber, pink, and tawny brown, set off by blue eyespots fringed with black. At thirteen I looked at it often and shivered; each time, the unnameable tug of the body.

Looking into its wings I saw the sweet, wet of the woods after rain, the ragged patches of soft moss we touched to our cheeks and lips, the slightest feather fallen from the wing of a sharp-tailed swallow. I saw mountains folding into each other and thunder and night and mist. Waves of rain passed through blue hills, sheer as desire. It spoke the language of my body and I listened eagerly, the way a hungry child listens to the language of red flowers.

During our last summer together, the summer of the swing and snowy mountains, Blue and I tried every night to find the Sphinx. We slept, whenever permitted, in a tent at the foot of her parents' garden and roamed the woods with our flashlights searching the spots we thought most likely. We'd return with pine gum on our fingers and flecks of bark in our hair, and climb into a sleeping bag together. We'd whisper and giggle together at the stickiness of our hands and fall asleep holding each other, intoning the Sphinx's name in hopes that it would find us. Dreaming the beautiful moth under the July moon.

And her neck smelled like the inside of a guitar.

It was August when something suddenly happened. Even now this is the only way I can think to say it: something happened. I suppose this is because that's the first thing my mother said when she came to my room early on a Sunday morning, before I was beginning to waken.

She came strangely and carefully, like someone bearing the most delicate thing in a small box, something struggling softly to be released. When I sat up in bed rubbing my eyes, she looked as if to place it next to me and quietly remove the lid to reveal what was inside.

"Something's happened," she said. And then, "Blue is..." She stopped.

"Her mother and father have been looking all night. And the police. They found her this morning ... in the playing field."

She put her arms around me.

"Someone took her, stole her away, you see? And then they left her there."

She told me all she could bear to tell me right then and tucked the blankets around my shoulders, then she sat beside me, sometimes looking off to wherever the delicate thing in the box had flown.

I slept again, my dreams full, as they would be for some time, of Blue. Blue on a breaking swing, falling through the dark oak branches, her body shattered on the ground beneath me. My arms outstretched. Empty.

Shortly afterwards I started stealing things and hiding them away. Small items from department and grocery stores when I went shopping with my mother or friends: a green candle, two ballpoint pens, a button from a coat hanging on a rack in Eaton's, a handkerchief with blue embroidery along one edge.

At home I took things from the kitchen and hid them in my room. Cutlery, food, a cup and dish. I still wandered the forest and marsh, but now with the sole idea of finding the Sphinx. It seemed more important than ever to find it, since I was convinced that was what Blue had been doing when something else, something dark that we hadn't suspected, hadn't measured the right magic for, had found her.

For a while, though I looked the same, I lived as if alone in my parents' house — a furtive, thieving, thirteen-year-old insomniac with a piece of cold, white neon in her heart.

The next winter we moved away.

My mother tells a story about me, and shows a picture taken the winter I turned fourteen, just before we moved.

The way she explains it, I got up early one morning in February, put on my jacket, toque, and mitts, and headed for the park, which was deep and fresh from an overnight snowfall.

There I engaged (she tells the "friend" who sometimes visits home with me) in the energetic and purposeful task of making snow figures — "angels" she calls them — the impression you leave after falling backwards into the snow and then fanning your legs and arms.

She says I made dozens of them and some of the neighbors even came out and took pictures, they found it such an interesting sight, as if all the angels in heaven had fallen to earth at once, and they'd chosen our park to do it in.

It's always at this point that my mother asks me what could have gotten into my head to do that. It's become somewhat of a rhetorical question finally, since whenever she asks I pretend I can't remember.

But I do. I remember making twenty-five figures altogether, and that in my mind they weren't angels at all.

Maybe one of these times when my mother asks I'll find some words to tell her — about the swing and the most desirable place, about dusk and the Moonlite Motel, about namelessness and knowing something forever. I'll tell her about the undeniable tug; about Blue and how I loved her.

"Cerisy's Sphinx," I hollered (just as Blue had, from her swing) and leapt up from the snowy field, from my flock of illusive, fluttering moths, and galloped off into the distant trees, my heart filled with moss and feather and mountains folding into each other.

Red Delicious

Lynne Yamaguchi

Its tang bites back
like the punch of leather
summer of my eleventh year.
The ball I gripped then,
fingers snug along the seams, slug
tucked into my father's glove,
gave just so: ripely.
That summer I hurled that ball
as far as mettle could reckon,
always farther, faster, harder.
This body is a shot I flung
the length of childhood,
its core cupped chest-deep,
forever caught like the first bite of apple
swallowed
scarcely chewed.

Summer Showdown

Pat Griffin

When I think of growing up in Maryland, I think of summer and baseball: hazy, hot days spent playing games that ended only when everyone was called home for dinner. When there weren't enough players for a full game, we played work-up or hot box or some other game we made up. Our gang had a core group who always played together. Kerry, Steve, Wayne, Billy, and Tom are the guys I remember most. Nine or ten other guys played with us too, but not every day. We were all in fourth, fifth, or sixth grade, and we all wore blue jeans, t-shirts, and sneakers. We had a special way of rolling the bills of our baseball caps, too, so that they rounded in just the right way.

I was different from the rest of the guys on two counts: I was a lefty and I was a girl. I expected no special treatment, though, and got none. I didn't need it. I could hit, catch, and throw as well as any of the guys, and I wasn't afraid to dive for a line drive or slide into the catcher. That seemed to be all that mattered. I had rules for myself, though, things that I didn't do that the guys did. I didn't fight, spit, or cuss. That seemed to be enough to preserve my female identity among all those boys.

I was a baby dyke, too, though I had no words then to describe what I knew to be true about myself. It was the late 1950s, after all, and I had never heard the word *lesbian.* I just had this sense that I crack

was different from friends in my Girl Scout troop and that I wasn't quite what most adults expected me to be. I staged little rebellions against those pressures of femininity intended to herd me into a frilly pink box: When my mother made me wear a new dress to my grandmother's Christmas party, I insisted on wearing my new Hopalong Cassidy two-gun holster set over it. When I was given dolls for my birthday, they became hostages that I rescued in heroic fantasy games.

thwack

My major rebellion was being an athlete. From early on I had a gift for sports, which developed into a passion for baseball. The closest I came to being fully me in that Donna Reed world of the 1950s was on the baseball diamond. And so I played ball with the guys, my sexuality expressed through the sensuality of athletics: the crack of the ball on the bat, the thwack of the ball in my glove, the taste of sweat on my lips, the stretch of muscle and the joy of a ball well hit or an impossible catch made.

The guys and I spent many hours together playing inning after inning in the hot sun on a field we carved out of a corner of Mr. Cronin's horse pasture. We built a backstop out of chicken wire and old barn boards we got from Tommy's dad. Kerry and Steve's mom made us canvas bases filled with sawdust. My dad cut us a regulation-sized plywood home plate. We played so much that we wore base paths in the grass. Our field felt like Griffith Stadium to us, Washington Senators' fans all.

sweat

Since we played together nearly every day, we were comfortable with one another. We knew who the hotheads were and who were the peacemakers. We had our clowns and hot dogs and the crybabies who whined about every little scrape or bump. We knew who could hit the ball the farthest and who the best fielders were. Some guys always brought the bats and others brought balls.

stretch

On one of those soft summer days, our gang was well into a game. A lot of us were playing that day, and our usual ragging and baseball chatter ricocheted comfortably around the field. Kerry had just caught a fly ball in left field for the last out of the inning when Bay Quinn showed up wanting to play with us.

As well as we knew one another, we knew Bay hardly at all. When he bent under the barbwire fence and walked onto the field, we all got quiet. We watched as he took a last drag on his cigarette and flicked the butt over the fence. We had never played ball with him. He was in junior high school, a "big kid" to us. He wore his hair like Elvis Presley, greasy and slicked back. (Our guys had crew cuts and I had pigtails.) He had the sleeves of his white t-shirt rolled up to show his well-developed biceps, and a pack of Camels bulged at his left shoulder. Instead of sneakers, Bay wore shiny track spikes that glistened in the sun like sharks' teeth. We'd heard rumors about him driving without a license and getting into trouble with the police. It was simple, really: Bay Quinn was older, tougher, and a hood. We had to let him play, because none of us had the nerve to tell him we didn't want him around.

He ended up on the other team, since they had been playing one short. Everyone was a bit subdued as we resumed play, but things loosened up a little after we got back into the game — until Bay came up to bat.

I was pitching that day. Bay stepped up to the plate and took two vicious practice swings, his bat whipping through the still summer air. As he settled into his stance, he looked toward the pitcher's mound. He smiled at me over his shoulder and flicked his bat back and forth. The smile was not friendly. It said, Get ready to duck. I'm going to take your head off. As he dug the toes of his shoes into the dirt, I watched the stiletto points of his spikes shine through the dust he kicked up. Finally, he was ready. The chatter from my team was tentative: "Come on, Patty, kiiiddd, put it in there, babeee."

I rocked, kicked, and threw the ball. Bay twitched his bat, stepped into the pitch, and swung mightily. I expected to hear the crack of wood on leather. What I heard was leather on leather. The ball was in Steve's catcher's mitt. Strike one. Bay looked at his bat in disbelief, spit in the dirt behind him, and dug himself in again. This time he wasn't smiling. I took the throw from Steve and looked back at Bay. I rocked, kicked, and threw again. It was a meatball, right down the center. He went for it with everything

This time he wasn't smiling.

he had, caught a piece, and fouled it off over the fence behind home plate. Bay swung so hard, he had to prop himself up with his bat to keep from going down. Strike two.

He reached down and rubbed dirt onto the bat handle. When he stepped back into the box, he snarled at me, "No girl is striking me out." I felt my jaw tighten and I thwacked the ball into my glove a couple of times. I had never felt like this before. This had become more than a simple pickup game, more than a play that would unfold and be forgotten by the next day. Though I didn't completely understand why, I knew that whatever happened next was important: something was on the line here for both Bay Quinn and me. All the guys felt it too. The field was quiet.

I tugged at the bill of my cap. I smacked the ball into my glove one last time, then gripped it, fingers light across the ball's seams. I looked at Steve's mitt, held up as my target. I didn't look at Bay. I could feel him there at the plate, radiating waves of hatred toward me. I stretched, rocked, kicked, and threw the ball as hard as I could. Bay's face contorted with anticipated effort and he swung so hard, I could hear his bat whistle through the air. Steve stood up as he threw the ball to third base and yelled, "Awright, Patty, kiiid!" Strike three.

I had struck Bay Quinn out! I wanted to jump up and smack my fist into my glove and yell something to celebrate, but Bay's glower and hissed cuss words warned me not to. Instead, I turned to second base and grinned at Wayne. Striking someone out had never felt so sweet. Bay Quinn was outraged that a girl had struck him out. None of the guys in my gang had ever acted like that. If I struck them out, it was just like when anyone else struck them out. With Bay, it was different, and I felt mean and superior in a way I'd never felt before after a good play. I had this giddy sense of triumph. Bay Quinn taught me something that day: I learned to appreciate the special malicious satisfaction there is in beating a guy who considers himself my better just because he's a guy.

The game continued. Bay had lost some of his power to intimidate, and we slid back into our comfortable chatter with only a small awareness now of the stranger among us. Bay came up to bat twice more before I left the game. On his second trip to the plate, I struck him out again. Actually, to be fair, Bay struck himself out. His first swing was another attempt to put the ball in the next county. His second and third swings were more tentative and a little late. By then, he was so worried about striking out that he made himself do it. It didn't matter what I served up as long as it was near the plate. Before he left the batter's box this time, he spit toward the pitcher's mound and shot me a look of pure hate. The second strikeout felt as fine as the first. I even risked a smile at him this time, probably a mistake, in retrospect.

The third time Bay came up, the sun was going down and the game was losing steam. It was almost suppertime and we were ready to load up our bikes and head home. Bay dug his spikes into the dirt and looked grimly determined to get a hit. He swung at the first pitch late and hit a short fly ball that fell into the outfield just behind first base: a single, nothing more. Tommy came in from right field and took the ball on the hop. I ran to cover second, since we were short a couple of players. Tommy made a routine throw to me, as we all expected Bay to hold on first. He didn't.

I stood on second base with the ball in my glove and watched with horror as Bay rounded first and, picking up speed, headed straight for me. My first thought was that it was a crazy thing for him to do. I had the ball. There was no way he'd safely make it into second. Then, with a flash of fear, I realized that he didn't care about being safe. Bay Quinn had turned into a locomotive steaming down the base path, spikes flashing in the late-afternoon sun, and I was on the tracks. Bay wanted to hurt me.

I suppose I could have jumped out of the way. I don't really know why I didn't. Partly, I just couldn't *not* go for the tag. Part of it was pure stubbornness: I wasn't going to back down now. It's also true that fear kept me from thinking fast enough to move. Plus, I was naive enough to think he wouldn't really run me down.

Bay didn't slide. He ran right over me. My last thought before the collision was "Don't drop the ball."

We hit the ground about four feet behind second base. I lay motionless in the grass with my eyes closed, unable to breathe for a minute, and listened to the guys running toward us. I heard Kerry yelling, "You're out, Quinn." Then Tommy: "Yeah, and don't bother to come back." I squeezed my glove hand and, sure enough, the ball was there. My foot throbbed and I felt a sharp pain when I moved my toes. I sat up to see a red stain spreading around a jagged tear in the top of my canvas sneaker. Bay had not only knocked me down; he'd spiked me, too.

The rest of the afternoon was a blur: a hasty bike ride home, Mom driving me to the emergency room, and five stitches in my foot. The doctor said that there was no permanent damage, but I couldn't play baseball for a few days.

I was back on the pitcher's mound in a week with a new pair of sneakers. The guys and I resumed our summer baseball rituals and continued them every year until so many of us entered junior high school that the games broke down for lack of players. Bay Quinn never did come back to play with us. I never saw him again, but the memory of that day has stayed with me. I learned about boys who think they're better than girls just because they're boys. I also learned that pride in my athletic talents makes beating guys like that especially satisfying. Most important, I became aware of something deep inside me that I did not then completely understand, an unexplored core that refused to let go of who I was in a world trying to force me to be something else. In the face of the Bay Quinns of the world, I learned that I loved me enough to take the hit, hold onto the ball, and come back for the next game.

come back for the next game
back for the next game
for the next game
the next game

About the Contributors

Tracy Alderman, originally from Syracuse, New York, moved to San Diego, California, in 1988 to avoid winter, learn to surf, and earn her Ph.D. in clinical psychology. She divides her time between writing; creating artwork; going to the beach; playing with her two cats, Opie and Garbo; and working as an associate professor of psychology.

Alison Bechdel has been creating the comic strip *Dykes to Watch Out For* since 1983. Six collections of her work and an annual calendar have been published by Firebrand Books. Her strip is syndicated in more than fifty publications in the U.S., Canada, and the U.K.

Henri Bensussen lives with her partner, the usual two cats, and a rabbit in San Jose, California. She daydreams of retiring and moving to Oregon, where she will devote herself to writing and gardening full-time.

Kris A. Billhardt is on the eve of forty in Portland, Oregon. Director of a shelter for homeless and battered women and kids, she is approached when jars need opening, bikes need fixing, or kids need rough-housing. She still runs, climbs, and plays ball, and dreams of being independently wealthy. This is her first published work.

Lucy Jane Bledsoe is the author of the fiction collection *Sweat* (Seal Press, 1995) and a children's novel *The Big Bike Race* (Holiday House, 1995). She is also editor of the latest lesbian erotica anthology from Alyson (1995). Bledsoe writes books for, and teaches creative writing to, adult new readers (literacy students). She's an avid cyclist, hiker, and skier.

Louise A. Blum is the author of the novel *Amnesty* (Alyson, 1995) and an associate professor of English at Mansfield University in Pennsylvania. Her work has appeared in *Sojourner*, as well as in three anthologies published by Crossing Press: *Lovers*, *Love's Shadow*, and *Breaking Up Is Hard to Do*. She lives in Wellsboro, Pennsylvania, with her spouse, Connie Sullivan, and their new baby, Zoe.

Linda Bourke gardens in Gloucester, Massachusetts, and gives bloody noses to anyone who laughs about the button up her nose. She writes and illustrates amazing children's books, but never with cotton from the top of a vitamin pill jar.

BRENDA BROOKS lives on Salt Spring Island in British Columbia, Canada. She has published two books of poetry: *Somebody Should Kiss You* (gynergy, 1991) and *Blue Light in the Dash* (Polestar, 1994).

JAYNE RELAFORD BROWN performs her writing and teaches college composition, literature, women's studies, and writing workshops "part-time." Brown's work has appeared in such anthologies as *Dykescapes*, *I Am Becoming the Woman I've Wanted*, *El Vuelo del Aguila/The Flight of the Eagle*, *Wanting Women*, *Ex-Lover Weird Shit*, and *Lesbian Love Poems*. She is the mother of three grown children, including a tomboy daughter, and lives with her life partner, a tomboy cyclist, in the suburbs east of San Diego.

GIOVANNA (JANET) CAPONE is a poet and fiction writer of Southern Italian descent. Her work has appeared in a variety of journals and anthologies. She is also co-editing a book on Italian-American gay men and lesbians. "Stingrays" is chapter three of her novel-in-progress *Olive and Lavender: The Story of an Italian American Lesbian*. She lives in Oakland, California.

TP. CATALANO is still a jock, stemming from her tomboy years. Only her bloomers have changed — to boxer shorts.

LAUREN RENÉE CORDER is a 29-year-old San Antonio teacher and freelance writer. The room where she writes is made of wood. Reminiscent of her childhood tree houses, it is her space in which to be unabashedly herself.

JEANNE CÓRDOVA was a founder of the California gay and lesbian movement, and is the author of *Kicking the Habit: A Lesbian Nun Story*. Her work also appears in the anthologies *Lesbian Nuns: Breaking the Silence*, *The Persistent Desire: A Femme-Butch Reader*, and *Dagger*. A journalist and commentator and the founder and former publisher of *Lesbian Tide*, Córdova lives and writes in Los Angeles below the "D" in the Hollywood sign.

MARIE ELIZABETH DOLCINI has been composting and editorializing for the past seven years in San Francisco, where she now plays soccer and accordion and tunes her car.

MARIANNE DRESSER is senior editor at an independent press and a writer and reviewer whose work has appeared in *Deneuve*, *Girlfriends*, *Dykespeak*, *Bay Area Reporter*, *Lesbian Review of Books*, and *San Franscisco Review of Books*. She lives in San Francisco. This essay explores germinal material that she hopes to develop into a novel.

Born and raised in Lowell, Massachusetts, DENISE K. EARLEY now resides in the mountain town of Steamboat Springs, Colorado. She has been journalizing since the age of twelve, writing sporadically of key life experiences.

A former proofreader for the State of Texas, ALLISON FAUST now freelances in Austin. Whether swimming, running, biking, or go-go dancing with the mostly defunct lesbian band Girls in the Nose, she succeeds in surrounding herself with tomboys: her girlfriend was voted Most Athletic Girl by her high school class in 1977. Faust's current projects include a collection of poetry, *Set My Porn to Music;* an undercover exposé on cafeteria workers (as Lu Ann Platter); and two novellas, *Volunteer Scholar* and *Country Hair*.

RHOMYLLY B. FORBES spent her childhood in Berea, Kentucky, where the events depicted in "A Day in the Life of the King's Musketeers" actually took place. She now lives near Washington, D.C., where she divides her time between writing, caring for her cat and three ferrets, singing with the Lesbian and Gay Chorus of Washington, co-priestessing a Wiccan training coven, and working to improve the quality of justice for women everywhere. Previous work has appeared in erotic publications, so she is pleased to finally have a story in print that she can show her parents and grandmother.

DIANE F. GERMAIN is a French-American feminist-lesbian social worker and creator of a strength group for women survivors of incest and childhood sexual abuse. She was jailed for protesting the objectification of women in the "Myth CaliPORNia Kontest" in 1986. She has been a staff cartoonist for *Hot Wire: The Journal of Women's Music and Culture*, out of Chicago, and Los Angeles's *Lesbian News* since 1987. She has created a computer clipart program of diverse images of women for feminists to enhance their desktop publications.

PATRICIA A. GOZEMBA lives in Salem, Massachusetts, and Honolulu, Hawaii (when she can). She never stuck a button up her nose or even thought of it until she met Linda Bourke. Now she dreams of being the button-nose bloody-nose fighter for "truth, justice, and the American Way."

PAT GRIFFIN is an associate professor in the social justice education program at the University of Massachusetts in Amherst. She plays third and first base on a team in a lesbian-identified softball league. She is currently writing a book about lesbians and homophobia in sports.

SUSAN M. HAFNER occasionally interviews and writes about women for the Rhode Island gay and lesbian newspaper, *Options*. She is a transplanted midwesterner who would like to quit her job and write a lesbian trash novel about a golf tomboy.

CHAIA HELLER is a poet and ecofeminist activist, educator, and theorist living in Hatfield, Massachusetts. Her poetry has appeared in numerous journals and anthologies including *Calyx*, *Sojourner*, and *Lesbian Culture* and *Women's Glibber* (both from Crossing Press). In addition, Chaia teaches ecofeminism at the Institute for Social Ecology in Plainfield, Vermont. Her book *The Revolution That Dances: Ecofeminism and the Politics of Desire* will be published by Aigis Publications in spring 1996.

CATHERINE HOUSER is an associate professor of writing at the University of Massachusetts, Dartmouth, but she is most proud of going four for five in last night's game.

KANANI L. KAUKA is the assistant editor of the *Lambda Book Report*. Her short story "Going Home" appears in the anthology *Out for Blood* (Third Side, 1995). Currently, her favorite tomboy activity is barbecuing.

KISA now lives in eastern Washington on her own land. At fifty-three, she is still creating her ideas on her homestead but confesses that cowboys have been replaced as her heroes by the wisewomen who live closely with the earth.

DIANA LE BLANC is a bicoastal vegetarian surrealist who contracts as a visual artist, filmmaker, poet, athlete, and hair sculptress with strong inclinations toward humanism, minimalism, Zen Catholic Native American spirituality, and multilingual conversation.

MIA LEVESQUE grew up on Long Island Sound in Connecticut. She now lives in Philadelphia with her family: Tracy, Sophie, and Dillan.

KAROL D. LIGHTNER is a longtime lesbian activist, writer, and speaker who now resides in San Diego, California, and works as a social worker for San Diego County. She has written articles for lesbian and gay newspapers, and is published in both editions of *Our Right to Love*. A staged reading of her play *The Rehabilitation of Jehanne D'Arc* was performed recently at the Writing Center in San Diego.

SHARON LIM-HING grew up in Jamaica, where "Alan and Me" is set, and now lives and writes in Boston. She is the editor of *The Very Inside: An Anthology of Writings by Asian and Pacific Islander Lesbian and Bisexual Women* (Sister Vision, 1994).

MARLENE H. LIPINSKI received her B.F.A. and M.F.A. degrees in art from the University of Wisconsin, Milwaukee. She is presently a professor of art at Columbia College, Chicago, where she teaches graphic and computer-aided design. She is the founder of Calhoun Press at Columbia College and Hypotheses Press, where she is currently designing, illustrating, and printing a children's book. She started writing in 1993, but has been an artist and a tomboy for as long as she can remember.

ANDREA LOWE lives in Vancouver, British Columbia, where she pursues her enduring passions of writing and photography. When not alarming women in public rest rooms with her oft-times sirlike appearance, she attends classic car events and contemplates the confusing realities of lesbian love.

ANN L. MCCLINTOCK was a tomboy in north central Montana and now lives in San Francisco. An all-star guard on her school's basketball team, she continues to enjoy athletics. She currently works in film and video production.

FRANCI MCMAHON was born in 1941 in Oregon from ranching and homesteading stock, and grew up in Washington State riding every chance horse that came her way. A lifelong student of the public library, Franci has always had three loves: horses, books, and women. A need to once again smell the sage-tinted air brought her from Vermont back to the west and to a discovery of the typewriter, on which she wrote *Staying the Distance* (Firebrand Books). Franci lives with her partner and two horses on the edge of Deerlodge National Forest in Montana.

S. JAYNE MELTON, having spent most of her life dodging the pigeonholes of prejudice and challenging society's stereotypes, is now enjoying the more satisfying challenges of kayaking the coast, rivers, and estuaries of Britain with her partner, Alison.

BETTY MOORE is a happy 63-year-old lesbian, retired, who is working on a novel at this time.

HILARY MULLINS lives in Oakland, California, with her partner, April, and their clan of cats. Her first novel, *The Cat Came Back*, won a 1993 Lambda Literary Award for young-adult fiction. She has a part-time job at an alternative weekly and is at work on another novel and her first screenplay.

MARIAH BURTON NELSON is the author of *The Stronger Women Get, the More Men Love Football: Sexism and the American Culture of Sports* (Harcourt Brace, 1994; Avon Books, 1995) and *Are We Winning Yet? How Women Are Changing Sports and Sports Are Changing Women* (Random House, 1991). A former Stanford and pro basketball player, she has won four national awards for her writing. She came out at nineteen, just in time to wear a button that said, "Teenage Lesbian."

BARB NETTER lives in Chicago with her cat, Max. She plays softball, loves women, and enjoys the friendship of some truly great friends. She supports her writing habit by doing theatre. Go figure.

Linda Niemann is the author of *Boomer: Railroad Memoirs* (Cleis Press) and works as a freight conductor on the Southern Pacific Railroad.

Denise Carmen Paquin, thirty years old, lives well, works hard, and bikes year-round in the Boston area. She invents delicious entrées and fabulous desserts. She would throw more dinner parties if her apartment were bigger. This is her first published work.

Pat Pomerleau-Chávez lives in Santa Rosa, California, with Sparky Chávez, an illegal dog. He tells stories and she writes them down. Once in a while, one of them is published, and that makes Pat and Sparky feel pleased, lucky, and nervous.

Dianne Reum uses her "Tomboy" character, who is based on her own childhood experiences, as a vehicle to expose what she calls that "socially acceptable abuse: tomboy torment." "Tomboy" can be seen on a regular basis in strip form in *Bluestocking*, a Portland-Seattle feminist newspaper, and in Canada's *OH...*, a quarterly women's comic published by B Publications, which featured "Tomboy" exclusively in its November 1994 issue.

Susan Fox Rogers is the editor of *SportsDykes: Stories from on and off the Field* (St. Martin's Press) and *Another Wilderness: New Outdoor Writing by Women* (Seal Press). Her work has appeared in the anthologies *Sister and Brother*, *Women on Women 3*, and *Leading Out: Women Climbers Reaching for the Top*. She still rock climbs but will no longer play smear the queer or strip poker.

Postmenopausal Elena Sherman, upset about seeing her life as a Jewish lesbian written out of history while she is still alive, has stopped writing her résumé and started writing her life. Having joined the ranks of the self-employed, she is finding she has a lot to say. She lives happily with her lover, a dog, and three and a half cats, and she eats spaghetti on Sundays.

Sally Sotomayor lives in California's Mendocino County and is committed to making female-affirming stories available to adolescent and preadolescent girls. "Marta's Magic" is part of a collection of such stories to be published someday in both Spanish and English.

After teaching physical education for nine years in the Chicago area, Kate Stoll hung up her whistle to write. When she isn't writing, she is busy with tomboy activities like coaching softball and field hockey, rehabing houses, and playing golf, in Houston.

Becky Thompson is a Canadian package car driver for UPS with dreams of becoming a pilot. She continues to catch frogs, ride bikes, and walk barefoot in the sand braless.

ANNA VAN EVERA lives in West Virginia — and likes it! She is the author of *Have You Ever? 391 Questions to Help You Know Yourself and Others* (Alyson, 1994).

BARBARA ANN WRAY was born in 1953 and grew up in Drexel Hill, Pennsylvania. She enjoys square dancing with her partner, Julie. She has a B.A. in German and an M.A. in information studies from Drexel University. Barbara has two children: Timothy, age fifteen and Alison, age six.

LYNNE YAMAGUCHI is a poet, writer, editor, and book designer.

THE EDITORS:

RIGHT: Lynne Yamaguchi (right), with sister; age 6, Kyoto, Japan, 1963

BELOW: Karen Barber, age 3, Dunellen, New Jersey, 1968

Good night, sweet tomboys, wherever you may be...

Sometimes, tomboy is a stance...